FEMINIST
POLICYMAKING
IN
CHILE

FEMINIST POLICYMAKING IN CHILE

LIESL HAAS

THE
PENNSYLVANIA
STATE
UNIVERSITY
PRESS

UNIVERSITY PARK,
PENNSYLVANIA

Library of Congress Cataloging-in-Publication Data

Haas, Liesl.
Feminist policymaking in Chile / Liesl Haas.
    p. cm.
Includes bibliographical references and index.
Summary: "Investigates the efforts of feminists in
Chile to win policy reforms on a broad range of
gender equity issues, from labor and marriage laws
to educational opportunities to health and
reproductive rights"—Provided by publisher.
ISBN 978-0-271-03746-2 (cloth : alk. paper)
ISBN 978-0-271-03747-9 (pbk. : alk. paper)
    1. Women's rights—Chile.
  2. Women—Government policy—Chile.
      3. Feminism—Chile.
           I. Title.

HQ1236.5.C5H33   2010
305.420983—dc22
2010018392

Copyright © 2010 The Pennsylvania State University
All rights reserved
Printed in the United States of America
Published by The Pennsylvania State University Press,
University Park, PA 16802-1003

It is the policy of The Pennsylvania State University Press to
use acid-free paper. Publications on uncoated stock satisfy the
minimum requirements of American National Standard for
Information Sciences—Permanence of Paper for Printed
Library Material, ANSI Z39.48-1992.

for RICH

CONTENTS

Preface and Acknowledgments ix

List of Abbreviations xiii

Introduction:
Feminist Policymaking and the
Struggle for Women's Equality 1

1
The Rules of the Game:
Explaining Feminist Policy Outcomes 21

2
Feminist Policy Reform in Chile 53

3
Success at a Price:
Passing Domestic Violence Legislation 97

4
The Limits of Framing:
Legislating Abortion Rights 119

5
Winning the Game:
The Legalization of Divorce 145

6
Conclusion:
The Future of Feminist Policymaking 169

Appendixes 185

References 203

Index 221

PREFACE AND ACKNOWLEDGMENTS

This project began almost twenty years ago. After graduating from college I spent two years as a community organizer in rural Chile, working with women's cooperatives in relatively isolated communities near Los Andes, north of Santiago. It's hard to remember now what I imagined the experience would be like, but as anyone who has done volunteer work can attest, the reality is almost always more challenging, more humbling, and ultimately more transformative than one expects. My two strongest memories from that time are of being overwhelmed by the generosity of my Chilean neighbors and of being taken aback by the political engagement and sophistication of people living such a rural existence.

I arrived in Pocuro at the end of 1990, shortly after the transition to democracy. The silos and fences around my house were still covered with graffiti from the 1988 plebiscite on General Pinochet's regime. Despite their isolation, the people in the village where I lived suffered significantly under the military government, particularly in the first years after the 1973 coup. Many of my neighbors had relatives who had been exiled abroad, or had spent time in prison, or had been tortured. Finally free to speak openly about their experiences, they poured out stories of the chaos of the Allende years and of the brutal repression that followed the coup.

I was initially shocked by the harsh conditions in which these women lived: dilapidated housing without heating, telephones, or, in many cases, indoor plumbing. Daily tasks like laundry were done by hand. Paid employment was scarce, and many men left for weeks at a time to work in mining or at the ski resorts, effectively leaving the women sole caretakers of the home and children. Yet many of the women made time to attend the cooperative meetings, where they spoke with great insight about their common struggles: of the need for better health care and birth control, of practical advice for defending themselves against domestic abuse (which was endemic in the area), of their inability to make the most basic financial decisions without the permission of their husbands, of the need for legal divorce. On multiple occasions women who by all appearances conformed to the role of traditional rural wife and mother argued passionately for the need for abortion "in extreme cases."

These were not women who had internalized or acquiesced in the limitations of their social roles. Many could clearly articulate their inequality but felt trapped not only by a *machista* culture but by laws that failed to guarantee their socioeconomic and political equality. I owe an enormous debt of gratitude to these women, who first opened my eyes to the reality of women's lives in Chile and whose tremendous hospitality and lasting friendship sustained me there and remain with me today.

In the years after my return to the United States, feminist representatives in the Chilean Congress introduced legislation to criminalize domestic violence, establish salary equity for women workers and day-care centers for their children, give married women more control over their salaries and property, and legalize divorce. Their early enthusiasm for policy reform waned, however, in the face of staunch political opposition. Sernam, the National Women's Service, established itself as a center for policy development on women's rights, but not without controversy—both from feminists outside the state and from political conservatives opposed to reform. The Chilean women's movement, which had played a central role in fighting for a return to democracy, struggled to redefine its mission and its relationship with the government.

My work with the women's cooperatives, together with the fledgling projects of the new democratic government, prompted me to consider whether, and how, women might change the inequalities that were so much a part of their lives. Could women effectively combat the cultural beliefs that limited their potential? How impenetrable were the structural factors—particularly the lack of legal protections to ensure women's equality—that sustained and perpetuated these beliefs? This book is my attempt to investigate the extent to which women in Chile have found political strategies to challenge discriminatory laws and to create the legal framework that will improve the concrete conditions of their lives.

I would like to acknowledge the financial support that made my research possible. Dissertation fieldwork was funded by the Ford Foundation/Duke-UNC Program in Latin American Studies and the J. William Fulbright Foundation. A write-up grant from the University of North Carolina Graduate School provided critical support during my final year of graduate school. A summer research grant from Western Michigan University in 2001 and grants from California State University, Long Beach, in 2002 and 2008 helped me complete my fieldwork and writing.

This book would not have been possible without the help and support of numerous people. I owe a special debt of gratitude to a number of people who were essential to the successful completion of my fieldwork in Chile. Alicia Frohmann and Teresa Valdes of Flacso-Chile provided critical feedback in the early stages of my research and were constant sources of encouragement. I am forever indebted to Gustavo Mendez, archivist at the Chilean National Congress in Valparaíso, who facilitated my access both to congressional documents (before they were online!) and to members of Congress. Special thanks are due Patricia Aguilera, who undertook the unenviable task of transcribing my interviews—and is still my friend despite it.

Dozens of congressional representatives, political party leaders, and members of Sernam generously allowed me to interview them—sometimes multiple times. Members of the women's movement allowed me access to their private archives, welcomed me to their meetings, and spent countless hours helping me understand their positions and their political strategies. I am grateful to the archivists at the National Episcopal Council, who helped me locate documents that shed light on the Catholic Church's involvement in policy debates and evolving relationship with the democratic government.

I would like to thank my advisor at UNC, Evelyne Huber, for her unfailing support, patience, and constructive feedback at every stage of this project. The other members of my dissertation committee also deserve thanks. Jonathan Hartlyn offered early support for my interest in studying women's rights in Latin America and provided encouragement not just for this project but throughout my graduate career. I am grateful to Lars Schoultz and John Stephens for their enthusiasm for my research and their willingness to give me honest feedback—positive and negative. Christian Smith never failed to offer helpful comments on my work, and I especially appreciate his willingness to cross disciplinary boundaries to serve on my committee.

I am particularly indebted to Gina Perez and David Carey, housemates in Pocuro and later fellow graduate students, for two decades of insightful and challenging conversations about Latin American history and politics. At UNC, Merike Blofield, Anne Marie Choup, Christina Ewig, Mary Rose Kubal, and Beth Whitaker were and are continuing sources of inspiration to me, and I am a better person and a better academic for knowing them. Merike Blofield generously shared her own field research from Chile with me, and our academic collaborations have made my own work much stronger. I want to thank my colleagues at CSULB who provided feedback and encouragement on earlier drafts of this work, especially Charles Noble, Larry George, and Teresa Wright. I am also grateful to the three reviewers of the manuscript for their very helpful critiques.

I am profoundly grateful to my family, especially my parents, Kathleen and Frederic, who raised me to love politics, my brother, Eric, and sister-in-law, Leslie, who share my love of Latin America (and California), and my sister, Katrin, whose work with a development agency focused on women's health is a constant reminder that academic work should mean something on the ground.

I am most thankful for my husband, Richard Haesly, who has supported me in every possible way over the many years of this project. His faith in me never wavered, even when my confidence did, and I bet he is even happier than I am that this book is finally finished. I promise the next one will go faster. And finally, to our children, Xavier, Carys and Juliet, whose unbridled joy for life helps me keep all of this in perspective.

ABBREVIATIONS

CEDAW	Convention on the Elimination of All Forms of Discrimination Against Women
Concertación	National Concertation for Democracy
Flacso	Latin American Faculty in the Social Sciences
MEMCH	Movement for the Emancipation of the Chilean Woman
NGO	Nongovernmental organization
PAL	Legislative Analysis Program
PDC	Christian Democratic Party
PPD	Party for Democracy
PRD	Radical Democratic Party
PRSD	Radical Social Democratic Party
PS	Socialist Party
PSD	Social Democratic Party
RN	National Renovation Party
Sernam	National Women's Service
UCC	Center-Center Union Party
UDI	Independent Democratic Union Party
WPM	Women's Policy Machinery

INTRODUCTION:
FEMINIST POLICYMAKING AND THE STRUGGLE
FOR WOMEN'S EQUALITY

> The fact that I am the one who is here tonight is a symbol of the change we have lived.
> —President-Elect Michelle Bachelet, victory speech, Santiago, January 15, 2006

On January 15, 2006, Socialist Michelle Bachelet was elected president of Chile.[1] Bachelet's election has enormous political and cultural implications for Chilean women and their ongoing struggle for full citizenship and equal rights. An avowed feminist, she signifies the progress that Chilean women have made since the transition to democracy in legitimizing issues of women's rights and in gaining a greater political voice. She demonstrated her commitment to expanding the gains Chilean women have made to date by appointing a cabinet that is 50 percent female, expanding women's access to contraception, and strengthening the implementation of domestic violence laws. In many ways, Michelle Bachelet's political success would seem to represent the public face of a deeper transformation of women's status in Chilean society.

---

1. Bachelet continued the rule of the Center-Left Concertación coalition, which governed Chile from the transition to democratic government in 1990 until 2010. (The posttransition presidents have been Christian Democrats Patricio Aylwin [1990–94] and Eduardo Frei [1994–2000], followed by Socialist Ricardo Lagos [2000–2006].) Yet the public support for Bachelet's candidacy in particular represented a dramatic shift from past Concertación presidents, who hailed from the old guard of their parties and had enjoyed national political careers prior to the 1973 coup. The popularity of Bachelet, a former political prisoner who spent years in exile during the dictatorship, indicates an increased willingness by Chileans to confront the country's authoritarian past more openly. (All translations from the Spanish are my own unless otherwise indicated.)

At the moment of the transition to democracy in 1990, the state of women's legal rights in Chile lagged far behind most of Latin America (in contrast to the strength of the country's economy, which led the region). Sexual assault laws mandated different punishments for sexual aggressors based on the social reputation of the victim, and sexual abuse within families was not legally recognized. Property rights laws gave disproportionate control over marital property, as well as complete legal authority over children, to the husband. The use of pregnancy tests as a condition of work contracts was commonplace, and pregnant girls were expelled from both public and private schools. Abortion was illegal in all circumstances, outlawed by the military government even when it would save a woman's life.[2] Divorce was also completely illegal, with no enforceable family support system in place, leaving many women and children economically destitute if a husband abandoned the family. Finally, legal distinctions were made between children born within and outside marriage, and fathers had no legal responsibility to provide for their extramarital children, leaving mothers solely responsible for these children's care. In light of the significant political influence Chilean women achieved as part of the opposition to authoritarian rule, members of the women's movement and observers of Chilean politics expected that women's political influence would increase as democracy in Chile became more firmly established. They predicted that women's political power would translate into policy reform on such issues.

Indeed, there have been a number of important advances in women's rights since the transition. Under pressure from the feminist community, the first democratic government created a National Women's Service (Sernam) to promote and oversee women's rights issues at the national level. Sernam and feminist representatives in the Congress have spearheaded a broad range of policy proposals to expand women's equality, touching on education, health, political representation, and the family. Among these proposals are notable successes, including legislation on domestic violence, sexual assault, day care, employment discrimination, and divorce. Women's political representation, while low, is on the rise across political parties, and support for a national quota law for women's representation is increasing. Perhaps more significant, congressional backing for feminist policy proposals has widened beyond the small core of feminist representatives who initiated the majority of proposals in the first democratic administrations. The same literature that

---

2. Between 1931 and 1989, "therapeutic" abortion was legal in limited cases (see chapter 4).

notes the political disintegration of the feminist movement also acknowledges the wide diffusion of feminist ideals throughout Chilean society—in the media, universities, political parties, and public opinion (e.g., Ríos Tobar 2003).

However, observers of Chilean politics dispute the extent to which Bachelet's election reflects broader progress in the country toward gender equality. In fact, a burgeoning literature on Latin American feminism displays deep ambivalence about the current status of women's rights in Chile. Much of the existing research emphasizes the ways in which Chilean democracy has fallen short of the expectations of Chilean feminists. The visibility of the women's movement in the struggle for democracy, and feminists' political clout at the moment of transition (Chuchryk 1994; Frohmann and Valdés 1993), have not, in the view of many feminists and students of Latin American politics, translated into sustained political influence over democratic policymaking.

A number of scholars emphasize the political dissolution of Chile's feminist movement[3] and women's movement more broadly (Baldez 2002; Franceschet 2005; Matear 1997). This dissolution has dramatically reduced the visibility of feminism as a source of political pressure for policy reform. While some of the reasons for this are internal in nature,[4] scholars have also pointed out the ways in which the democratic transition itself and the institutional political structure that resulted have undermined women's participation and limited the opportunities for far-reaching policy reforms (Alvarez 1998, 2000; Ríos Tobar 2003; Waylen 1996a). The creation of Sernam, a cabinet-level women's rights agency, established a permanent location for women's rights advocacy within the state. However, both members of feminist organizations and feminist representatives in the Congress lament their secondary role in Sernam's policymaking efforts (Franceschet 2003; Richards 2004; Schild 1998; Waylen 1996a).

This high-profile election of a woman to national political office thus brings with it several questions. If women seem to be at once succeeding and

---

3. The feminist movement, which is a subset of the broader women's movement, seeks the transformation of the system of gender domination. As there is no single, unified feminist community in Chile, many scholars speak of "feminisms" or feminist movements. See Alvarez 2000; Baldez 2002; Blofield and Haas 2005; Frohman and Valdés 1993; Ríos Tobar 2003.

4. Several factors have negatively affected the feminist community since the transition to democracy, among them financial difficulties, exhaustion and lack of generational replacement, depletion of leadership to the political parties, and difficulty strategizing movement activism to fit the democratic political context.

failing in their quest for equal rights, how can we make sense of the conflicting characterizations of the state of women's rights in Chile? In this book I analyze women's political success since the transition to democracy by focusing on what is inarguably a core component of progress on women's rights: the passage of legislation that promotes the goals of the feminist movement. While legislative policy is not, of course, the only measure of a society's openness to women's rights, it is a critical component of any larger program of political, cultural, and economic transformation of women's status. The feminist movement that arose under the dictatorship (1973–89) articulated a well-developed agenda for political change, and the political parties vying for representation in the new government promised to respond to that agenda. How has this professed commitment to women's rights played out in practice? To what extent have feminists been able to implement the political demands they developed over the previous sixteen years by influencing public policies on women's rights? By looking at legislative attempts to promote women's equality, we can evaluate the political responsiveness of the Chilean government to citizen claims for equal treatment, which goes to the heart of democratization.

Chile as a Bellwether for Women's Rights in Latin America

Formal legislative change makes a fundamental difference in the lives of women at all levels of society. Whether women have the option of civil divorce and therefore a right to alimony and child support, whether married women have control over their own property and income, whether sanctions exist to protect women from violence in the home and sexual harassment in the workplace, and whether women earn comparable wages for their work are of crucial importance for women's social, political, and economic equality. While legal advances alone cannot eliminate discrimination against women, laws that expand women's rights both reflect and reinforce broader processes of cultural change. The process by which de jure protections are translated into de facto rights may be frustratingly slow, but it is a necessary and critical component of lasting change.

Chile provides the opportunity to explore the ways in which feminists can learn to play by the institutional rules to increase their policy success. The political strategies feminists use are themselves constantly evolving. The outcome of one attempt to influence policy will influence actors' perceptions of what is possible and thus the strategies they choose for the next round. The outcome of each policy proposal, and the strategies that surround it, shape the political opportunity structure for future endeavors. As we examine these changing political strategies, it becomes clear that success itself needs to be more clearly defined. Beyond merely calculating whether a given legislative proposal ultimately becomes law, we need to consider the form of the proposal. Is it radical or conservative? Sweeping in breadth or narrowly focused? We must also examine how the policy process includes or excludes various groups and thereby shapes the expectations of those actors for future engagement with the state. Ultimately, what should we count as a "good" proposal or law? How realistic are hopes for radical change, and how necessary is compromise? The chapters that follow illuminate the ways in which the debates about these issues influenced how Chilean feminists have engaged in the political process since the return of democratic government in 1990.

In Latin America there has been notable progress on women's rights in recent years, particularly in the areas of domestic violence, political participation, the family, and basic civil rights. The women's movements that arose in the 1970s and 1980s politicized these issues and successfully pressured governments for significant legal changes. Nevertheless, women's continuing legal inequality in Latin America remains entrenched in numerous anachronistic laws still in force throughout the region.[5] In many countries there are restrictions on the types of work women can perform, husbands retain primary authority over children and marital property, and rapists can be acquitted if they marry their victims. Even where progressive laws are on the books, barriers to implementation and enforcement continue to pose obstacles to reform. Among other, more strictly institutional problems with implementation, judges, lawyers, and law enforcement officials need to be sensitized to the issues so that they become willing to enforce new laws. Women need to be informed about their legal rights in order to claim them.

The women's movements that emerged in response to military dictatorships throughout Latin America developed a feminist critique of women's social, political, and economic inequality as part of their larger opposition to military rule (see Chinchilla and Haas 2006; Frohmann and Valdés 1993; Jaquette 1994; Kirkwood 1986). In response to women's active and influential participation in pro-democracy movements, posttransition governments and

---

5. As Htun (1998, 3) notes, in Latin America "it is often only when laws lag social practices by decades that they become uncontroversial enough to be changed."

political parties across the region courted women voters and declared themselves in favor of women's equality. Throughout the region, government ministries have been created to pursue women's rights at the state level, and the implementation of quota laws in a number of countries has increased women's legislative representation. Yet despite these auspicious beginnings, much of the research undertaken since the transitions to democracy has focused on the fragmentation of social movements and the resistance of political parties and the state to incorporating both women and a feminist policy agenda (e.g., Baldez 2001; Franceschet 2005; Matear 1997; Richards 2004; Waylen 1994, 2000). In the face of political resistance to demands for women's equality, strategies for advancing women's rights increasingly focus on influencing the programs of the political parties and the policymaking process itself. In this area advocates of women's rights have met with success as well as failure.

Chile is a fascinating example of the triumphs and continuing challenges in the evolution of women's rights in Latin America, as it combines the region's most traditional laws on women with one of the largest and most influential women's movements in the region. Chile provides a critical case study for the major factors that have been cited in comparative research as key to successful policymaking on women's rights. That is to say, Chile has a feminist movement with an articulated policy agenda, supportive political parties, and an executive agency focused on women's rights. However, the diversity of comparative cases and the numerous additional factors that appear to affect policy success—from the larger cultural context, to the economic level of development, to international pressure, to the structure of the electoral system and even internal party electoral dynamics—have made it difficult to assign relative weights to each factor in a given case or to generalize across cases. There are multiple paths to policy success. The complexity of the policymaking process in general, the multiplicity of actors involved inside and outside government, and the diversity of the larger political and cultural contexts force us to conclude that what constitutes a propitious political context varies across time and space.

The most compelling policymaking puzzle involves the variation in policy success within countries. To the extent that the macrostructural or institutional variables identified in the literature are case specific, they cannot explain this variation. What constitutes a positive political opportunity structure for feminist policymaking often varies within countries across policy areas, as different coalitions of forces will coalesce around particular political issues (Stetson and Mazur 1995; see also Blofield 2006; Htun 2003).

Understanding this fact is an important step in helping to uncover the highly dynamic political environment surrounding efforts to develop feminist policy proposals. Chile complicates the scenario further by revealing significant variation in success even within specific policy areas. The mix of success and failure within policy areas in a single country means that we need to reexamine our assumptions about individual cases. This book concludes that there is tremendous room for politics on women's rights issues, and therefore room for actors to improve their policy success rates over time. This proves to be true even within a largely static macropolitical structure, and even on issues where success has been elusive in the past.

The evolution of policy reform on women's rights in Chile since the transition to democracy reveals the trade-offs and compromises behind the incorporation of feminists in democratic politics. The behavior of key actors represents a critical and underexamined factor in the fate of feminist policy proposals. The effort to move beyond a macrolevel analysis of party systems or women's policy machinery (WPM) to look at the strategies feminists use within those systems to advance their cause offers a much needed advancement in our understanding of feminist policymaking.

The Feminist Policy Agenda in Chile

Feminist legislation seeks to eliminate all forms of economic, political, social, and cultural inequalities between women and men. In so doing, feminism seeks women's full and equitable incorporation as citizens. Early in the first posttransition democratic administration, drawing on the policy agenda developed by the feminist community under the dictatorship, congressional advocates for women's rights and the leadership of Sernam began to develop a wide-ranging policy agenda, touching on a number of critical women's rights issues. Over the past eighteen years, sixty-four legislative proposals have been introduced to expand women's legal equality, across policy areas as diverse as the rights of domestic workers, intrafamily violence, sexual harassment and assault, sex and wage discrimination, the educational rights of pregnant students, protections for pregnant workers, day care, paternity law, marital property rights, therapeutic abortion, and divorce (see appendix 1).[6]

---

6. These issues have been introduced as legislation in various forms, some narrowly focused and some more sweeping in scope, but all the bills defined as feminist in this study deal with topics first advocated by the feminist community. As the ideals of feminism are diffused beyond

Legislative reform tends to move at a glacial pace. With this in mind, a number of observations can be made from an initial analysis of women's rights legislation. To begin, the range of policy proposals is impressively broad. It is also apparent that, while the majority of proposals were introduced by congressional representatives, the executive women's ministry, Sernam, has enjoyed a much higher success rate with its own legislative projects.[7] Eight of nine bills introduced by Sernam eventually became law,[8] whereas, between 1990 and March 2008, only nine of fifty-three congressional bills were successful.[9] It is worth noting that Sernam's bills were often successful where congressional efforts on the same issue had failed. This was the case with bills on sex discrimination, paternity laws, and marital property rights. Considering the range of topics covered by congressional versus executive bills, it is clear that the most controversial proposals—namely, abortion and divorce, which have been the subject of multiple proposals—have only been introduced by congressional representatives. Despite the overall low success rate of congressional bills, they enjoyed greater success beginning in the second administration (1994–2000). This corresponds with an increase in cross-party sponsorship of the bills. Finally, the past few years have witnessed the passage of legislation that had been dormant for many years and the introduction of new proposals, including new legislative proposals on reproductive rights and abortion, arguably the most politically controversial women's rights issues.

Beyond the mere fact of a bill's success or failure, it is important to consider the alterations that a bill may undergo before it garners enough political

---

an original group of self-defined activists, and as the importance of women's equality becomes more accepted culturally and politically, we should not be surprised to see legislation that is feminist in character supported, or even drafted, by representatives beyond the narrowly defined feminist community. Describing legislation as "feminist" is thus not a simple matter of whether all the representatives who introduce a particular bill define themselves as feminist or of the degree to which feminists outside government publicly demonstrate in support of every bill. Rather, the identification of a bill as feminist rests on the character and goal of the legislation itself, which must aim to eliminate some form of discrimination against women.

7. This parallels the larger pattern of Chilean legislation, where executive proposals are more successful than congressional efforts. See Siavelis 2000.

8. An additional executive bill introduced by President Bachelet in 2006 (Law 20.172) also passed.

9. My comparison of the success rates of congressional bills includes those introduced between 1990 and 2008. Given the slow pace of the legislative process, it should not be surprising that little progress has been made on the most recent bills. These recent bills are nevertheless included in the study to illustrate the issues currently under debate, the broadening support for the proposals at the point of introduction in Congress, and the increasing political willingness to legislate on particularly controversial policy issues (such as reproductive rights).

support for passage. Some bills pass the Congress in a form relatively faithful to their original composition; others are radically transformed through negotiation and compromise and ultimately "succeed" in a version that may counter the original purpose of the bill. The case studies that follow evaluate the degree to which the women's rights bills that have passed Congress have done so in a version that the Chilean feminist community considers a victory.

Methodology

Research on gender and politics has expanded from single case studies (e.g., Alvarez 1990; Baldez 2001; Franceschet 2005; Thomas 1994) to small-N comparative studies (Blofield 2006; Chant and Craske 2002; Htun 2003; Mazur 2001; Stetson 2002) and quantitative analyses (Kittilson 2006; Krook 2010; Weldon 2002). This trend has allowed researchers to identify broad, regional, or systemwide patterns that have strengthened, and in some cases challenged, the conclusions of individual case studies. The trade-off in such comparative work, however, often involves the privileging of system-level economic, institutional, and sociopolitical variables and a difficulty in examining variation within systems, including individual behavior. Furthermore, because work on multiple cases must limit itself to a few policy areas, the policy patterns that emerge may well be endemic to the issue areas examined.[10] By focusing on the universe of relevant policy proposals in a given country and tracing variation in these patterns over time, I explore the role of individual and group strategy on policy outcomes and generalize these dynamics beyond a limited range of policy areas. My conclusions regarding the potential for policy movement within a given system, in turn, have broad implications for general research on feminist policymaking.

Tracing each stage of development in the policy process pushes the analysis beyond reliance on one sector or interaction within the legislative process

---

10. For example, Weldon (2002) concludes that religion does not play a significant role in policymaking, but her analysis is limited to domestic violence legislation, an issue much less likely to provoke the opposition of conservative religious leaders than divorce or reproductive rights. Blofield (2006) compares policy reform on divorce and abortion in Chile, Argentina, and Spain and finds the institutional power of the Catholic Church, relative to other political and social actors, a key explanatory variable.

and allows me to contextualize the impressions and recollections of individuals at various points in the process. This kind of detailed analysis is invaluable in separating fact from fiction (and impression from reality) in terms of who influences policy proposals on women's rights, how much, and at what point in the process. This type of analysis lends itself particularly well to policy predictions, or to evaluations regarding the type of action necessary to increase the success of these kinds of policy proposals. Illuminating the microlevel factors at work, and their interaction with the country's larger sociopolitical and institutional structure, contributes to our understanding of the opportunities available for policymaking in a variety of systems.

This analysis requires a gender and politics framework because I explore the way that policy success depends in large part on the creation and negotiation of gender stereotypes at work in both society and the state. I find that the ways in which women's roles are constructed, and how those constructions are manipulated politically, play a key role in the success or failure of proposals to advance women's equality.

The variation in the success rate of policy proposals in general, and within specific issue areas (such as paternity laws, property rights, violence against women, education, and divorce) suggests that there is no easy formula for successful feminist policymaking, but rather that we must look at the tradeoffs and compromises made along the way if we want to understand the advantages and disadvantages of various strategies. For example, what are the short- and long-term political consequences for feminists when they seek allies within the political opposition, when a sweeping bill is sacrificed in terms of a more politically viable but more conservative version, or when linkages to a broader feminist community are forsaken for the efficiency of professional organizations better versed in the mechanics of the policy process? What is the long-term impact of the final version of a bill on efforts to improve on it later? Over time and across policy area, how have feminist policymakers attempted to balance the often competing loyalties of the feminist community, their electoral constituency, and their party and coalition? How has feminist activists' participation in the policy process shaped their expectations of state response and their willingness to engage in future actions? The outcome of each legislative proposal, and the strategic dynamics surrounding it, will affect in critical ways the future interaction of interested actors in the policymaking process.

In limiting its focus to the legislative process, this study does not evaluate explicitly the implementation of new public policies on women's rights. I contend that the passage of new laws expanding women's rights represents a critical step in the struggle for gender equality, and not simply in symbolic terms. Even in those cases where new policies are underfunded or are slow to be implemented, the successful creation of public policies that expand women's rights both legitimizes women's rights inside and outside the state and creates a legal basis for later expansion of those rights. In this respect, the issue of implementation is examined indirectly in the case studies, where, on a number of issues, lack of government follow-through on policy reforms has sparked renewed legislative efforts to clarify and strengthen existing law.

Data Collection

The cases examined in this work represent all legislative proposals promoting women's equality that were introduced into the Chilean Congress between 1990 and March 2008. These sixty-four bills were proposed during the first five democratic Congresses, a period that coincides with the first four posttransition presidents.[11] The proposals cover a wide range of issues, touching on health, education, labor, the constitution, and foreign relations. Eight congressional committees were involved in reviewing women's rights legislation, and several executive ministries lobbied for one or more of the proposals. The broad range of actors and institutions involved in proposing or supporting women's rights legislation provides wide-ranging insight into the policymaking process in Chile.

In limiting my case selection to feminist legislation, it is important to explain what is and is not included in the case study. Feminist legislation, or feminist policy, seeks to advance women's equality by eliminating legal distinctions that limit women's political, economic, social, or cultural rights vis-à-vis men.[12] This is a critical point, because not all legislation proposed in Chile that focuses on women's rights has sought to expand those rights—a number of bills have sought further restrictions on women's equality and were introduced by representatives on the right specifically to counter feminist proposals already introduced. For example, in response to feminist

---

11. March 2008 marks the midpoint of the fifth democratic Congress. Deputies elected will serve until 2010. March 2008 also marks the halfway point of Bachelet's presidency.

12. Of the many definitions of "feminist" circulating in academic work, I find Stetson and Mazur's definition particularly relevant to this study: "an ideology, policy, organization or activity . . . that has the purpose of improving the status of women as a group and undermining patterns of gender hierarchy" (1995, 15).

bills seeking to legalize divorce, conservative representatives introduced two bills to restrict further the options for legal marital annulment (the only means of ending a marriage until 2004). And in response to calls from feminists for debate on abortion and the introduction by a Socialist deputy of a bill to decriminalize abortion, deputies and senators from the conservative National Renovation Party (RN) and Independent Democratic Union Party (UDI) introduced three separate bills proposing greater sanctions for women who seek abortions and those who perform them. These bills are not included in the formal case study because they do not seek to advance women's legal rights, but they are included in the discussions of policymaking as illustrations of the conservative political and cultural forces opposing feminist proposals.

The sixty-four bills included in the study focus on the specific areas in which Chilean women are disadvantaged socioeconomically relative to men. These are issue areas that have been the focus of feminist organizations in Chile as well as of the international women's movement generally. Such areas include (but are not limited to) the legal status and rights of married women, specifically regarding property rights, legal authority over children, and protection from domestic abuse; access to education and health services, including reproductive rights; and the position of women in the labor force. As discussed in the following chapters, there is significant variation in the degree to which the rights of Chilean women have been addressed in each of these areas since the transition to democracy.

The qualitative data analyzed for this study include more than a thousand pages of legislative debate, archival material from the Congress and from the private archives of members of the Chilean women's movement, and more than fifty interviews with legislative representatives, party leaders, Sernam members, and members of the feminist community. The analyses in chapters 3–6 are based on archival research and in-depth interviews undertaken in Santiago and Valparaíso (the site of the Congress) from August 1996 through July 1997, June through August 2001, and November 2008. Reconstructing the path through Congress of the bills that I investigate required the systematic evaluation of all related documents published by the Chamber of Deputies, the Senate, and executive ministries, including the original drafts of the bills, committee reports and floor debates, and the final versions of the bills that passed Congress. Included in this analysis are the evaluations of pending legislation issued by academic institutions, as well as by policy institutes and lobbying groups affiliated with the Left, Center, and Right. I analyzed the evolution over time of party positions on issues by studying party documents (including position papers, election campaign materials, and reports from party meetings) from 1989 to 2001. Executive interviews focused on the leadership of Sernam, as well as the members of the ministry involved in developing and lobbying for legislative proposals on women's rights. Congressional interviews included members of all the major political parties and targeted party leaders and committee chairs as well as the main proponents and opponents of the legislation.

I traced the development of women's rights issues within the feminist community primarily through the archives of Flacso-Chile (Facultad Latinoamericana de Ciencias Sociales), ISIS International, Casa de la Mujer–Valparaíso, and La Morada, as well as through private archives of members of the women's movement. In addition to extensive interviews conducted with members of feminist community, I attended numerous conferences, seminars, and organizational meetings of both NGOs and non-NGO women's organizations in Santiago and Valparaíso.

An analysis of reporting on women's rights in the country's three main newspapers (*El Mercurio*, *La Época* [now defunct], and *La Nación*) from 1989 to 2006 and in interviews with journalists helped me gauge the extent of media coverage of women's rights issues as well as changes in the media's framing of feminism and feminist topics. I investigated the position of the Catholic hierarchy on this legislation through archival work at the Archdiocese of Santiago and the Chilean Episcopal Council and through interviews with church leaders. Public opinion is more difficult to tap, because the opinion surveys undertaken since the transition have not focused specifically on most of these issues. Public opinion has been surveyed, however, on some of the most important questions, such as divorce, abortion, and women's political participation generally. Where surveys of public opinion on women's rights are available, the results have been incorporated into the analysis.

In examining the proposed legislation, I have considered the relative success of each of the bills at several distinct moments in time: during the development of the legislative initiative, during passage by committee in the Chamber of Deputies, during passage on the floor of the Chamber, during passage by committee in the Senate, and during passage on the floor of the Senate (and subsequent passage into law). In tracing the fate of each bill, I focus on three broad clusters of factors: executive factors, including the broad institutional powers of the president and Sernam; legislative factors, including party position and discipline as well as coalitional considerations; and civil society factors, including the participation and influence of groups that support and oppose feminist policy proposals.

Explaining Successful Feminist Policymaking

Two primary factors pose obstacles to the success of feminist policy proposals: the institutional structure of the Chilean political system, which mitigates against cooperative policymaking between the executive and Congress, and the strength of the conservative opposition to women's rights, which enjoys disproportionate political influence within the political system. While the rigidity and undemocratic nature of Chile's political institutions and the continued strength of conservative cultural forces have been well documented in such works as Siavelis 2000, existing research tends to treat both as largely static forces. By contrast, an examination of feminist policymaking reveals a political environment that is highly dynamic. Over the past eighteen years, feminists within the political system have learned to navigate more effectively within this challenging institutional and cultural context.

The interesting question is under what conditions feminists have used the state to advance the cause of women's rights. Particularly, how are feminists in Chile learning over time to win politically in what is a new institutional setting for the country and a new political setting for many women? Over time, feminists have evolved more sophisticated ways to frame feminist proposals and have negotiated more strategically with the political opposition on the content of feminist proposals. This has led to an improvement in institutional cooperation between congressional feminists and Sernam. It has also broadened the appeal of, and support for, feminist proposals across party lines within the Congress.

My analysis of feminist policymaking emerges from an examination of the feminist legislative bills introduced between 1990 and 2008. Of the sixty-four legislative proposals analyzed in this work,[13] three issues most clearly represent both the range of success among feminist policy initiatives as well as the political dynamics that govern negotiation on feminist bills: domestic violence, abortion, and divorce. In the case studies that follow, I examine the most significant legislative efforts in each of these areas: the 1994 Intrafamily

---

13. The final bill analyzed was introduced in June 2009, after the period examined here. It is nevertheless included because it represents a major legislative success of the Bachelet administration (see chapter 6).

Violence Law (introduced in 1991), the (unsuccessful) therapeutic abortion bill (introduced in 1991), and the 2004 divorce law (introduced in 1995), as well as subsequent efforts to improve upon these earlier proposals. I chose to look closely at these three bills because these policy issues have been an important focus for the feminist community. Each issue has been the subject of multiple legislative proposals. Finally, the bills provide broad variation on the two main factors that explain policy success: institutional cooperation and strategic framing. As a result, each had a different trajectory and outcome. Moreover, the dynamic of each one influenced subsequent strategies on later bills. In sum, this is a story about political learning, and about how feminists learn to maneuver on a challenging institutional and cultural terrain.

By investigating how feminists in Chile have learned to play by the institutional rules to increase their policy influence, I address a number of debates about gender and politics and state feminism, including the impact of feminist movements, and effect of the percentage of women elected to office, the variable support for feminist policy across the ideological spectrum, the importance of institutional structure on policy outcomes, the role of women's policy machinery, the influence of autonomous civil society organizations that oppose feminist policy initiatives, and the political relevance of public opinion.

Outline of the Book

Chapter 1 evaluates existing hypotheses about the determinants of feminist policy change. To date, comparative work on this topic has focused primarily on the advanced industrial nations, although work on Latin America is increasing. In this chapter I examine the strengths and weaknesses of existing work on the policy impact of feminist movements, women's policy machinery, political parties and ideology, electoral systems, studies of critical mass, the role of religious institutions in promoting or opposing policy change, and public opinion. In each case I identify the gaps in our understanding of feminist policymaking and clarify where further research can shed light on the dynamics of policy change. In addition, I introduce an underexamined factor in the comparative literature: the role that institutional balance of power plays in creating effective or dysfunctional policymaking dynamics within the state. This is a critical factor in Latin America, where, historically, strong executives often dominate the legislative process. Policymaking opportunities are shaped by the varying strength of these factors across cases and their interaction around concrete policy issues.

Chapter 2 applies these hypotheses to the Chilean case by analyzing the evolution of the policy agenda on women's rights since the transition to democracy. Centrally important to this analysis are the executive, legislative, and civil society factors that influence the policymaking process. An overview of the democratic transition is followed by a detailed explanation of the institutional structure of the Chilean political system. This discussion includes the effects of the electoral system, the existence, until 2005, of "designated" (unelected) senators, the committee structure, the institutional balance of power between the executive and legislative branches, and the structure and ideological affiliation of the political parties. I then analyze the growth and transformation of the Chilean women's movement, and the feminist movement in particular, as well as the relationship between Chilean feminists and their major political opposition—the political Right and the Catholic Church. I examine the way in which both political conservatives and the institutional church gain representation and influence within Chile's political and cultural institutions, and I consider their ability to block or overturn feminist policy proposals.

The main factors pinpointed in the comparative research as affecting the shape of feminist policy, such as social movements, parties, and executive women's agencies, are critical in Chile as well. In addition, I focus particular attention on the critical role of intergovernmental relations in forming stable policy networks and in developing successful policy initiatives. My contribution to this question illuminates two interrelated factors: first, that institutional balance of power has a major impact on the success of feminist policy proposals. It affects the way the major actors identified in the larger literature, such as social movements in favor of policy reform, groups in civil society opposing change, political parties, and executive agencies, can influence policymaking on a given issue. Second, as actors learn to play by the institutional rules, policy success increases over time. Examining the interaction of actors' political strategies with a given political and institutional context affords significant explanatory and predictive power in understanding the evolution of feminist policymaking in Chile since the return of democracy.

The next three chapters analyze particular policy cases so as to illustrate the larger dynamics of feminist policymaking. Chapter 3 focuses on efforts to reform laws on domestic violence. The case of domestic violence legislation reveals poor institutional cooperation between congressional representatives and Sernam and illustrates the intensity of debate on the question of how much to compromise with the political opposition. An early bill (introduced in 1991) clarified the consequences of Chile's posttransition institutional structure—namely, competition over bill ownership between Congress and Sernam and a consequent lack of interbranch coordination on policymaking—and the exclusion of much of the larger feminist community from the policy process. The bill eventually passed Congress, but at a huge cost in terms of both the relationship among the key players and the content of the proposal itself. In the end, inadequate levels of institutional cooperation, together with moderate efforts to strategize negotiations on the bill's content, led to a moderately successful piece of legislation. Later legislative efforts in this area have focused on strengthening and expanding the provisions of the original law.

In a broader sense, the case of domestic violence legislation demonstrates the effects, both positive and negative, of a high level of executive involvement with a bill. Sernam's success in promoting legislation illustrates the importance of executive support for a bill, but executive support does not easily or automatically translate into cooperation with congressional feminists. Congressional representatives and members of the women's movement complained that executive involvement with the domestic violence bill resulted in a more conservative bill than was necessary, one that many considered worse than nothing. The conflict over efforts to legislate on domestic violence confirmed the suspicions of many feminists about Sernam and influenced subsequent attempts to promote feminist policy reforms. The experience of legislating on domestic violence, together with Sernam's resistance to supporting legislation on divorce or therapeutic abortion, persuaded congressional feminists that they would need to increase their efforts to legislate independently of Sernam.

Chapter 4 examines congressional efforts to decriminalize therapeutic abortion. In one of the last acts of the military government, abortion was criminalized even in cases where it would save the life of the woman. In 1991 congressional representatives introduced a bill to decriminalize therapeutic abortion in a narrow range of circumstances. This effort reflects two lessons learned from the earlier experience with domestic violence legislation. First, given Sernam's resistance to policy reform on particularly controversial issues (most notably, abortion and divorce), the bill was introduced in the absence of any executive support. Second, the bill's sponsors made a concerted effort to frame abortion as a family issue rather than strictly as a women's rights issue, in an attempt to expand congressional support. The absence of both executive support and broad political backing within Congress, together with a lack of public support for the measure by feminist groups outside government and strong opposition from political conservatives and the Catholic Church, killed the bill in committee. In the end, strategic framing of the initiative could not compensate for the lack of institutional cooperation and for the general resistance across the political spectrum to legislating on abortion.

Nevertheless, the case of the therapeutic abortion bill, along with other independent legislative efforts, provided further lessons for feminists. Representatives became convinced of the importance of marshaling public support for legislation prior to its introduction, the necessity of strategically framing feminist initiatives to build political support beyond self-defined feminist representatives and the parties of the Left, and the need to build a more cooperative relationship with Sernam. In the short term, these lessons bore fruit in subsequent efforts to legalize divorce. Over the longer term, lessons gleaned from the first attempts to decriminalize abortion led to the creation of broader legislative coalitions in support of reproductive rights and renewed efforts to reform policy in this area.

The final case study, divorce, is examined in chapter 5. Efforts to legalize divorce in Chile demonstrate how executive involvement, even late in the game, can save a stalled initiative. The ultimately successful divorce bill was introduced in 1995. In the absence of executive support, it made extremely slow progress through Congress, and the bill's supporters were forced to agree to substantive changes to appease congressional conservatives. Five years after its introduction, the executive branch offered active support for the bill, and it passed the Congress eighteen months later, in a version close to the original. Better framing by congressional supporters, and the active solicitation of support and participation from the larger feminist community, helped to pass the bill in the Chamber of Deputies and to keep it alive for years in a hostile Senate committee.

We see two distinct stages in the efforts to legislate divorce, which confirm the relevance of institutional cooperation between Congress and Sernam: the necessity of strategic compromise with the opposition, and the importance of broader public support. In the first stage, low support from the executive meant extremely slow progress through Congress, but strategic framing and negotiation by the bill's supporters prevented it from being killed in committee. In the second stage, a change to Socialist leadership at the national level and at Sernam led to a shift by the ministry in support of divorce legislation. As a result of executive pressure on the Senate, the bill not only eventually passed Congress but its supporters were able to reverse some of the conservative changes that had been made in committee. In this second stage, high levels of executive support and sophisticated negotiation by the bill's congressional supporters and their strategic mobilization of public opinion led to the passage of a sweeping reform bill. The case of divorce demonstrates the possibility of passing progressive legal reforms even on the most controversial policy issues.

Chapter 6 summarizes the results of the research and considers the implications of these patterns of policymaking for attempts to legislate progressive change on women's rights in Chile. I then address the degree to which Michelle Bachelet's election as president altered the fundamental dynamics of feminist policymaking in Chile. In the case studies, I identify the strength of the executive branch as a key factor in creating either productive or conflictive policymaking patterns with other political actors, from congressional representatives to feminists in civil society. To what extent did Bachelet's administration bolster the development of policy networks between the state and civil society and strengthen efforts to reform laws on women's rights?

I conclude the book by discussing the degree to which my conclusions can be generalized for the study of women and politics within Latin America and in comparison with other regions. I argue that the study of feminist policymaking in Chile challenges existing theories on women and politics, including the implicit assumption in much research that feminists will automatically cooperate to promote feminist policy. The relationship among feminists within various sectors of the government merits examination not only across Latin America, where conflicts between executives and legislatures have a long history, but in advanced industrial nations as well. I conclude that Latin American cases like Chile thus function both as critical case studies (George 1979; Ragin and Zaret 1983) for theories developed in advanced industrial countries and as theory-generating cases that contribute to our global understanding of feminist policymaking.

Most important, by focusing on feminist learning over time, I am able to demonstrate the dynamic nature of feminist policymaking, even within significantly constrained political contexts. By examining the details of the policymaking process itself and comparing the failures and successes in Chile, this work offers new insights for our global understanding of women's political participation and women's rights.

1

THE RULES OF THE GAME:
EXPLAINING FEMINIST POLICY OUTCOMES

> It is far better to see the state as a site of struggle, not lying outside of society and social processes, but on the one hand, having a degree of autonomy from these which varies under particular circumstances, and, on the other, being permeated by them. Gender inequalities are therefore buried within the state, but through part of the same dynamic process, gender relations are also partly constituted through the state.
> —Waylen 1996b, 15, citing Pringle and Watson 1992

To explore the question of how feminists in Chile learned to strategize politically to promote women's rights within the state, we must consider a wide range of political factors that affect their ability to influence state policy. While every case study presents a unique set of opportunities and obstacles for policy reform, comparative research has identified a number of conditions that are likely to play a role in creating an auspicious context for feminist policymaking.

Any attempt to understand the determinants of feminist policy change must confront two sets of challenges. The first involves the highly dynamic nature of the policy process itself. Multiple actors inside and outside the state attempt to influence the policymaking process, and the strength of these actors varies across cases. Within a given country, the shifting strength of different political parties, as well as the larger stability of government institutions, fundamentally shapes the opportunities for policy change. Within this context, critical actors are more or less successful in their ability to exploit available political opportunities. More complicated still is the fact that political opportunities shift within countries, not only over time but across policy areas. Effective political strategies may not be transferable from one policy area to the next. Finally, past success or failure will affect future strategy decisions, creating a policy context that is constantly in flux.

A second series of challenges emerges from the subjective perceptions of the political actors themselves. Particularly in an area such as women's rights, which arouses strong passions among proponents and opponents, actors' evaluation of their effectiveness in influencing policy shapes their future willingness to participate in the policy process. How do feminists within and outside the state define successful policy reform? What were their original expectations for change in a given case? Did their participation leave them more or less confident about their ability to shape government policy? What role do political leaders play in shaping expectations for reform?

Before an issue can be seen as a legitimate domain for public policy, it must first be seen as a political issue. Organized women in civil society are most often responsible for the politicization of women's rights issues. The policy impact of women's movements, and feminist movements in particular, makes a logical starting point for any analysis of feminist policymaking. But the larger political context in which these movements operate shapes movement strategies and the possibilities for policy reform. Within the state, research from cases across the globe identifies several institutional factors that enhance the prospects for feminist policy reform. The existence of an executive agency specifically focused on women's rights can significantly broaden the opportunities for feminists to influence state policy, although the influence of these agencies varies widely across cases. In addition, the strength of the political Left within the government is often key, although the Left is not monolithic in its support for women's rights. Many proponents of women's rights assume that increasing the number of women in office will increase government attention to women's rights, but as more women from across the political spectrum win election, one cannot assume their support for feminist proposals. To these institutional components I add the importance of balance of power among branches of government, which often determines the origin and trajectory of proposals for reform, as well as the degree of policy cooperation within the government. Outside the state, feminists battle with opposition to women's rights from powerful cultural forces like religious institutions. These struggles are influenced by, and in turn influence, larger patterns in public opinion on women's rights.

This chapter evaluates the importance of each of these factors for feminist policymaking. Of crucial importance are not only the "inherent" powers of each actor or institution but their power in relation to other actors interested in shaping the policy process. The interaction of these factors, and the individual strategies of the actors involved, determines the political opportunities for feminist policy reform.

The Impact of Feminist Movements

How critical is a mobilized, politically engaged feminist movement for successful policymaking on women's rights? Earlier research on Latin America identified women's movements as key players in the struggles for democracy across the region (e.g., Alvarez 1990; Frohmann and Valdés 1993; Dandavati 1996; Jaquette 1994). Organized feminists in particular were able to translate women's political momentum into influence over the political programs of new democratic governments. But more recent work laments the apparent dissolution of feminist movements in the wake of the return to democracy. Can significant policy reform take place in the absence of a mobilized feminist constituency?

Defining Influence

A broad range of comparative literature on women and politics concludes that an active women's movement, and specifically a feminist movement, is a critical force for policy change (e.g., Conway, Steuernagel, and Ahern 1995; Banaszak 1996; Bashevkin 1996; Bergqvist et al. 1999; Bystydzienski and Sekhon 1999; Caul 1999; Costain 1992; Disney and Gelb 2000; Ferree and Martin 1995; Freeman 1975; Gardiner 1997; Murphy 1997; Simon and Danziger 1991; Stetson 1995; Stetson and McBride 1995, 2000; Turshen and Holcomb 1993). This general conclusion holds true across geographic region and level of development, although the degree of movement influence varies widely across cases. The bulk of research examining the impact of feminist movements on public policy comes from the advanced industrial democracies, where the longer period of unbroken democratic governance has facilitated the development and political participation of an organized civil society.[1]

---

1. The bulk of studies on gender and policymaking in Europe focus on the gendered character of the region's welfare states. Work such as Hobson and Takahashi 1997; Huber and Stephens 2000; Lewis and Astrom 1992; Mazur 2002; O'Connor 1993, 1996; Orloff 1993, 1996; O'Connor, Orloff, and Shaver 1999; and Sainsbury 1994, 1999 address a range of questions regarding the influence of women's movements on the development of the welfare states and on the gendered effects of welfare state policies.

Whether the focus is a national government or a supranational organization such as the European Union, this literature is replete with examples of movement influence over policy. For example, Hoskyns (1996a) examines the role of European women's movements in influencing EU policy on employment. She finds that while the complexity of the EU bureaucracy, with its multiple points of entry and negotiation, complicates women's activism, movement activity has been critical to the EU response on women's rights issues: "Activism outside the EU, and not specifically directed at it, has been at least as important in effecting change as anything done from inside" (22). In political systems as dissimilar as the United States and Sweden, Elman (1996) found that pressure from women's movements was the key to government action on domestic violence. Similarly, Geller-Schwartz (1995) concludes that the most successful feminist policy formation by Canada's Council on the Status of Women followed focused political pressure by feminist organizations.

The participation of feminist movements in democratic politics is a more recent phenomenon in Latin America, where in many countries women organized politically in the 1970s in response to authoritarian rule. This political context influenced the major focus for feminists in those countries, as well as the way in which those issues were framed. In Latin America, women's movements argued for a return to democracy and a respect for human rights, and also for "democracy in the home."[2] This connection between women's rights and the larger political context was most explicit in the decision to link the violation of human rights under the dictatorships to the violence women suffered in the home. In Argentina, Brazil, Uruguay, and Chile, domestic violence became the first major policy issue that feminist movements pursued following the transition to democracy.

In the decades since the democratic transitions in Latin America, a wealth of research has developed on the women's movements that emerged under authoritarian rule and their attempts to engage politically with the new democratic governments (Alvarez 1990; Craske 1999; Dore 1996; Escobar and Alvarez 1992; Franceschet 2005; Jaquette 1994; Staudt 1997, 1998; Waylen 1996a, 2000). Like the movement literature from the advanced industrial nations, research on Latin American women's movements emphasizes the historical context in which the movements emerged, the particular

---

2. "Democracy in the country and in the home" became a rallying cry of the Chilean women's movement (see Frohmann and Valdés 1993).

catalysts that politicized women in each country, the variety of perspectives of movement members, and the priority issues in each case. While this research is not uniformly optimistic about the openness of democratic governments to organized feminist interests, it does conclude that under specific circumstances feminist movements can exert a profound influence on politics (see, e.g., Dore 1996; Fitzsimmons 2000; Stephen 1997; and Wieringa 1996).

Across Latin American cases, one of the most noteworthy victories for feminist movements was the creation of national-level ministries devoted to women's rights.[3] In addition, feminists throughout the region have organized around a wide range of policy issues, from sexual assault to educational reform. Alvarez's (1990) seminal research on the Brazilian women's movement credits movement activism with the creation of federal and state agencies for women's rights as well as policy reforms on issues like domestic violence and sexual assault. More recent work by Blofield (2006) and others investigates the combination of factors, including media access and links to political parties, that have allowed feminists in countries like Argentina to push for policy reform even on the most contentious issues, such as abortion.

In her cross-national study on domestic violence policy, Weldon (2002) goes so far as to argue that the strength of an autonomous women's movement is the most important factor in state adoption of feminist policy.[4] Yet despite the consensus of this literature, the tremendous cross-national variation in both movement strategy and state response poses a challenge to the search for theories on the policy impact of movement activism that can be generalized to other cases. The central question becomes not whether but under what conditions feminist movements will have an impact of policymaking. In order to answer this question, we must first examine the very notion of "influence."

Costain (1998), Feree and Martin (1995), and Weldon (2002) are among those who argue for an expansive definition of influence (see also Brownmiller 1975; Elman 1996; and MacKinnon 1989). Such work contends that, just as a women's movement cannot be reduced to the professional feminist organizations that may dominate policy debates on women's rights, policy

---

3. See, for example, Alvarez 1990 on the Brazilian case, Richards 2004 and Waylen 1996a on Chile, and Francescet 2003 on Argentina.
4. Weldon focuses only on government policy that addresses violence against women. Although she does not include posttransition Latin American democracies in her study, these Latin American cases do bolster her central argument that women's movements have influenced government policy on domestic violence.

influence cannot be reduced to a direct hand in the drafting of legislation. Weldon in particular emphasizes that the very emergence of feminist issues for public debate begins with women's movements, and that much of their ultimate influence rests on their impact on public opinion, the shaping of political discourse, and the politicization of women's rights issues. In her comparative examination of domestic violence policy, Weldon argues that if we focus only on a much later moment in the process—the drafting of policy proposals—we miss much of the influence that women's movements bring. "Feminist activists are responsible for developing the very concept of violence against women, and it is hard to imagine the issue framed as a public one before the women's movement transformed public discussion of what had previously been seen as a private matter" (2002, 64–65).

One can easily concur with Weldon that women's movements are a "necessary condition for the articulation" (61) of women's rights issues as political issues, and nevertheless acknowledge that such a broad definition of influence makes comparative measurement and analysis of feminist policy influence extremely challenging. Cultural differences across countries (and even across particular policy areas), the evolution of public opinion, and shifting political opportunities for movement activism are long-term, multicausal factors that are difficult to quantify and compare across cases. Ríos Tobar (2003), for example, notes that feminism seems to be gaining cultural and political influence in Chile at the same time that the feminist movement has become less visible. Htun (2002) finds that a number of progressive policies on women's rights have emerged in Brazil despite the strikingly low representation of women in Congress. Influence also varies across policy area (see Stetson and Mazur 2000), and even within policy areas over time, as I find in the case of Chile. Finally, much of the movement's cultural or political impact may not be apparent for many years. While it is clear that feminist movements may have a significant impact, once the definition of influence expands to encompass diffuse and largely immeasurable concepts like shaping discourse or raising awareness, it becomes impossible to assess comparatively the movement's actual policy effect.

Further complicating this task is the fact that the entire terrain of feminism is currently undergoing dramatic evolution. The diversification of feminist organizations within the context of globalization and transnationalism makes the very definition of "feminist movement" increasingly problematic. Alvarez (1998, 295) argues that Latin American feminism (reflecting global trends) has become an "expansive, polycentric and heterogeneous field of action that spans into a vast array of cultural, social, and political arenas." In her analysis of Chilean feminism, Ríos Tobar concludes that the multiplication and "diversification" of issues have led to an increase in the number of women mobilizing along feminist lines, but that at the same time a common focus has given way to an explosion of groups organizing around narrowly specific issues. Ríos Tobar explains that women increasingly balance multiple political identities, of which gender is only one. She concludes that the result of these trends is to question "the very notion of a unified feminist subject, and with that, the possibility of concerted political actions. . . . While the growing plurality and heterogeneity sets the stage for greater participation of women who traditionally had not mobilized around a gender identity, it also causes fragmentation and a lack of articulation among feminists" (2003, 266–67).

While acknowledging the importance of the broad cultural impact of feminism, which ultimately affects public opinion and political discourse on women's rights, my research employs a narrower definition of influence. I examine direct involvement in the policy process, ranging from protest and other extragovernmental activities focused on a particular policy issue to direct participation in the drafting of legislation and lobbying for it.

In this way my work draws on earlier research by Stetson and Mazur (2000, building on Gamson 1975), who argue that researchers need to consider the impact of women's movements in general, and feminist movements in particular, in three interrelated areas: agenda setting (problem framing and definition), the accessibility of the policymaking process, and the content of resulting policies. Results may include "substantive responses" (i.e., changes in policy in response to movement demands) and/or "procedural acceptance" (i.e., whether the state accepts women's organizations as legitimate players in the policymaking process). Stetson and Mazur explain that this latter requirement includes increasing the descriptive representation of women in the policymaking arena, not simply allowing women's organizations access to the process.[5]

Engagement with the State

Within this narrower definition of influence, we need to consider the actual dynamics that govern movement participation in politics. When we move

---

5. Stetson and Mazur consider four possible outcomes for a given case: (1) dual response (the state accepts individual women or groups into the process and changes policy); (2) co-optation (the state accepts groups into the policymaking process but doesn't not alter policy itself); (3) preemption (policy satisfaction without group representation); and (4) no response.

from a focus on general and indirect policy influence to consider the direct impact of feminist groups on policy development, a more complicated, and less optimistic, picture of feminist influence emerges. A number of factors internal to the movements affect their orientation toward formal political participation. To begin with, there is a range of opinion on the merits of engagement with formal politics. Second, groups that want to participate in the policy process are often unable to do so successfully. Effective political participation depends in part on the particular resources and expertise of the groups themselves, but also on the institutional structure of the state, which largely determines how much access is granted to outside groups.

Feminist movements in most countries have struggled with whether, and how, to engage with the state. "Autonomous" groups prioritize independence from government control, but usually at the cost of political influence. On the other hand, feminist groups that work too closely with the state, by joining political parties, unions, or the bureaucracy, or even by accepting government subsidies to assist with policy development, risk government cooptation of the feminist agenda. A strictly autonomous stance is not the norm for feminist organizations, whether in Europe, North America, or Latin America.[6] However, independence from government cooptation remains a concern across regions, and research is divided on the influence independent feminist groups exert on the policy process.

In examining the debate over strategy in advanced industrialized countries, Stetson and Mazur conclude that in "high state feminist" countries, women were active participants in outside feminist groups as well as in established trade unions and parties. Furthermore,

> women were equally attracted to newer autonomous women's liberal movements and to the mainstream political and moderate reform-oriented groups they eschewed. While the radical feminist groups concentrated on consciousness-raising among women at the grass-roots level and thrust gender-based discrimination on to the public agenda, the moderate feminist groups directly pressured political party elites and politicians to establish and operate feminist women's policy machinery. Thus, even though the two groups were often in conflict, their combined influence set the stage for more effective state feminist offices. (1995, 290–91)

---

6. In Chile the autonomous wing of the movement was particularly strong, and it undercut the overall impact of the broader feminist community. See chapter 2.

Other work confirms the complicated balance between independence and engagement with the state while presenting a less sanguine picture of the relationship between feminists inside and outside government. Gelb and Palley (1996) find that disruptive, protest-oriented strategies hurt the negotiating efforts of feminists inside the state. Conversely, Christensen (1999) uses the case of Denmark to argue that the incorporation of women into the state undermines the movement outside. Christensen explains that when Danish parties created women's organizations in the 1960s, the larger autonomous movement "dissipated." When the parties closed these organizations in the 1970s, the movement was revitalized (Kaplan 1992; Weldon 2002).

Comparative research has also raised concerns that the political orientation of women who choose to work within the state may in some cases cause further conflict with the feminist base. Hoskyns (1996a) argues that policymaking within the EU is controlled by neoliberals, who are unable to respond to critiques by feminists (or by regionalists, environmentalists, and so on). She concludes that a "dissonance" has developed between "Eurocrats" and political activists, which has in turn deepened divisions within the European women's movement. Given the neoliberal orientation of the EU, Hoskyns argues that state policies have benefited mostly educated middle-class white women. This has undercut cross-class coalitions among feminist women and weakened the class solidarity of middle-class feminists (21).[7]

Researchers like Banaszak (1996), by contrast, contend that working within the state need not lead to a moderation of the movement's agenda. Drawing on Freeman's (1975) work on the U.S. women's movement, Banaszak concludes that when feminists working in the state "perceived that opportunities within the state were closed, they were equally willing to take to the streets. Moreover, some of the actions that occurred within the air-conditioned halls of government were by no means moderate" (31). Banaszak stresses the "overlapping" nature and composition of feminist groups inside and outside the state and the often dynamic interaction between them. She concurs with Freeman (1975, 230) that "there is clearly a symbiotic relationship between feminists within our government institutions, feminists operating in the private sphere, and even feminists who are openly opposed to and/or alienated from the American political system." In a similar vein, Mackay's (1996) work on the Zero Tolerance Campaign in Scotland demonstrates that

---

7. Such work seems to bolster earlier theories of social movement activism (such as Piven and Cloward 1993), suggesting that a movement cannot expend resources building formal organizational structures without undermining its ability to serve as a vehicle for protest.

it is possible for activists to engage with the state without compromising the movement's policy goals. Mackay explains that Scottish activists and feminists within local government were able to agree on a broad, radical definition of violence against women and to coordinate their actions in support of legal reform on the issue.[8]

Feminist concerns about state cooptation of the feminist policy agenda have taken on greater weight as the terrain in which feminist organizations try to influence government policy has shifted in favor of "professional" feminist organizations and NGOs. This shift has been particularly dramatic in Latin America, where transitions to democracy in the 1980s, combined with the UN's focus on gender, created an unprecedented opportunity for feminists to participate in politics. Alvarez (1998, 153) coined this process the "NGOization" of the women's movement, and its effect on the orientation, strategies, and self-definition of the feminist movement in that region has been profound. Ríos Tobar explains, "These processes have forced Latin American feminists not only to modify the practices that they had originally developed to confront a hostile authoritarian context, but also to professionalize their activities and organizations and develop specialisms. Hence, the politics of confrontation have been transformed into the politics of negotiation, requiring intricate knowledge of policy making processes. . . . The script for interaction has changed, and in the process pushed those involved to change their strategies to secure influence in the future" (2003, 259).

Not surprisingly, this shift has exacerbated tensions within feminist movements. Chinchilla and Haas contend that this "NGOization" has had contradictory effects on Latin American feminism, draining leaders from grassroots organizations and reducing the political influence of the larger movement:

> The visibility and availability of NGO feminists, together with their access to technical expertise and funding, increasingly put them in a position of being the ones consulted by governments and national and international institutions. . . . In the absence of mechanisms of consultation and accountability to respond to the new organizational context, this growing inequality in access to resources and official sites of power and the "crisis" of representation that resulted led to

---

8. See Cichowski's (2000) discussion of this and other European cases.

conflicts about "who speaks for whom" and how democracy and citizenship can be guaranteed among feminists as well as in the society at large. (2006, 268)

Alvarez believes that Latin American feminist NGOs per se do not have to be de-radicalizing or demobilizing to the feminist movement but can form a vital link between the base and policymakers: "Feminist NGOs' political hybridity enabled them to play a critical role in 'advocating feminism' by advancing a progressive gender policy agenda while simultaneously articulating vital political linkages among larger women's movement and civil society constituencies" (1999, 182). She cites the issue-oriented "advocacy networks" that proliferated in Latin America in the 1990s as an example of such hybrid organizations, in that they focused both on lobbying governments and on grassroots mobilization. She warns, however, that when feminist NGOs become too narrowly focused and cut off from the base, they can become the "vehicle of choice" for nonradical government gender policies and can thereby undermine the larger goals of the feminist movement.

It is thus necessary to identify contexts that bolster this type of advocacy, as opposed to factors that encourage feminist NGOs to "de-hybridize" their identities and strategies. Alvarez concludes that states narrow the scope of NGOs' work and undermine their linkages with the feminist base in three primary ways: governments tend to treat NGOs as "gender experts," limiting their political participation to largely technical policy advice; they assume that NGOs are "surrogates for civil society"; and they subcontract with feminist NGOs to carry out government women's programs, which undermines NGOs' ability to criticize government policy and advocate for more sweeping reforms. Franceschet (2005) argues that in Chile closer alliance between feminist NGOs and the state has meant less independence from the state when debating policy issues.

In addition to the orientation of women's movements toward the state, analyses of feminist policy development must consider how the structure of the state itself shapes access and determines the type of outside engagement that is possible. Across a range of issues, scholars have considered the degree of access different states allow outside actors, as well as how engagement with the state alters the policy agenda of the movements themselves.[9] For example, Stetson and Mazur (2000) analyze the interaction of the state and

---

9. Influential work in this area includes McAdam, McCarthy, and Zald 1996 and Tilly 1985.

the women's movement in the United States and France and find the United States a more "hospitable environment" for feminist policymaking because the relatively decentralized policy process there allows the large and well-organized women's movement to explore multiple points of access and influence.[10] By contrast, France's smaller and more autonomous women's movement must confront a more centralized state with a less open policy process.

Ríos Tobar concludes that the "form and effect" of movement impact depend in large part "on the state's capacity and will to repress dissident groups; institutional norms and procedures that regulate the emergence of social organizations; specific policies aimed at civil society; symbolic referents and discourses constructed by public institutions; the legitimacy of non-institutional actors to represent their interests; as well as strategies for inclusion or exclusion of certain issues and actors from public debates." She asserts that "the question is not whether the state intervenes directly in the organization of civil society, but what role it plays in establishing the rules that condition political life" (2003, 261). Franceschet (2003) argues that state structure plays a critical role in determining the net effect of transnational activism within a particular country. Where a well-organized and well-funded feminist movement exists, and where political institutions are responsive to pressure from outside groups, the creation of global agreements on women's rights can spur national governments to make needed reforms. Small and resource-poor groups, however, and organizations in less democratic institutional settings, may find that their participation in transnational conferences leaves them on the sidelines of relevant domestic debates.

In sum, feminist activism operates within a highly complex and constantly evolving political and cultural terrain. Movement activism may provoke state response, but this response will in turn affect internal movement dynamics and shape future political strategies. As Banaszak, Beckwith, and Rucht explain,

> The formation, modification, or elimination of particular public policies changes the organization of government, moves people in and out of institutions, and creates a web of operating rules and norms that determine the functioning of the state. These type of changes, whether

---

10. Comparative research suggests that decentralization poses advantages and disadvantages for women's activism: it allows potentially greater access to the state, but that access is complicated by multiple points of entry and negotiation.

profound or minute, sometimes even in areas far removed from the social movement's focus, may alter the movement-state intersection by changing the supply of movement activists interested in positions within the state or by altering the demand of the state for movement activists. (2003, 33–34)

Opportunities and Obstacles Within the State

If feminists are to influence policy, the state not only must be accessible to outside feminist organizations but must be open to discussion and debate on women's rights issues. The permeability of the state with respect to feminist issues depends on several factors, not least the existence of a state agency specifically designed to monitor women's rights. In addition, the number of women elected or appointed to office, the strength of the Left within the Congress and the executive branch, and the institutional balance of power between branches of government are critical factors in creating opportunities for feminist policymaking.

Women's Policy Machinery

Arguably, the most obvious sign of institutional openness to feminist policymaking is the existence of an executive agency for women's rights. Situating a permanent institution within the state to monitor and promote women's rights creates enormous potential to increase gender equality, most obviously in the area of policy reform. Such "women's policy machinery" may take many forms, and its effectiveness will depend on its internal structure, including its ideological composition, its level of independence (particularly budgetary), its relationship with the rest of the bureaucracy and with the legislature, and the level of access it grants to outside groups. Women's policy machinery (WPM) exists throughout Europe, Canada, and Australia, as well as in much of Latin America. Feminist policy research from across these regions is focusing increased attention on the role that executive-level agencies devoted to monitoring women's rights may play in affecting government policy.

A central conclusion of the research from postindustrial countries (e.g., Bacchi 1996; Elman 1996; Gardiner 1997; Mazur 1995, 2002; Sawer 1995; Stetson and Mazur 1995, 2000; and Valiente 1995) is that without a specific agency devoted to monitoring women's rights at the national level, government policy tends to address gender only in areas such as employment and family leave, usually as a side note to policies developed without a gender focus and, most important, without a broader, integrated vision of women's rights in mind. For example, work by Polakow (1993) and Vogel (1993) on employment and maternity policy in the Unites States focuses on the enormous implications of child- or family-centered versus woman-centered policy, and on the social and economic consequences of government failure to provide adequate social welfare support to women. In her review of research on maternity policy in the United States, Chapman (1997) quotes Polakow's conclusion that U.S. policy worsens poverty among single mothers by promoting "an economy that relegates many women to the status of second-class, secondary-sector workers," and then fails to provide "family support systems such as exist in every other major industrialized democracy: guaranteed maternity leave; universal health care; affordable, safe, subsidized housing; a universal child allowance; and fully subsidized, high-quality care" (97).

Well-functioning WPM can help ensure that government policies across issue areas consider both the gendered dynamics of socioeconomic problems and the gendered impact of potential government policy solutions. At the same time, a key challenge in the creation of executive-level WPM is to link the institution to other relevant government agencies. Otherwise, such agencies can become ghettoized within the government, without influence or input into policies that are seen as the domain of other ministries (such as education, health, or labor). Furthermore, while such agencies can help monitor and promote women's rights from within the state, conservative governments can also co-opt these agencies and make them blocking agents for progressive policies initiated by other government agencies or outside groups.[11]

Stetson and Mazur (1995, 2000) have undertaken the most systematic attempts to date to evaluate the effect of WPM on policy outcomes. They conclude that "strong movement action does not necessarily lead to a strong state response in the absence of intervention by women's policy machineries." But WPM influence depends in turn on the leadership within the ministry, the relationship WPM forms with the women's movement, and the

---

11. The possibility of this latter scenario is a focus of Valiente's (1995) research on the Women's Institute in Spain.

strength of the Left within the government (2000, 598).[12] Stetson and Mazur demonstrate that WPM has, in some countries, "taken up certain demands from second-wave feminism in policy proposals and brought feminist activists into the state, as staff members, sectoral representatives, and individual experts" (600). These feminists can form a critical link between the state and feminists in civil society. Stetson and Mazur (1995) conclude that the most effective feminist policymaking takes place where the relevant WPM has policy influence over the government, and where the structure of the agency allows for policy access by feminist groups.

Stetson and Mazur's 1995 study found the most successful WPM in Australia's Office on the Status of Women (OSW), the Netherlands' Department for the Coordination of Equality Policy, and the Equal Status Councils in Norway and Denmark. All four were created by Social Democratic governments, together with pressure from each country's women's movement. In each case WPM was well integrated into the bureaucracy and had strong links to other agencies, which facilitated the coordination of feminist policy development across a number of government sectors. By contrast, in the less successful cases of Ireland, France, and Spain, left-wing governments created the WPM, but there was little outside pressure from the women's movement. Furthermore, the WPM in these cases was not set up to coordinate policy effectively with other government agencies. In Canada and Germany feminist pressure from outside the state is strong, but the WPM itself has little influence within the government. The decentralization of both political systems complicates coordination among WPM, the women's movement, and the rest of the government. Finally, in Italy, movement pressure was almost nonexistent, and Socialists were a minor player within a Center-Right governing coalition.[13]

---

12. Stetson and Mazur analyze the cases along two dimensions: whether the agency advocates feminist goals on the issue, and whether it is effective in changing "the frame of the policy debate to reflect these feminist goals" (2000, 602). The result is four categories: (1) "insider," where both conditions are met; (2) "marginal," where the agency asserts the goals of the women's movement but is unsuccessful in gendering public debate; (3) "nonfeminist," where the agency is not an advocate for feminist goals but does insert other gendered terms into the policy definitions of the issue; and (4) "symbolic," in which neither condition is met. The authors conclude that "insider" agencies consistently lead to a strong state response, that "marginal" and "nonfeminist" agencies lead to inconsistent and weak state response, and that "symbolic" agencies provoke no state response (600–602).

13. For more detail on the most successful cases, see Sawer 1995 and Sawer and Groves 1994 on Australia; Outshoorn 1995 on the Netherlands; and Bystydzienski 1992, 1995 and Borchorst 1994, 1999 on Norway.

Across cases, even the most successful WPM has struggled to build a strong working relationship with feminists in civil society. For example, Sawer's 1995 work on the Australian OSW argues that feminists outside the state often misunderstood the constraints faced by "femocrats" within the government, including their need to forge alliances and to make compromises on policy, and that members of the movement often blamed the feminists within the state for weak government policy. Sawer explains that femocrats are often unable to publicize details of the policymaking process that would help clarify their role in pushing for feminist policy. "Femocrats may be blamed for government policies they have been powerless to change and miss out on credit for policies that are changed. They may be attacked for decisions that are, in fact, least-worst outcomes. . . . Those inside often felt aggrieved by the lack of understanding and support from those outside, particularly as they themselves were constantly under suspicion from the rest of the bureaucracy because of their assumed closeness to the women's movement" (34–35). Over time, as feminists outside the state reevaluated their expectations of the political process, and feminists within the state became more accessible to the women's movement, the relationship between the Australian women's movement and the OSW improved significantly, to the point that Stetson and Mazur (1995) classify it as a case of "high state feminism." In Latin America as well, feminists have struggled to build cooperative relationships with the WPM created to advocate for them (Craske 1999; Friedman 2000; Franceschet 2003; Haas 2000; Htun 1998; Waylen 1996b).

In Latin America, a number of countries have created WPM over the past two decades, and a burgeoning literature examines their effectiveness (e.g., Alvarez 1990; Baldez 2001; Blofield and Haas 2005; Chinchilla and Haas 2006; Franceschet 2005; Friedman 2000; Jaquette 1994; Randall and Waylen 1998; Richards 2004). While the policy impact of these agencies varies widely across the region, Latin American WPM faces challenges. Cultural and political opposition to WPM agencies remains higher in Latin America than in the advanced industrialized democracies. The political reticence in addressing feminist issues is compounded by larger problems of institutional instability in some countries, as well as by ongoing economic crises, which lower the priority of women's rights for the government.

To a greater degree than in the postindustrial democracies of Europe, Canada, and Australia, the legitimacy of WPM is still subject to much debate in Latin America. The ambivalence toward WPM agencies, particularly by political conservatives, is reflected in the varying degrees to which WPM exists in the form of independent agencies that can focus solely on women's rights. Some agencies are independent ministries, such as the National Council of Women's Rights in Brazil, Venezuela's National Council for Women, and Costa Rica's National Women's Institute. Elsewhere the agencies fall under the jurisdiction of other executive ministries. This is the case with Chile's Sernam, which falls under the jurisdiction of the Ministry for Cooperation and Planning. Other examples include Bolivia's Subsecretary for Gender (under the National Secretariat for Indigenous Issues, Gender, and Generations),[14] Nicaragua's Women's Institute (under the Office of the President), and Colombia's Council for Youth, Women, and the Family (under the Office of the President). Where women's agencies are subject to the direction of other agencies, their ability to promote women's rights within the government is limited. Yet independent agencies, like Chile's Sernam, are considered low-status ministries (with correspondingly small budgets), and they struggle to legitimate the theme of women's rights to the rest of the bureaucracy. As indicated by the titles of some agencies, in a number of cases women's rights agencies are combined with ministries or subministries that focus on children and the family. Where this is the case, it is logically more difficult for government officials to promote policies that expand women's equality outside their traditional roles within the family.

In federal systems, agencies may exist at both the national and state levels, as is the case in Argentina and was for a time the case in Brazil (the National Women's Rights Council has been disbanded, but a similar council continues to exist at the state level). In Uruguay and Peru national women's ministries survived only a few years in the 1990s, before being abolished following a transition to more conservative government.

In Latin America the advantages of having a powerful executive agency pursue women's rights initiatives are counterbalanced by the potential dangers such agencies pose if changes in government administration lead to the restaffing of an agency with nonfeminists. In both Argentina and Venezuela strong executives were able to promote women's rights through the national women's agencies, often over the heads of a reluctant Congress. In the Venezuelan case, Friedman (2000, 73) argues that "the fate of the [women's] agency [is] largely dictated by the will of the president." In recent years, however, Argentina's Council for Women's Rights has been plagued by difficulties and is largely inactive at present. The executive power of Chile's

---

14. Bolivia's ministry was abolished after the election of Evo Morales in 2005.

Sernam helped it push through legislation that had previously been introduced by feminist representatives but had died in committee. At the same time, the agency clashed with feminists in Congress, who advocated a more expansive policy agenda. When women's rights issues are habitually pursued through the executive branch, other potential avenues of feminist policy influence, most notably the legislature, tend to be closed off. In Uruguay and Peru, for instance, the closing of the national agencies left feminists without open access to the political system.

In keeping with the conclusions of the European literature, leadership is a key factor in Latin American cases, as is the overall ideological orientation of the agencies (Baldez 2001; Franceschet 2005; Haas 2000). Latin American WPM has also tended to be able to take on a more ambitious agenda when the Left has been more influential within the government overall. For example, Baldez (2001) explains that in Spain, long-term government control by the Socialist Worker's Party led to an effective working relationship with the Women's Institute (see also Valiente 1995). It is therefore important to examine the overall role of parties and political ideology in enhancing the visibility of feminist policy issues.

Political Parties and Ideology

Adoption by the political parties of a feminist policy agenda is a critical requirement for sustained political attention to women's rights. Research is unanimous in its conclusion that, across electoral and institutional systems, the political Left is a more hospitable political environment for feminists (Bacchi 1996; Beckwith 1992; Ellickson and Whistler 2000; Elman 1996; Lovenduski and Norris 1993; Rozell 2000). However, analysts disagree on the degree of natural affinity between feminism and the Left and on the ease with which leftist parties agree to adopt feminist policy positions. Huber and Stephens (2000) and Pierson (2000) argue that women's rights issues in western European democracies have consistently been promoted and supported by Social Democratic parties and organized labor. Similarly, Norris's (1997) comparative examination of the effect of increasing numbers of women in European parliaments finds that party ideology was the major determinant in the approval of gender quotas for women's representation, with disproportionate support from leftist parties.

Yet while the Left appears more open ideologically to women's rights issues than the Right, the relationship between feminists and the Left is neither simple nor straightforward. Case studies from Europe as well as Latin America find that gender issues provoke strong internal disagreement within left-leaning parties and organized labor. Traditional leftist parties, like unions, have historically harbored traditional views on women and have prioritized issues of class over gender inequality. Elman (1996) contends that even as the Left appears more open than other political groups to women's participation, parties on the left still work to control the activism of women members. Hoskyns finds that conflict between trade unions and the women's movement in the EU weakened both movements (1996a, 18). She argues that economic hard times make policymakers less amenable to feminist policy proposals, such as calls for equal pay or day care. Haas (2001) argues that feminists within Brazil's Workers Party engaged in intense struggle with other party members over the party's position on women's rights issues.[15] Nevertheless, the Left historically has encouraged women's political participation. This has given women the opportunity to agitate for change from within the political parties. Much of the openness to women's rights we see globally on the political left is the result of intense work by feminist party members to force incorporation of these issues into party platforms.

Other research distinguishes between "traditional," or Old Left, parties, which are not consistently supportive, and the New Left parties that have emerged as the primary focal point for women's political advancement. Caul's (1999) quantitative study of party representation finds that the "New Left," in particular, is an important variable in women's parliamentary representation. Drawing on Ingelhart (1997), Caul argues that the New Left's "postindustrial" issues distinguish it both from the Right and from traditional leftist parties and unions. Additionally, New Left parties lack the "entrenched hierarchies" of the Old Left, and this facilitates women's advancement.

Latin American cases confirm that women's primary access to the system comes through the parties of the Left, particularly the newer, more eclectic leftist parties that have emerged in many countries since the transitions to democracy (see Alvarez 1990; Blofield and Haas 2005; Haas 1999, 2001; Jaquette 1994; Waylen 1996a). Yet here, too, feminists struggle even within New Left parties to force the adoption of feminist policy concerns.

Eventual support for feminist policy depends on the successful negotiation of these issues by feminist activists within the parties and unions, bolstered by outside pressure from the women's movement. Comparative

---

15. See Weldon 2002 for a broad review of this literature.

research (such as Matland and Studlar 1996) concurs that political parties focus on women's rights largely in response to pressure from women activists within the parties. Caul (1999, 2001) similarly finds the presence of women activists a direct positive influence on party willingness to promote female candidates and to support women's rights issues.

If parties respond to pressure from women members, this leads naturally to a consideration of the effect increasing numbers of elected women may have on policy, both within political parties and within legislatures at large. How easily do women win elective office across political systems? And what difference do they make once in office?

How Many Women Does It Take to Influence Policy? Quotas and the Impact of Women in Office

Throughout Latin America, women struggle within conservative cultures to gain leadership positions within political parties and to be promoted as candidates. Across the region, women's legislative representation remains extremely low. Comparative work on women's representation demonstrates that women have the greatest success in gaining office in party-list proportional representation systems (Caul 1999, 2001; Jones 1998, 2004; LeDuc, Neimi, and Norris 1996; Norris and Lovenduski 1994; Matland and Taylor 1997; Rule and Zimmerman 1994). Yet even in the most auspicious institutional settings, male party members have used a variety of tactics to avoid promoting women candidates, including the placement of women in low-level (unelectable) positions on party lists, withholding funding for women's campaigns, and blocking access to party leadership positions.

In the belief that more women in office will translate into more government attention to women's rights, feminists in many parts of the world have successfully pressured democratic governments to institute quotas for women's representation. In most cases these quotas mandate that a certain percentage of candidates for legislative office from each political party must be women. A wealth of comparative research now confirms that quota laws, when properly designed and implemented, have a positive impact on women's representation in both advanced industrial and developing countries (Bacchi 1996; Bergqvist et al. 1999; Craske 1999; Dahlerup 1988; Hofmann 1994; Jones and Navia 1999; Leijenaar 1997; Matland 1998; Matland and Taylor 1997; Peters 1999). For example, Kolinsky (1991, 1993) and Lang (1989) conclude that women's representation in the German Bundestag increased dramatically following the adoption of quotas in the 1980s.[16] Guadagnini (1995) finds a similar positive impact in the Italian case, and Bystydzienski finds further confirmation in the case of Norway (1992, 1995). Quantitative cross-national analyses of the effects of gender quotas, such as Caul 2001, Jones and Navia 1999, Matland 1998, Peters 1999, and Rule 1987, strengthen these conclusions by showing the positive effects of quotas across a wide variety of industrialized countries and, in the case of Matland 1998, across both developed and developing nations.

Across electoral systems in Latin America, women's representation remains extremely low (Craske 1999; Diaz 1995; Haas 2001; Matland and Taylor 1997; Randall and Waylen 1998). In response, feminist representatives have pushed for minimum quotas for women's representation. Over the past decade, half of Latin American countries have established some form of so-called gender quotas for elected offices.[17] A notable success story is Argentina, where feminist pressure resulted in the region's first adoption of national-level quotas, in 1993, which have strengthened women's legislative representation (see Htun and Jones 2002; Jones 1996, 1998). Costa Rica's gender quotas, instituted in 1997, mandate that 40 percent of candidates on party lists must be women—the highest threshold in the region. This has resulted in a significant increase in the number of women in the legislature (de Figueres 2002). Where national-level quotas are politically or institutionally unfeasible, specific political parties have acceded to women's demand for greater representation by instituting minimum quotas for women candidates. Party-level electoral quotas now exist in Chile, Venezuela, Colombia, Bolivia, and Mexico, and feminists in other countries are pressing for their adoption (see Baldez 2004).

Behind the push for gender quotas lies the assumption that electing more women to public office will make a difference in government policy. In what specific ways are women seen to affect the policy process? Research from the United States, Canada, and western Europe suggests that as the number of women in the legislature increases, governments pay more attention to women's policy demands (e.g., Bystydzienski 1995; Lovenduski and Norris 1993; Matland 1993; Tremblay 1998). Much of this literature focuses on the "interests" of women legislators versus their male counterparts. Bashevkin (1996),

---

16. All German parties except the Christian Democrats currently employ some system of quotas. The most dramatic are found in the SDP, which instituted a 40 percent minimum for female party officers in 1988 and for female candidates in 1998. See also Caul 1999.

17. Eleven Latin American countries have instituted quota laws. Worldwide, fifty nations have done so. See IDEA's international quota database at http://www.quotaproject.org/.

Galligan and Temblay (2005), and Mansbridge (2005) are among the researchers who argue that female legislators pay relatively more attention not only to narrowly defined issues of women's rights but also to issues like education and health, for example, and less to defense. Swers (2002) and Thomas (1994) demonstrate that this distinction manifests itself most clearly on issues that dominate legislators' time (for example, committee choice and sponsorship of legislation), while party affiliation appears to trump gender concerns on simple roll-call votes.

Researchers further suggest that women legislators exert an additional, indirect influence on policy by sensitizing male representatives to women's rights issues. Mansbridge argues that the presence of an underrepresented group sensitizes others to their concerns (2005, 627). She cites evidence that the presence of women legislators leads male legislators to show greater awareness and responsiveness to women's rights issues. Kittilson concurs, citing evidence that women's presence changes focus and policy (2006, 642). Similarly, Wägnerud's (2006) research on Scandinavian legislatures finds that political parties altered their positions in response to the presence of female legislators.[18] Building on Ingelhart and Norris's (2003) claim that cultural change necessarily precedes institutional change, Kittilson further notes that quotas, by raising the number of women in office, encourage cultural change in attitudes about women's leadership—both on the part of male policymakers and in the public at large (the "contagion effect").

Yet the evidence for women's policy impact is both ambiguous and contradictory. Most researchers argue that a "critical mass" (more than 30 percent)[19] of women legislators is necessary to create caucuses or subcommittees that can focus consistent attention on women's rights issues. However, Bratton (2005) finds that in legislatures with fewer women representatives, individual women feel more responsible for promoting women's rights legislation. Bratton theorizes that as the number of women in the legislature increases, individual women representatives feel less personal obligation to prioritize the issue. Indeed, research from Scandinavia, where women achieved significant presence in national legislatures without mandatory quotas, indicates that evidence of gendered policy interests seems to dissipate as a representative's time in office increases (Wägnerud 2006).

---

18. Bratton and Ray (2002) find intriguing evidence in Norway at the municipal level of a correlation between the percentage of women elected to office and the percentage of children in state-funded child-care facilities.

19. For more on the concept and impact of critical mass, see Studlar and McAllistar 2002.

Other works, such as Weldon 2002, argue that assumptions about women's policy preferences rely on essentialized notions of "women's interests," and that women as a group show more variation in political ideology than do women and men within a given political party. Mansbridge (2005) shows particular concern for the tendency of quotas (and, by extension, discussions of why more women need to be in office) to reify socialized gender differences between women and men. She argues that the affinity for certain types of policy flows comes from the personal experience of legislators, not from inherent biological differences between the sexes.

Many of the difficulties in investigating the existence of a gendered set of political interests are due to the imbalance in the number of women elected from different ideological backgrounds. Much of the theoretical and empirical research on women's political behavior predates the widespread use of quotas and concentrates instead on instances where women have gained political office without this institutional help. Globally, as noted above, women have had much more success in gaining political office through the parties of the Left. (Not surprisingly, leftist and left-leaning parties also demonstrate greater openness to gender quotas than other parties do.) As a result, it remains unclear whether female politicians gravitate toward particular policy concerns because of political ideology, gender identity, or some combination of the two. As more conservative women are elected to office, research has begun to focus on women's political diversity and its impact on women's rights policy.

Recent work on political participation and activism by conservative women (such as Bacchetta and Power 2002; Baldez 2002; and González and Kampwirth 2001) confirms women's political complexity and warns against easy assumptions about the effect of women's political presence. Since quotas require all parties to increase the number of women on the ballot, assumptions about women's "natural" policy concerns need to be reexamined across the ideological spectrum. That said, there is evidence that women across parties are generally more interested in "women's issues" (however defined) than are men in their parties. Indeed, some initial research suggests that conservative women may become more open to feminist issues with more time in office. Krook concludes that "sensitizing" doesn't occur only with male colleagues but also with women representatives who do not identify themselves as feminists. "Quota policies in many countries have led to a shift not only in the political agenda but also in the gender consciousness of female representatives and the political engagement of female constituents.

More specifically, a growing amount of evidence suggests that the experience of holding political office exerts transformative effects, both on women who firmly believe that they have never been the victims of sex discrimination and on women who have known nothing else but lives as second-class citizens" (2006, 111). Nevertheless, much more research is needed to untangle the question of how women representatives balance the sometimes competing loyalties of gender, party ideology, and political constituency. As the overall number of women elected to a given legislature increases, political conflict among women, as well as opportunities for cross-party alliances in support of women's rights policies, also increases.

However, the viability of gender quotas as a political issue depends not only on supportive parties but on the institutional structure of the electoral system. While national-level quotas have been successfully implemented in parts of Europe and in a few cases in Latin America, their broader application in Latin America has been limited by both political opposition and institutional structures not conducive to their use. While gender quotas provide one avenue for increasing women's representation, they remain a controversial solution to women's underrepresentation, even among feminists and the parties on the left.[20]

Finally, in addition to questioning the existence of women's inherent policy concerns, we must avoid assuming that women's influence is merely "additive," without regard for the broader context of politics, in which party strength, balance of power, constituency concerns, and electoral competition fundamentally affect how legislators focus their efforts. We must distinguish among the expressed interests of women representatives, the behavior of women in office, and their policy impact. Passion for women's rights issues, without access to key committees, broader party support, or the resources to craft viable legislation, will not result in successful policy. Even where quotas or other strategies have increased the percentage of women running for office, women's participation in Latin American legislatures remains low, as does their access to key positions of influence within national legislatures and political parties.

---

20. Opponents of quotas argue that they are inherently undemocratic, that there are not yet enough qualified women candidates in many countries to fill quota requirements, and that women elected under quota laws will confront charges that they were elected only because of an artificial system of candidate selection.

Outside Pressures on State Policy

Outside the state, the opposition to feminism competes with women's movements for influence over state policy. This opposition is often religious in nature, and in Latin America the Catholic Church represents the strongest organized opponent of feminist policy change. The political power of the church depends on several factors beyond the general religiosity of the population. The institutional power of the church, particularly its formal and informal links to political parties, helps determine the leverage the church is able to exert over the policy process. In the countries of Latin America, where the church has historically played a significant political role, struggles between feminists and church leaders have important consequences for overall public opinion on women's rights issues.

The Role of Religion in Framing Debates on Women's Rights

Comparative research has shown that national culture is an important variable in the political viability of proposals to promote women's equality. Religion, in particular, has played an important role in framing public debate on contentious policy issues. Cultural variations in social norms and traditions are correlated in some ways to the level of industrialization but also vary across nations at similar levels of economic development. In countries where religious institutions have significant political influence, they often serve as obstacles to the reform of laws that affect women's rights.

Compared to the substantial literature on institutional politics, relatively little recent work has been done on the effect of religion on politics in western Europe, although the work that has been done argues forcefully for the continued influence of religion on politics in the region (e.g., Castles 2006; Dogan 1995; Mahon 1996; Mazur 2002; Van Kersbergen 1995).[21] Characteristic of such research are Valiente's 1997 work on Spain and Gardiner and Leijenaar's 1997 analysis of Ireland and the Netherlands, both of which explore the impact of historical and cultural perceptions of women on the implementation of EU equality policy. The Irish case in particular is often noted as an outlier among European countries precisely because of the continued strong political influence of the Catholic Church.

---

21. See also Lipset and Rokkan's classic 1967 work on religious cleavages in European democracies.

Research on Latin American politics has focused more attention on the role of religion on the subject of gender and policy (most recently, see Blofield 2006; Blofield and Haas 2005; Fleet and Smith 1997; Grau et al. 1997; Haas 1999; Htun 2003). Religion exerts a more powerful cultural and political role in Latin America than it does in Europe, and the strength of the institutional Catholic Church in much of Latin America constitutes a major impediment to feminist policymaking. While the strength of the church varies widely across Latin America, the church plays a significant role in influencing public debate on social policy in most of the region.[22]

Posttransition Latin American politics has challenged the widespread assumption that political and economic development will lead to secularization. In countries where the Catholic Church played a crucial role in the defense of human rights during periods of authoritarian rule, the church has, since the transitions to democracy, attempted to parlay its increased visibility and the respect it earned as part of a democratic opposition into political influence over the policymaking of democratic governments (Blofield and Haas 2005; Fleet and Smith 1997; Haas 1999). In her cross-national study of policy reform on domestic violence, Weldon (2002) finds that religion is an insignificant factor, but I argue that this is due to her operationalization of religion as a variable in her analysis.[23] As Blofield (2006) demonstrates, one sees extensive policy variation across majority-Catholic countries, even on the most contentious policy issues for the church, such as abortion and divorce. A key explanatory factor in Blofield's comparative analysis of social policy in Spain, Chile, and Argentina concerns the level of media control by the Catholic Church. In countries where media access and ownership by the church is high, such as Chile, this represents a powerful tool for shaping public opinion on social and political issues.

My research on Chile also suggests that the key factor in charting the religious impact on the policy process is not only, or even predominantly, the level of popular religiosity or the historically dominant denomination, but the political power of the institutional church(es). While religious belief (or lack of belief) no doubt plays a role in shaping public opinion on policy

---

22. For a comprehensive overview of the political influence of the Catholic Church in Latin America, see Gill 1998.

23. Weldon does not distinguish between levels of expressed religiosity in the general population and the institutional power of particular churches. In addition, since her study is limited to violence against women, an issue on which churches are less likely to oppose policy reform, her analysis underestimates the degree of opposition on more contentious policy issues, such as divorce or reproductive rights.

issues, there may be a significant disconnect over the short to medium term between levels of religiosity at the popular level and the political influence of religious institutions. One sees this clearly in the case of Mexico, where popular religiosity remains relatively high but where constitutional limitations on the political power of the Catholic Church have made it difficult for the church to translate the majority religious affiliation of the population into policy influence. Since 2000 the Mexican church has been gaining political influence with the rise of the conservative National Action Party, with its philosophical and historical links to the Catholic Church. There is also interesting variation in church influence in Brazil, Chile, and Argentina, owing in part to the role the church played during the military governments. In Chile and Brazil the church played a strong role in defending human rights, whereas in Argentina significant sectors of the hierarchy supported the military government. Since the transitions, the Chilean and Brazilian churches have remained influential political players, whereas the Argentine church has suffered a loss of public confidence and political power under democracy.

The Catholic Church is, of course, just one example, albeit the most relevant one for Latin America (and Europe). In other regions, from the Middle East, to Southeast Asia, to Africa, religious leaders and institutions are important players in debates on women's rights.[24]

Public Opinion

Finally, we must consider the effect of public opinion on government policy. There are several relevant dimensions of this question. On the one hand, we can consider the effect of organized women's movements on public opinion. The social movement literature on Latin America discusses this question extensively. For example, Jaquette's (1994) work on women in transition politics demonstrates that women's movements in Latin America helped shape public perceptions, first, on issues of human rights during the dictatorships. Later, these same women's movements helped raise public awareness on issues such as domestic violence. Another relevant area of research examines the ideological differences that may exist between women and men (the so-called gender gap) (e.g., Baldez 2008; Iverson and Rosenbluth 2006; Jelen, Thomas, and Wilcox 1994; Norris and Ingelhart 2001). Iverson and Rosenbluth (2006) conclude, for example, that the gendered nature of workforce

---

24. One could argue that this is increasingly the case in the United States as well.

participation helps explain the gender gap on issues like government employment policy. When we try to gauge the general effect of public opinion on government willingness to address women's rights, however, research is decidedly sparser.

Public opinion research in Latin America is expanding at an enormous pace, both through multicountry studies like Latin Barometer and through country-specific polling agencies like CEP in Chile. Unfortunately, these studies have focused little attention on women's rights issues. Nevertheless, we can identify some broad trends in the evolution of public opinion in this area. Despite the overall dearth of data, there are clear indications that public opinion in Latin America has become more liberal in recent years. Research indicates that on certain issues public opinion in favor of policy reform has had an impact on legislative behavior. Haas (2000) argues that overwhelming public support for legalizing divorce in Chile helped counteract the opposition campaigns of political conservatives and the Catholic Church. Progressive politicians were able to win conservative support for divorce by threatening to "go public" with conservative opposition. Even on such issues as abortion, where there is little public demonstration in favor of expanded rights, public opinion data have captured a surprising level of support for liberalizing the law (see Blofield 2006; Grau et al. 1997). As I argue in chapter 4 of this book, public opinion polls in favor of reforming abortion law have bolstered congressional efforts to expand reproductive rights in Chile.

In other cases, the liberalization of public opinion has seemed to follow policy change on women's rights. Blofield (2006) demonstrates that public support for abortion rights in Spain followed, rather than led, government efforts to decriminalize abortion. Ríos Tobar (2003) notes that changes in public opinion on women's rights are evident in the increasing press coverage devoted to feminist issues, as well as in the growing number of women's studies centers in Chilean universities, although it is unclear how much this has translated into a general shift in public opinion. More generally, Norris and Ingelhart (2001) find that as women's visibility in public office increases, public opinion shows greater comfort with the idea of women in leadership roles (which may translate into support for women's rights issues). Finally, the role of the media in shaping public perceptions on women's rights issues is key, and therefore the degree of media concentration in conservative hands, including church ownership of media, is an important factor (Blofield 2006).

Policy Networks and the Challenge of Cooperation

Overcoming the institutional and cultural obstacles to more effective feminist policymaking requires the coordinated effort of feminists across the state and civil society. Multifaceted alliances among feminist representatives in legislatures, women's organizations, and women's ministries are the best hope for creating multiple access points within the state for feminists and sustained attention to issues of women's rights. Comprehensive policy reform on women's rights has resulted from an alliance of women's rights advocates in political parties, the bureaucracy, and organizations representing the women's movement (Conway, Steuernagel, and Ahern 1995; Gardiner 1997; Htun 2003; Lovenduski and Norris 1993; Lycklama, Vargas, and Wieringa 1998; Mazur 2002). The comparative literature details the many challenges feminists face in penetrating political parties, in developing influential WPM, and in launching effective lobbying campaigns from within the women's movement. But existing work has paid comparatively little attention to the difficulties feminists encounter in coordinating with one another to pursue feminist policymaking.

Beyond the institutional factors discussed above, we need a deeper analysis of the role that institutional balance of power plays in creating an auspicious (or inauspicious) policymaking dynamic. In Latin America in particular, powerful executives have a long history of conflict-ridden relationships with legislatures, and as a result the governmental balance of power and interbranch relations have a profound impact on feminist policymaking. Across the region, different sectors of the state possess different degrees of power to shape the policy agenda. The relative strength of the executive and legislative bodies in initiating successful policy on women's rights, the balance of power among political parties, and the necessity of party alliances all have a significant impact on the type of dynamic that develops within the state on a given policy issue. This in turn affects the ability of outside feminist organizations to permeate and influence the state.

Although the political Left tends to be most supportive of women's rights, participation in a coalition government will force the Left to temper its agenda in negotiating with its governing partners. But Laver and Shepsle explain that policy is not simply the result of an averaging of party positions. Rather, as the coalition parties distribute their members throughout the government ministries, policy in a particular area often reflects the ideological position of whatever party heads the relevant ministry. Laver and Shepsle contend that the policy output of a governing coalition will thus "vary by portfolio. . . . Policy reflects not an amalgam or blend of party preferences, but a set of fixed points that varies according to which party controls what ministry. Coalitions may articulate a platform for the purposes of campaigning, but the informational and procedural advantages inherent to ministerial positions means that actual policy implementation depends on the will of particular politicians" (1996, 8).

Even where there is close ideological agreement between branches of government, in systems where both the executive and the legislature can introduce legislation, conflict may arise over ownership of policy initiatives. This is particularly a factor in Latin America, which has a history of powerful executives and of conflict between executive and legislature (Carey and Shugart 1998). Congressional representatives jealously guard their power and may resent losing control of policy proposals to the executive branch. Electoral concerns encourage representatives to make a name for themselves through policy work, and representatives may resent playing a supporting role in the executive's legislative plans. If conflict between the branches becomes public (as it did on occasion in Chile), this may negatively affect feminist activists' perception of the merits of political participation.

A particular challenge with feminist policymaking is that the issues cross traditional policy lines; as a result, policy networks are not as stable as in other areas. The effectiveness of the policy networks that feminists develop will therefore vary not only across countries but across policy areas within countries. Depending upon the particular issue, a government ministry may be more or less open to reform, legislators may have considerable, or inadequate, levels of expertise on the issue, and constituencies within civil society may be more or less mobilized to push for change. In addition, the political opposition may be well organized against the proposed reform, indifferent, or even somewhat supportive. The political dynamics surrounding a particular policy area are not stable even within a given country.

The case of Chile illustrates that even within a specific policy area, the policymaking dynamic is constantly in flux because feminists adjust their political strategies based on the outcome of earlier attempts at legislative reform. There is an implicit assumption in much of the institutional literature (e.g., North 1990) that political actors will easily comprehend the formal and informal "rules of the game" and will adjust their behavior in order to maximize their political advantage. But the case of feminist policymaking in Chile demonstrates that political actors must learn over time, through trial and error, how to "win" in a particular institutional context. In Chile, constitutional reforms enacted during the dictatorship fundamentally altered the institutional landscape. Even politicians who were active prior to the 1973 coup were faced with a new set of political rules upon their return to government in 1990. Many feminists became involved in formal politics for the first time after the transition, and they faced a particularly steep political learning curve.

This study explores the political learning that has taken place among Chilean feminists and the consequences of these lessons for feminist policymaking. Over time, feminists in Chile have learned to maneuver more successfully within the country's institutional context. They have developed strategies to broaden the appeal of their proposals across political parties, and they have evolved more sophisticated responses to the political and cultural opposition. But the compromises and negotiations that have been part of feminists' success are themselves the subject of deep disagreement within feminist circles. Thus feminists must develop mechanisms not only for dealing with the opposition but also for maintaining effective policy alliances with other feminists.

By examining the evolution of feminist policymaking across issue areas, we are able to evaluate the impact of particular political strategies on the chances for reform. What, for example, was the difference between the divorce bill that passed in Chile and the previous ones that did not? Why do feminists in Congress continue to introduce legislation to expand reproductive rights, despite the failure of previous efforts? How does the success or failure of a given proposal affect the willingness of feminists outside the state to participate in the political process? And how do feminists balance the desire for transformative change with the pragmatic demands of democratic politics?

2

FEMINIST POLICY REFORM IN CHILE

> We legislators are the representatives of the citizenry, not their masters.
> —Christian Democratic senator Jorge Lavandero,
> August 13, 2003, during Senate debate on divorce

Any attempt to evaluate the opportunities for progressive policymaking on women's rights in Chile must situate the analysis within the context of the institutional constraints on policymaking endemic to the Chilean political system. This chapter outlines the specific institutional powers of the main policymaking actors and discusses the incentives and disincentives for cooperative policymaking that flow from the institutional imbalance of the Chilean system. While some institutional structures are more conducive than others to allowing key actors to assert themselves in the policy process, and while some historical moments are more propitious than others for social movements that aim to influence the state, within any political context, particular actors and specific strategies are also key. Structural and institutional limitations may constrain the actions of particular groups, but we know that actors can help to create the kinds of political conditions that allow further action to occur.[1] The goal is to explore both sides of this dynamic—structure and agency—and the dialogue between them. Given how slowly macrostructures change over time, the critical story concerns the strategies that actors develop within a given political system, and their subsequent successes and

---

1. See Baldez 2002 on the concept of a tipping point for social movement activity, for example.

failures. This chapter breaks open each of the main arenas for policymaking action—the executive branch, the legislature, and civil society—and evaluates the maneuverability of the main actors within the policymaking process.

The broad dynamics of the Chilean case, in which demands for women's rights emerged in the context of dictatorship, are typical of much of the region. Ongoing tensions with sectors supportive of the past military regime, cultural resistance to women's equality from various political and social sectors, and continuing economic difficulties exemplify the challenges of advancing a feminist policymaking agenda in Latin America. At the same time, the relative strength of the Chilean party system, the overall stability of the political system two decades after the democratic transition, and the existence of a clearly articulated mandate for change from feminists in civil society make the Chilean case an excellent first application of comparative theory to Latin America.

The return of electoral democracy in 1989 ushered a new institutional structure into Chilean politics. An analysis of feminist policymaking since the transition reveals that political actors do not automatically comprehend the most effective strategy for gaining political advantage in a given institutional context. Rather, successful political strategy evolves over time, with repeated political interactions. The striking breadth of feminist proposals introduced since the transition to democracy demonstrates the commitment of Chilean feminists, inside and outside the state, to policy reform. In Chile, however, both institutional structure and cultural opposition to feminism constrain the opportunities for progressive policymaking on women's rights.

For example, feminists working within the political system have learned that executive support is a critical factor for legislative success but that this sponsorship often comes at the cost of losing ownership of legislative initiatives and control over their content. Framing feminist proposals in language that appeals to cultural conservatives and compromising on the content of legislative initiatives can help build support for passage, but the resulting laws may be ineffective and may offer little improvement over the status quo. Feminist groups in civil society have learned that the price of access to the policy process is often self-censorship of the groups' political critique of state policy. Over the past two decades, feminists in Chile have learned to strategize more effectively within a complex political landscape, where institutional balance of power, governing alliances, contrasting party ideologies, and a disorganized civil society combine to shape the opportunities for policy reform.

Overview of Contemporary Chilean Politics

A number of institutional factors determine the government's ability to initiate and support feminist policy. These factors include the degree of support for women's rights on the left, from Christian Democrats, and on the right, the relationship between Congress and the executive (particularly Sernam), women's access to power within the Congress, the strength of the political opposition, including the Catholic Church, and the political strategies of feminist groups pressuring for policy reform.

Historically, Chilean parties have had a reputation as highly disciplined. Traditionally, there have been three distinct political-ideological tendencies in Chilean society (Left, Center, and Right), and it is clear from the party breakdown in appendix 2 that this trend continues.[2] However, the electoral law created by the 1980 constitution establishes a binomial system with a modified d'Hondt vote-counting scheme, which has the effect of forcing the parties to form broad electoral coalitions.[3] Today the parties in Chile are in the ideologically awkward position of representing three distinct ideological currents within two broad political coalitions: the Center-Left Concertación and the Right.[4] In current democratic politics, issues of internal party discipline are therefore complicated by the need for parties to find areas of compromise with one another in order to maintain the stability of these broad alliances. This is especially true within the Center-Left parties of the governing Concertación. While the leaders of the Left parties within the Concertación have officially voiced their support for the government's current economic policies (see Constable and Valenzuela 1991), there is significant

---

2. The continuation of party loyalty in Chile, despite the seventeen-year absence of party politics, is discussed at length in Scully 1995.

3. The 1980 constitution transformed the basis of the electoral system from multimember districts to binomial districts. Parties or coalitions present open lists of candidates for each district. The first seat is given to the list that wins the most votes and to the first-place candidate on that list. The second seat is given to the second-place list and to the first-place candidate on that list. For both candidates from one list to capture both district seats, the total percentage of votes won by that list must be double that of the second-place list. In this way it is possible for a second-place candidate overall to lose a district seat if the first-place candidate is on the same list. This system benefits the second-place party or coalition, which in the case of Chile is often the Right. In many districts the Right is able to gain half the seats with much less support than the first- and second-place (Concertación) candidates. The effects of the electoral system on representation is discussed in Linz and Stepan 1996; Scully 1995, 1996; and Siavelis and Valenzuela 1996.

4. The parties of the Right have formed an electoral coalition in each of the posttransition congressional elections, although under different names (Democracy and Progress in 1989, Union for Progress in 1993, and Union for Chile since 1997).

disagreement at the party level on social issues between the Left and the Christian Democrats. Within the Left, there is greater willingness to discuss issues of women's rights and a higher degree of ideological unity on these issues than among Christian Democrats. These tensions play out within the Congress, and also between Congress and the executive branch, where the Center-Left coalition divides the leadership of government ministries across the parties of the coalition (see Baldez 2001). Feminist policymaking thus depends in large part on the successful negotiation of interparty disagreements on women's rights, conflict within the governing coalition over policy priorities, and interbranch competition for legislative prerogatives on important policy issues. These institutional factors in turn shape the access granted to outside groups such as feminist organizations.

The Importance of Executive Power

The success rate of the executive's legislative efforts relative to those of the Congress has been the driving dynamic behind feminist policymaking since the transition to democracy, shaping the strategies and expectations of all actors involved in the process. Historically strong, the executive branch in Chile increased its strength under the 1980 constitution, and it plays an influential legislative role in democratic politics.[5] The constitution limits congressional power over critical policy areas, most critically budget making and constitutional reform (see Baldez and Carey 1999). Additional forms of executive influence over the legislative process include the power to introduce bills and the ability to force debate on a bill by declaring it "urgent." Informal tools of influence include the executive's superior resources, technical expertise, and support staff, which result in executive bills that are often more competitive than congressional versions. Other informal executive powers include strong lobbying ability and access to congressional committees during debates. These executive tools can be used to various degrees, or not at all, to influence a bill's movement through Congress. In the case of bills that take years to pass Congress, the executive often chooses to intervene only at particular moments. The less congressional support a bill has, the more the executive's power matters in keeping the bill alive in committee until sufficient support for passage can be built.

---

5. The dominance of the executive is evident not only on issues of women's rights but across policy areas (see Siavelis 2000).

Either the executive or Congress may introduce a bill.[6] Before the constitutional reforms of 2005, however, the legislative calendar was divided into two periods: the ordinary session ran from May 21 through September 18, while the rest of the year was considered part of the extraordinary legislative session. During the extraordinary session, only executive bills or congressional bills chosen by the executive for sponsorship (*patrocinante*) could be discussed in Congress. Even debate on congressional initiatives was restricted during the four months of the ordinary session. During the shorter ordinary legislative period, legislative initiatives not included in the executive's list of priorities could be discussed, but only after any outstanding bills from the executive list had been dealt with. This division of the legislative calendar affected feminist legislative efforts for most of the period examined here. The 2005 reforms allow congressional bills to be discussed throughout the year, but, as noted below, the executive can use additional tools to push its favored projects to the top of the agenda.

Linz and Stepan (1996), Scully (1996), and Siavelis (2000, 2002) have noted that in the first decade after the transition to democracy, the executive in Chile did not resort to exercising the degree of legislative power granted by the constitution, and my research confirms this. The authors cite a number of factors that account for the unexpectedly consensual tone of executive policymaking, including an emphasis on political stability in the years following the transition and the need to negotiate with the Right in the Senate, where the Concertación has not held a governing majority. Of the sixty-four bills examined in this study, twenty-three were included in the extraordinary session at least once. Seven of nine executive messages introduced by Sernam prior to 2005 were included in the extraordinary sessions, as were seventeen of thirty-five congressional bills during the same period.

A more significant, and still relevant, tool of executive influence is the use of "urgency" labels to force debate on specific bills. The president may apply or remove urgency labels to a bill at any time in the legislative process, and different levels of urgency stipulate different time periods within which debate on a bill must take place.[7] Congress has thirty days to debate a bill labeled with a "simple" urgency, ten days for a "summa" urgency, and only three days for an "immediate" urgency. In the last case, the bill would be

---

6. An executive bill is called a *mensaje* (message), and a congressional bill is a *moción* (motion).

7. Article 71 of the constitution. Under the 1925 constitution, Congress voted to accept or reject executive urgency labels. The 1980 constitution eliminated this congressional power.

discussed in general and in particular simultaneously, shortcutting the usual legislative procedure for debate.[8] Because the executive may make unlimited use of urgencies, they have the potential to play a determining role in setting the legislative agenda. If an urgency label expires before Congress debates the bill, the executive can simply reapply it. Congress may not debate other legislation until all urgent bills have been discussed, and if the executive continually reapplies an urgency label, this functions as an executive filibuster, effectively preventing other legislative work from taking place. For example, in the case of a bill introduced in 1993 to reform rape laws (Law 19.617), the executive declared the bill urgent fourteen times before it passed the Chamber in 1995, and the bill was declared urgent several more times in the Senate before finally passing that house in late 1998.[9] More recently, a bill on femicide that enjoys strong support from President Bachelet (bill 4937) has been declared urgent thirteen times in a little more than a year since its introduction. Only ten bills in this study have been declared urgent at some point in the process, but six of eleven executive bills have been declared urgent.[10]

The general lack of formal executive support for congressional bills stems in large part from the fact that the executive has so much power to legislate on its own. In addition to its greater formal powers, it has more resources and better technical assistance to write and lobby for bills. The superior staff available to the executive means that in the case of a bill that proposes sweeping legal reform, the executive is often able to write a more complete and technically more coherent bill. On a high-priority issue, the executive may decide that it makes more sense to introduce its own bill.

---

8. Bills are subject to two rounds of debate in each chamber. The "general" round determines whether a majority of the members present favor legislating on the issue the bill addresses. If the bill passes this round, it is returned to the committee for modification, followed by the "particular" round of debate, which requires a vote on the particular form of the bill passed by the committee.

9. Because the executive is often willing to extend urgency labels or reapply them rather than allow the time for debate to expire, it is unclear how influential these labels alone are in forcing bills through Congress. Siavelis (2002) argues that with respect to all legislation, the use of urgency labels is not sufficient to determine the success of a bill. It must be remembered, however, that such labels are often applied precisely to the most controversial bills, such as the 1993 sexual assault bill mentioned above. Therefore, although Siavelis finds only a slightly higher rate of passage for urgent bills, this result alone is not sufficient to prove the lack of importance of this executive tool.

10. Of course, bills that have not yet passed may be declared urgent at some point in the future. Nevertheless, the greater frequency of urgency labels for executive bills is striking.

Chile's Servicio Nacional de la Mujer

Sernam was created in 1991, following Chile's transition to democracy. As an arm of the executive branch, the National Women's Service is the specific political institution that crafts executive bills on women's rights. Sernam has ministerial rank and an independent budget. While it is part of the executive branch, Sernam depends on the will of the president for inclusion of its bills in the extraordinary legislative session and for the application of urgency labels to bills that are stalled in Congress. Sernam is meant to oversee the policies developed by other government agencies, but it also develops its own projects, largely independently of the rest of the government. In this sense, Sernam's institutional structure allows it to take a cross-sectoral approach to women's rights, promoting its own projects and coordinating policy with other branches of the bureaucracy. Sernam's legal reform program, which is the focus of this book, is one of its four priorities. In addition, Sernam established a program for female heads of households, a program to prevent violence against women, and a network of information centers on women's rights issues.

The fate of Sernam is closely linked to the politics surrounding the democratic transition itself.[11] In the case of Chile, this included the forced cooperation of historically incompatible parties—the Left and the centrist Christian Democrats—to prevent the Far Right from gaining office. In her analysis of Sernam's first administration, Waylen (2000, 792) argues that the "institutional constraints generated by the terms of the transition" have limited Sernam's influence within the government and complicated its relationship with the women's movement. The strongest political support for Sernam came from the Left, but the Left parties were a minority in the governing coalition. The centrist Christian Democrats, who were deeply divided on many issues of women's rights, represented the largest party in the coalition and also held the presidency in the first two democratic administrations (1990–2000). Baldez (2001) and Blofield and Haas (2005) explain that these institutional arrangements limited the policy options available to feminists, making sweeping progress on women's rights unlikely.

Sernam's independent budget has increased over time. Prior to Bachelet's election, Sernam's budget was low even by global standards, and it relied for

---

11. For a comparative discussion of the effects of such transitions on women's political power, see Alvarez 1990; Jaquette 1994; Jaquette and Wolchik 1998; and Staudt 1998.

the bulk of its funding on international sources.[12] Bachelet increased Sernam's budget by 30 percent, much of it earmarked for the creation of domestic violence shelters. Nevertheless, international funding from sources such as the United Nations Development Fund for Women remains an important component of Sernam's budget.

Sernam enjoys significantly greater financial resources than feminist members of Congress do (see chapters 4 and 5); nevertheless, the ministry's budget limitations constrain its ability both to develop legislative proposals and to ensure the implementation of new laws. For example, Provoste (1995, 21) concludes that the Intrafamily Violence Law, a major legislative proposal that was passed in 1994 (Law 20.066), has been fundamentally undermined by the lack of money earmarked by the government for implementation.

The low level of funding Sernam receives relative to other ministries is indicative of the overall low priority of the agency for the rest of the government. Sernam's low status is also reflected in its difficulty in gaining access to the rest of the bureaucracy. Sernam's various attempts to encourage voluntary coordination with other ministries, such as Health, Education, or Labor, which also develop legislation relevant to women's rights, have met with little enthusiasm. Sernam has no power to force a participatory role for itself in projects outside its immediate jurisdiction. However, Franceschet (2003) argues that, beginning under Minister Bilbao (1994–98), Sernam became more successful in forging lasting links with other ministries.

Despite its relatively low funding, Sernam enjoys significantly higher resources than members of Congress do, employing experts in areas such as women's health and labor participation, as well as lawyers who draft and lobby for bills. As a result, Sernam is often able to write technically superior bills on complex legal issues, relative to congressional efforts. For example, both Sernam and feminist representatives drafted bills to expand property rights for married women, but Sernam's version was more comprehensive and technically sound. As part of the executive branch, Sernam enjoys access to congressional committee members during debates and often addresses the full Chamber of Deputies or Senate when a particular bill goes to the floor

---

12. In earlier research Baldez noted that Sernam received four times as much funding from international sources as from the Chilean government. The worldwide average for WPM is less than 1 percent of the government budget (Stetson and Mazur 1995), but Baldez (2001, citing Valenzuela 1998) explains that Sernam's funding at the time was less than .1 percent of the total government budget. For statistics on the funding of different types of women's organizations, see Baldez 2001, 15.

for a vote. This level of access, unavailable to feminist members of Congress outside the relevant committees or to feminist NGOs, affords Sernam an opportunity to influence negotiations on a bill at the key stages of its movement through the Congress. Such access also suggests that Sernam has the potential to serve as a critical link between the feminist community and Congress.

The people who fill Sernam's top positions are politically appointed. Reflecting the power balance within the Concertación, its first two ministers were Christian Democrats and its subdirectors were Socialists. After his election in 2000, Socialist president Ricardo Lagos appointed a Socialist to head Sernam.[13] As political appointees, Sernam's top directors must strike a somewhat precarious balance between the agenda of the feminist policy community and the more conservative agenda of the Concertación, in which the Christian Democrats were the largest party until 2002 (appendix 2). A common complaint among feminists is that the top appointees at Sernam are not women with links to the feminist community. This was the case not only with the first two Christian Democratic ministers, Soledad Alvear and Josefina Bilbao, but with Lagos's appointee, Adriana del Piano, as well. In addition to considering the policy preferences of the feminist community, Sernam must take into account the potential opposition of the Far Right and conservative sectors of the Catholic Church when deciding what issues to pursue.

The potential for a ministry like Sernam to alter perceptions of women's rights and to affect policy on women is great, even in a relatively conservative social and political climate such as that of Chile. Laitin (1986, cited in Baldez 2001, 6) concludes that "institutional design can alter or at least suppress certain cultural patterns and practices, even the most primordial ones." In the case of Chile, however, a number of researchers have concluded that Sernam's difficulties in influencing government policy are primarily a reflection of the Chilean government's overall weak commitment to women's rights and feminist policy proposals (Cáceres et al. 1993; Guzmán, Hola, and Ríos 1999; Hola and Pischedda 1993; Frohmann and Valdés 1995; Macaulay 1998; Matear 1997; Molina and Provoste 1997; Schild 1998; Valenzuela 1998; Waylen 1997). Waylen (1997) concludes that most of Sernam's action has

---

13. To date, the ministers of Sernam have been Christian Democrats Soledad Alvear (1990–94) and Josefina Bilbao (1994–2000), Socialist Adriana del Piano (2000–2002), Independent Cecilia Pérez (2003–6), and, under President Bachelet, Christian Democrat Laura Albornoz (2006–9), and Socialist Carmen Andrade (2009–March 2010).

therefore been on the least controversial issues, although, as discussed in the following chapters, my research indicates that Sernam's involvement with more controversial issues has increased in recent years.

Waylen (1996a) argues that Sernam's leaders recognized early on that poverty-alleviation programs aimed at poor women would be easier to sell politically than proposals that challenged gender relations. Baldez (2001, 18) hypothesizes that Sernam's apparent reluctance to take on the most controversial issues of women's rights is at least partially due to its Christian Democratic leadership in the first two administrations, given the opposition of conservative Christian Democrats to feminist policy proposals. Baldez suggests that Sernam might exhibit a greater willingness to propose (or at least support) more radical proposals under Socialist leadership, but my research suggests that even under more progressive leadership Sernam is restricted by the larger balance of power within the government.[14]

This political tension means that there are certain issues, like the legalization of divorce, that Sernam favored but would not explicitly support while under Christian Democratic leadership.[15] In these cases Sernam is limited to speaking informally in favor of a bill and offering limited, informal support to representatives. There are also issues—most notably the legalization of abortion—that, because of both the general political atmosphere and the ideologies of Sernam's Christian Democratic ministers, the Ministry did not support in any way.[16] Minister Josefina Bilbao joined feminists in protesting the imprisonment of women who have abortions, but she stopped short of advocating the decriminalization of abortion. During the 2000 presidential campaign, Ricardo Lagos indicated his willingness to reconsider the ban on therapeutic abortion, but in the face of strong opposition he backed down from this position. The current administration of Sernam has also declined to speak publicly about liberalizing Chile's abortion law.

Appendix 1 makes clear that Sernam has had much greater success than feminist representatives in passing feminist policy. Eight of nine bills introduced by Sernam eventually became law,[17] whereas only nine of fifty-three

---

14. Sernam came under Socialist leadership in 2000, with the election of Ricardo Lagos to the presidency. My research suggests that no dramatic change has taken place in its orientation or activities as a result. The one exception was Sernam's willingness, under Socialist ministers, openly to support congressional efforts to legalize divorce (see chapter 5).

15. In 2000, when Sernam came under Socialist leadership, it began to campaign publicly for the congressional divorce bill pending in the Senate (see chapter 5).

16. Since 1989 abortion has been completely criminalized in Chile, even in cases where it could save a woman's life (see chapter 5).

17. Two additional women's rights bills introduced by the executive branch (the Office of the President) also became law (Laws 20.172 and 20.418).

congressional bills between 1990 and March 2008 were successful. This is most notably the case on issues where both Sernam and congressional representatives introduced bills on such issues as paternity, discrimination on the basis of sex, day care, the rights of domestic workers, marital property rights, and sexual assault. Although Sernam's bills on sexual assault and paternity took more than five years to pass Congress, earlier congressional efforts never made it out of committee. Both Sernam bills benefited from numerous urgency labels, perpetual inclusion in the extraordinary legislative sessions, and the constant presence of Sernam's lawyers in committee debates. When Sernam's bills are declared urgent and Sernam is prepared to lobby hard for their passage, a committee will attend to the executive bill at the expense of a previously introduced congressional proposal on the same issue.

This does not imply a complete lack of executive interest in bills that originate in Congress. A number of congressional motions have received lower levels of executive support in the form of lobbying by Sernam or inclusion in extraordinary legislative sessions, and cooperation between Sernam and feminist legislators is increasing. A 1994 bill to ban the expulsion from school of pregnant students, and a 1995 bill (which became law in 1996) mandating the creation of day-care centers for certain categories of workers, are early examples of congressional motions that received Sernam's explicit support. In addition, after 2002, Sernam made a concerted effort under the leadership of Cecilia Pérez to lobby for the congressional divorce bill then stalled in Senate committee; Sernam's assistance was critical in its eventual passage in 2004. Minister Laura Albornoz, with the support of President Bachelet, has offered support for a number of congressional bills, including a bill to institute gender quotas (bill 3206), introduced in 2003, and a bill on femicide (bill 4937), introduced in 2007. Without some level of executive support from Sernam, feminist bills are much more vulnerable to becoming perpetually stalled in Congress.

Sernam's assistance can come at a price, however. In some cases Sernam's involvement with a bill has influenced the framing of the issues involved. The most dramatic—and consequential—example of this is the intrafamily violence bill, which was introduced in 1991 and became law in 1994. In exchange for its support, Sernam insisted on reframing the issue of domestic violence more conservatively than had been the case in the original version of the bill (see chapter 3). On controversial issues, however, it is more common for Sernam to avoid legislating on the topic altogether than to draft a conservative bill. Only congressional representatives have introduced bills liberalizing laws on abortion and divorce, for example.

Feminist representatives feel that the downside to Sernam is that it usurps Congress's legislative power. Indeed, Sernam's success as a policymaker poses clear disadvantages for other actors involved in legislative policymaking on women's issues. Over the long term, if an arm of the executive branch, staffed by political appointees, takes the lead in developing policy proposals on women's rights, the ability of elected congressional representatives to address those issues is severely hampered. In addition, such institutional arrangements leave the ability to promote women's rights vulnerable to the election of a conservative president and subsequent changes in Sernam's administration. In the short term, however, owing to Sernam's technical resources and lobbying power, the ministry's support for a particular bill adds considerably to its chances for success. PPD deputy Adriana Muñoz, one of the most active feminist legislators, explains the ambivalence feminist representatives feel toward Sernam: "The government is very strong, it's very strong . . . and the Parliament is like, I'd say, a necessary element for the functioning of democracy, but it doesn't have the importance and weight it should have in the creation of the legislative agenda. Parliamentary bills are generally absorbed, like additions. . . . [The executive] improves the legislative proposals a little, for sure, but there we lose ownership of the proposals, and we end up just cited as the source of inspiration."[18]

Party Position and Congressional Support for Feminist Policy

The overwhelming institutional power of Sernam relative to the Congress and, as a consequence, its greater success in passing feminist bills have failed to dampen the desire of congressional representatives to pursue an aggressive policy agenda on women's rights. Between 1990 and April 2008 congressional representatives introduced fifty-three feminist bills (appendix 1). Sernam, along with the executive branch overall, was much less active during this period. The difference in the level of activity is particularly striking between 2002 and April 2008, when only one executive bill—designed to give

---

18. Adriana Muñoz, interview by author, Valparaíso, June 5, 2001. Muñoz was first elected to Congress in 1990 as a member of the Socialist Party. When she lost her re-election bid in 1994, she switched to the Party for Democracy (PPD), and was reelected as a PPD deputy in 1998. (Muñoz's relationship with the Socialist Party is discussed in chapter 4.)

mothers direct access to child-support payments—was introduced (by President Bachelet, not through Sernam). The bill passed in 2007 (Law 20.172). By contrast, Congress introduced nineteen bills expanding women's rights during the same period, including a bill on therapeutic abortion (3197), two others on reproductive rights more broadly (3702 and 4277), a bill proposing no-fault divorce (4985), another to establish electoral quotas for women's representation (3020), bills to provide paternity leave following the birth or adoption of a child (4465), and bills to strengthen various provisions in the Intrafamily Violence Law (4106 and 5200). One of the reproductive bills (4277) originated in the Senate, suggesting increased openness to feminist policy in the upper house. Other bills addressed less controversial issues, including raising the minimum age of marriage (5241), expanding the right of mothers to nurse infants at work (4212), and banning salary discrimination (4356). While none of these bills has passed committee in either chamber, the bills themselves suggest some encouraging developments: an increased willingness to tackle controversial policy issues, the strengthening of cross-party legislative alliances, and an increase in the number of representatives interested in pursuing women's rights legislation. For example, a group of male representatives drafted and introduced both the Senate bill on reproductive rights and the Chamber bill on therapeutic abortion (3197); the latter included support from representatives on the right.

Given that this growing attention to feminist issues occurred within the context of a Bachelet administration and an increase in congressional seats held by the Left, an obvious question is why these bills have not been successful to date. Indeed, the increase in bills and their more radical content suggests that representatives have been trying to seize upon a particularly opportune political moment. Yet congressional supporters of women's rights face a number of challenges to successful policymaking, even in such seemingly auspicious circumstances.

The balance of power among the political parties, within both the Concertación and the opposition, is a critical factor shaping the political opportunities for policy reform. While the Left increased in strength after 2002, this period also saw dramatic growth by the ultra-right-wing UDI, which remains staunchly opposed to most feminist initiatives. The Christian Democratic Party and the RN, the moderately right-wing party, both lost seats beginning in 2002, decreasing the number of potential allies of feminist policy outside the Left (appendix 2). Even within the Left, attention to women's rights has depended upon sustained pressure by feminist party members.

While women's representation has increased since the transition to democracy, this growth has not been dramatic, and much of it has taken place within the Right, where even women representatives feel ambivalent about feminist policy. In addition, the larger institutional structure of Chilean politics, specifically the imbalance in power between the executive and legislative branches, works against effective congressional policymaking.

Within this complex environment, Congress's attempts to craft successful feminist policy depend upon strategically navigating relations with Sernam (and at times another executive ministry as well), with each representative's party and larger coalition, and with the opposition. The relative absence of feminists from key review committees means that they are unable directly to push their projects forward for debate. Additionally, the greater conservatism of the Senate often necessitates greater modifications to bills that manage to pass the Chamber of Deputies. Finally, these considerations must also be weighed against the constituent concerns of each member of Congress, which in the case of feminist representatives includes both an electoral constituency and the feminist community. Despite the growing diffusion of feminist ideas throughout Chilean society (Ríos Tobar 2003), opposition to reform remains strong within sectors of the population, and the Catholic Church and conservative organizations retain significant political influence.

Ideology and Women's Rights Policy

Consistent with global research on party politics and women's rights, the Left in Chile has been the most steadfast proponent of feminist policy reform. Since 2000 the Left has grown in strength, both through the election of two Socialist presidents (including Michelle Bachelet, who is also a self-declared feminist) and through an increase in the number of congressional seats held by the two Left parties within the Concertación, the Socialist Party (PS) and the Party for Democracy (PPD). Nevertheless, the Left must balance its support for women's rights against the demands of coalitional unity. The Left's major partner in the governing coalition, the Christian Democratic Party (PDC), is decidedly less enthusiastic about far-reaching feminist reforms. Outside the Concertación, the Far Right has grown in strength as well. While occasional support for feminist initiatives can be found within the RN, the UDI has been a consistent opponent of reform. As the Left's strength has grown in recent years, it has consistently sought to make its policy mark within a coalition long dominated by the Christian Democrats, while the Far Right (gaining strength at the expense of the moderate Right) seeks to halt this progress.

The Left

The PS and the PPD are the only parties that have adopted an official position in support of equal rights for women. Nevertheless, it has been a struggle within these two main parties of the Left to bring up women's rights issues for debate and to create party consensus on specific subjects. Feminists within the parties have been largely responsible for putting the issues on the table, and over time both parties have become more open to discussing them. As a "New Left" party, the PPD is generally the more open of the two. Although divisions among individual party militants do exist, the PPD and PS are the only major parties to have developed party-level agreements on issues of women's rights before specific bills come up for congressional debate. The parties even officially favor the (limited) legalization of abortion, an issue that the other major parties avoid at all costs. In fact, since the transition to democracy, support for women's rights legislation appears to have expanded more rapidly among male representatives on the left than among women outside it, judging by the introduction of several bills by male representatives alone and by the consistent support of a number of male representatives for feminist proposals.

With a few notable exceptions, such as the 1995 divorce bill (Law 19.947), representatives on the left have spearheaded all the congressional bills examined here. In addition, the Left as a whole was united or nearly united in support of almost all the bills. Exceptions were the 1991 abortion bill, where, despite a party position in favor of the limited legalization of abortion, the Left did not lobby for the bill (see chapter 4), and the 1992 congressional bill on sexual assault, which was introduced by María Angélica Cristi, then a deputy from the RN, and did not garner the support of the Concertación.[19] Nevertheless, despite general support for most of the bills, the degree of active support by the Left varied from case to case. This is understandable

---

19. In 2003, Cristi switched her party allegiance to the more conservative UDI. Bill 871 represents an ambivalent case of support for feminist policy, as Cristi developed the bill in isolation from feminist representatives. The Cristi bill refused to acknowledge the existence of sexual assault within the family, framing the issue instead as one of "stranger" assault. The Cristi bill failed to elicit broader support from her party or from feminist legislators, and Cristi later helped introduce a more expansive bill on sexual assault.

given that women's rights are generally a low priority for parties on the left, despite their official position of support. It falls to the relatively low number of feminist representatives to introduce and promote these bills, and these representatives cannot muster equal support or enthusiasm from the rest of the party for every bill on women's rights. Regardless, support by the Left was much higher overall than in the case of centrist and right-leaning parties.

The Socialists and the PPD form a united left-wing caucus (*bancada*) in the Congress, and the two parties vote as a bloc on virtually all the bills on women's rights that have reached the floor. Voting as a bloc in favor of these bills serves the important function of highlighting the difference between the Left and the Christian Democrats, in terms of both ideology and party unity. However, as is clear from the party distribution in the Congress (appendix 2), more than the support of the Left is needed to pass legislation. The alliance of at least a substantial portion of the Christian Democrats on controversial issues is necessary to build majority support for any women's rights bill.

The Christian Democrats

As the governing party between 1990 and 2000 and the largest party in the Congress until 2002, the PDC was long the dominant force within the Concertación. The support of a significant section of the Christian Democrats was—and continues to be—critical for a bill's success. This support has not been easy to come by. As a centrist party with historically strong links to the Catholic Church (Blofield 2006; Fleet and Smith 1997; Haas 1999; Scully 1995), the Christian Democrats are deeply divided on social issues that involve the family and sexuality and often challenge traditional gender roles. The party has had considerably more difficulty than the parties on either the left or the right in forming an opinion on these issues. At times the PDC has attempted to craft a party position on a particular bill, but individual representatives have more often been left to vote their consciences.

The PDC is split between a more traditional, conservative faction and a younger, more progressive wing (Blofield and Haas 2005; Haas 2000; Siavelis 2000). Because of this conservative-progressive split within the party, party unity on bills that would expand women's rights is relatively rare. This is particularly true in the Senate, where the conservative wing of the party is dominant. Together with the greater strength of the Right in the Senate, bills that do make it through the Chamber often become stalled in the upper house. The debate surrounding the 1993 paternity bill (Law 19.58) is an excellent illustration of the conservatism of Christian Democratic senators relative to deputies. The bill, which became law in 1998, sought to equalize the rights of children born within and outside marriage. While most Christian Democrats in the lower house supported the bill early on, a number of Christian Democratic senators contributed to stalling the bill in that chamber. Siding with the Right in the upper house, these representatives argued that the bill would undermine the sanctity of the Chilean family (Haas 2000).

The degree to which the party will rally support behind a bill varies by issue: on social issues with a predominantly economic focus, there is broad consensus; on issues that focus on sexuality or question gender norms, there is less agreement. The Christian Democrats were united on a number of the least controversial bills, such as one increasing the minimum wage for domestic workers, but the party was sharply divided on bills addressing divorce, abortion, and even paternity.[20] Fewer female representatives are elected from the PDC than from either the Right or the Left (appendix 3). Furthermore, among the women in the party rank and file, feminists are a minority.[21] Unlike the parties of the Left, therefore, the PDC contains few women willing to pressure the party to expand women's rights. Although these issues are generally avoided at the party level, specific representatives, most notably Deputy Mariana Aylwin (and Ignacio Walker, to a lesser extent), have pushed the boundaries of party ideology, particularly with their introduction of bills to legalize divorce.[22] With the exception of these bills, Christian

---

20. As discussed below, these divisions mirror the Catholic Church's position on political issues. The Chilean church usually takes a progressive political position on economic and human rights issues and a conservative one on issues of family and sexuality (see Blofield and Haas 2005; Haas 1999).

21. The view that feminists make up a minority of party militants was echoed repeatedly in interviews with male and female PDC members.

22. Aylwin served in the Chamber of Deputies from 1994 to 1998. During this time she was extremely active in promoting women's rights legislation, often working on proposals with left-wing deputies Fanny Pollarolo and María Antonieta Saa. Aylwin drafted the 1995 divorce bill—the bill that angered the party's conservative wing and publicized internal party divisions—with fellow Christian Democrat Ignacio Walker. Although Saa was an extremely popular representative in her Santiago district, weeks before the 1998 congressional elections the party leadership switched her to another district, where she was not well known. With little time to campaign in the new district, Aylwin came in third in the election, losing her seat in the Chamber. Many representatives feel that moving Aylwin to another district was an attempt by the party leadership to punish her for her outspoken position in favor of legal divorce. (Ignacio Walker was not subjected to the same disciplinary measures.) Aylwin later served as education minister in the Lagos administration between 2000 and 2003.

Democratic representatives have not taken the initiative in drafting and introducing legislation expanding women's rights, although in many cases progressive sectors of the party supported a bill after its introduction.

The Right

The political Right is usually divided on these bills, and not infrequently united in opposition to a proposal, as was the case with the pre-1995 divorce bills, the 1991 abortion bill, and the 1993 bill prohibiting discrimination on the basis of sex. On a number of bills, the Right united in opposition to particular aspects of the legislation. This was the case with an amendment to Sernam's sexual assault bill, which decriminalized voluntary homosexual relations between adults (Law 19.617).[23] The most conservative elements of the Right also protested a bill banning mandatory pregnancy tests for women workers (Law 19.591) and the bill to protect pregnant students from expulsion (Law 19.688).

The political Right comprises two primary parties, the Independent Democratic Union and the National Renovation Party. The UDI is the right-wing party most closely linked to the former military government, although it has worked hard in recent years to rebrand itself as a populist party and to distance itself from the legacy of Pinochet. In the first three posttransition Congresses, it was also the only major party without female representatives, although that too has changed in recent years, as the party began to promote women candidates as part of its larger effort at modernizing its image.[24]

The UDI has mounted the strongest opposition to women's rights legislation in the Congress. The few bills on women's rights that UDI representatives have introduced (alone or as part of an alliance with RN

---

23. Under the previous law, homosexual activity between consenting adults was legally equated with sexual assault.

24. Beginning in 2002, the UDI began an active campaign to promote women candidates for office. This dramatic change reflects the party's efforts to deflect criticism that it is "antiwoman." UDI representatives, interviews by author, Santiago, July 6, 2001. The increase in the election of women is most significant at the local level, where the UDI has heavily promoted female candidates for mayor. In the 2000 municipal elections, for example, the UDI ran—and elected—more women candidates than any other party (18 percent of the UDI mayoral candidates elected were women, compared to 13 percent for the RN, and 9 to 11 percent for the parties of the Concertación). See Hinojosa 2004. By 2006 noticeable change had also taken place at the national level, where four women candidates from the UDI were elected to the Chamber of Deputies (appendix 3). For more on the UDI's efforts to promote female candidates and court female voters, see Hinojosa 2004.

representatives) have sought further restrictions on abortion and divorce. They introduced these proposals to counter bills to legalize abortion and divorce that had been introduced earlier by representatives on the center-left.[25] This pattern has held true for the parties' female representatives, some of whom have spearheaded bills to restrict further women's reproductive rights (these bills are discussed in chapters 4 and 5).

The strength of the Right in general, and of the UDI in particular, is considerably greater in the Senate than in the Chamber of Deputies, in terms of both numbers and the ideological intensity of members. Officially, UDI representatives are free to vote their consciences on particular bills, but in practice the party tends to vote as a unified bloc, especially on such contentious issues as divorce.

In the Chamber of Deputies, UDI support for a particular women's rights bill tends to come only after a majority of representatives from other parties have already declared their support. For this reason UDI support has not been necessary for the actual passage of the bills, although strong UDI opposition in committee or on the floor can significantly complicate the modification of a bill. The bills on paternity, sexual assault, and intrafamily violence were significantly stalled by UDI opposition.

The position of the RN is more complicated. Although a conservative party, the RN is split between two distinct factions: an older group that ideologically allies itself most often with the UDI, and a younger group that is willing to break ranks to ally with the conservative sector of the Christian Democrats and, increasingly, with the Left. One of the first clear examples of this split within the RN emerged during the 1996 debate on divorce in the Chamber of Deputies, where nine of the fifty-eight votes in favor of the bill came from RN deputies.

With regard to feminist policy proposals, the RN is therefore less predictable than the UDI. Unlike the UDI, members of the RN have introduced bills (or signed on to them) that aim to expand women's rights. In some cases, such as the Abandonment and Family Support Law (Law 19.741), which provides child support for abandoned spouses, and a 1994 bill protecting the right of pregnant students to remain in school (Law 19.688), RN representatives co-sponsored a bill with representatives from the Concertación. In general, on many issues of this type, parts of the RN can be brought on board if some concessions are made on the bill.

---

25. For more detail on the various proposals to expand and limit abortion rights in Chile, see Blofield 2001 and 2006.

Furthermore, some evolution in thinking on the issue of women's rights is evident in this party. While a few women within the party, most notably former deputy Lily Pérez,[26] were widely recognized as being on the liberal end of the party spectrum, the broadening support for feminist legislation within the RN includes men as well as women. In recent years several RN deputies have even co-sponsored legislation with the Left (notably without any support from the Christian Democrats) to promote reproductive rights and to decriminalize therapeutic abortion (such as bill 3197).

The Number of Women Elected to Congress

Within the Concertación coalition, support for women's rights legislation correlates with the level of women's representation in the parties. Even within the progressive parties of the Left, attention to women's rights has resulted from sustained pressure from party feminists. Although low overall, women's success in winning elected office is greater within the Left than among the Christian Democrats. This is due to the greater openness of the Left to the participation of women, an attitude reflected in the PPD's and the Socialist Party's setting of quotas for women's representation as candidates for internal party office.[27] Nevertheless, the Left has failed to promote high numbers of female candidates for Congress, and, as shown in appendix 3, women's representation in Congress remains low across parties. The Concertación elects more women to office than the Right does, but, as noted above, in recent years the UDI has begun promoting conservative women to office.

While women's representation in Congress remains quite low (appendix 3), it has increased since the transition to democracy. The number of women elected to the Chamber of Deputies from the Concertación rose from four (out of 120) in 1990 to nine in 2006. During the same period, the number of women elected to the Chamber from the Right rose from three to seven. Reflecting the UDI's recent promotion of women candidates, in 2006 more women were elected from that party (four) than from the more moderate

---

26. Arguably the best-known female representative on the right, Pérez served in the Chamber of Deputies from 1998 to 2006. In 2006 she was defeated in her bid for a Senate seat. Pérez was known for her outspoken views in favor of legal divorce, expanded contraceptive rights, and activism against HIV/AIDS.

27. In both parties women must hold at least 30 percent of internal party offices. (Neither gender can surpass 70 percent representation in internal party posts.)

RN (three). In all, women's representation in the lower house rose from seven to eighteen during this period. In the Senate, women's representation remains extremely low. Currently, there are two women in the Senate, one from the PDC and one from the UDI.[28] The dearth of women legislators makes sustained attention to women's rights extremely difficult, particularly in the upper house. Most of the women's rights bills in the first two administrations were spearheaded by a small group of committed feminists from the Left.

Give the strong conservatism of the UDI, which extends for the most part to its women representatives, the increase in the number of women elected to Congress from the party is unlikely to lead to more support for women's rights issues. By contrast, women representatives from the more moderate RN have shown some openness to feminist policy proposals. Beginning in the second democratic Congress (1994–98), feminist representatives on the left were able to form alliances with a few women representatives from the RN. For example, women representatives from the RN supported legislation to institute child-support payments for abandoned spouses (Law 19.741) and to increase the penalties for sexual harassment and sexual assault (1419). In other cases, women from the RN offered outspoken support for feminist bills once they came to the floor for debate, as was the case with the intrafamily violence bill. More recently, the 2003 bill on gender quotas (3206) was supported by two women representatives from the UDI.[29]

Despite women's low representation in Congress, Chile's high incumbency rate (see Carey 2002) means that women who do get elected become increasingly expert legislators over time. This learning process has been critical, because most of the women elected to the Congress, particularly in the first administrations, were not lawyers and had no previous experience in elected office. Despite their lack of legislative experience, feminist representatives were eager to pursue the reform of existing laws on women's rights, and the women's movement had already discussed and prioritized a number of issues, including violence against women, women's health and reproductive rights, and the legalization of divorce. However, in addition to their low numbers overall, feminist representatives found themselves largely shut out of the main congressional committees that reviewed feminist proposals.

---

28. The Christian Democratic senator is Soledad Alvear, the first minister of Sernam.
29. These two UDI representatives, Rosa González and Carmen Ibáñez, failed to win reelection in 2006.

Given the overall low number of women in Congress, gender quotas have become an increasingly contentious issue in recent years. Three bills to institute gender quotas have been introduced in Congress, the first in 1997 (bill 1994) and more recently in 2002 (bill 3020) and 2003 (bill 3206). Bachelet pledged her support for the most recent bill, which as of this writing has still not been put to a floor vote in the Chamber of Deputies. While ideological opposition to gender quotas exists (and not only on the right), arguably the biggest obstacle to their implementation is institutional. Gender quotas work best in high-magnitude districts, where parties can more easily accommodate women candidates without creating as many obvious conflicts among other candidates. In Chile the combination of binomial districts with multiparty electoral coalitions means that parties must already undertake difficult negotiations to determine which party from each coalition may run candidates in each district. Further restricting candidate choice by mandating gender quotas would cause conflict across the parties, including those on the left, which have instituted a more flexible system of gender quotas. Nevertheless, support for gender quotas is increasing in Chile. The first two quota bills were supported only by representatives from the Concertación. The most recent bills, while similar in content, garnered support from representatives across the political spectrum.

Women's Access to Power in Congress

As in the U.S. Congress, the committee system in Chile plays a critical role in determining what legislation will be debated in Congress. In addition to their low numbers in the Congress, feminists until recently have had little access to the primary review committees. This has hampered their ability to push their projects to the floor. In response, feminists have managed to exploit the Family Committee (created in 1994) to force feminist policy onto the congressional agenda. Feminists have also been underrepresented within the larger leadership structure of the Congress, although in recent years they have made some important gains in this area.

The Review Committees

Bills that pass through the Chilean Congress undergo two rounds of debate. The first, or "general" round, follows the first report by the review committee and gauges broader congressional support. If a bill is passed in the general round, it is returned to the committee for more detailed review, at which time representatives on or off the committee, as well as the executive, may offer amendments. Following a second committee report, the floor votes the "particulars" of the bill, often item by item. If it passes this round of debate, the bill moves to the second house. Getting a bill out of committee for the first round is the most crucial step of the process. Each party (or caucus) is assigned a specific number of seats on each committee, based on the percentage of its seats in that chamber. Negotiations then take place within each party or caucus to determine which representatives will be assigned to each committee, subject to the approval of the president of that chamber. While the support of party colleagues is critical in gaining assignment to an influential committee, seniority as such does not determine committee assignments. Because of the low number of feminist representatives in Congress and their relatively weak position within their parties, few sit on the committees that most often review the relevant bills.

The Chamber of Deputies received sixty-one of the sixty-four bills under review here (the other three bills were introduced into the Senate and failed to pass that chamber). The Chamber of Deputies sent these bills to one or more of nine different committees: Constitution, Family, Labor, Human Rights, Education, Foreign Relations, Internal Affairs, Health, and Finance (in some cases, bills were reviewed by more than one committee). However, the majority of the bills have been sent to three of these committees: Constitution, Family, and Labor. As seen in appendix 4, the Constitution Committee has been given jurisdiction or co-jurisdiction over thirty-two of the sixty-one bills; the Family Committee has received twenty-one of the bills, and Labor has received ten. The twenty-four feminist bills that either originated in the Senate or were reviewed there after passing the Chamber were sent to Constitution, Labor, Education, Foreign Relations, or Finance. But here again, the Constitution and Labor committees are key: the Constitution Committee received thirteen of twenty-four bills, and the Labor Committee received eight. The access (or lack of access) of feminist representatives and their allies to these particular committees is thus a critical factor in the fate of these bills.

The party breakdown of each committee reflects the changing fortunes of the parties and coalitions over time.[30] Women are dependent upon the decisions of the party leadership in their committee assignments. In the first

---

30. The number of committee chairs allocated to each party is based on that party's proportion of seats in the Congress. The party and coalition leadership determine the committee place-

posttransition Congress (1990–94), a time when feminists were particularly eager to launch a legislative agenda, no women were assigned to the Constitution Committee in either house. The committee chair in the Chamber of Deputies was Hernán Bosselin, a conservative Christian Democrat, who was a staunch opponent of feminist proposals.[31] Conservatives dominated the committee in the Senate, although the single Socialist member, Hernán Vodanovic, was also the chair. From 1994 to 1998, one woman, Christian Democrat Martita Wörner, joined the Chamber committee. Although not one of the most active feminist members of Congress, Wörner generally supported legislation to expand women's rights. The bulk of committee members did not share her perspective, however, and the committee became significantly more conservative following the 1998 elections. This general pattern held until 2006, when two active feminists, María Antonieta Saa and Laura Soto, both from the PPD, joined the committee. Saa and Soto found consistent support for feminist proposals among two male colleagues on the committee, Juan Bustos (PS) and the committee chair, Jorge Burgos (PDC). The committee also includes a number of strong conservatives, however, including UDI representative Marisol Turres, who have blocked feminist proposals from debate (see chapter 4). Although the current Constitution Committee is the most ideologically progressive since the transition to democracy, strong proponents of feminist legislation still account for only four of the committee's thirteen members.

Another key committee for women's rights legislation has been the Labor Committee. In the first democratic administration, the Chamber's Labor Committee was less conservative than the Constitution Committee. Socialist deputy Adriana Muñoz, one of the most active feminist representatives, chaired the committee from 1990 to 1994. RN deputy Marina Prochelle, who supported the least controversial bills on women's rights, was also an early member. The potential for Muñoz and, to a more limited extent, Prochelle to promote feminist policy objectives was constrained by the relatively small number of bills relating to women's rights that were reviewed by that committee, as well as by the lack of support of other committee members. Muñoz failed to win re-election in 1994, and the 1994–98 Labor Committee was more conservative. Like the Constitution Committee, the growing

---

ment of each representative. Incumbency plays a smaller role in committee assignment than it does in the U.S. Congress.

31. In addition to blocking feminist proposals from debate, Bosselin wrote his own counterproposals, including a 1991 bill restricting civil annulments of marriage (see chapter 5).

strength of the Left in Congress in recent administrations has created a more progressive ideological balance on the committee. Following the 2006 elections, Muñoz returned to the committee as chair and was joined by four other consistent supporters of feminist legislation: Christian Democrat Carolina Goic, PPD representative Ximena Vidal, and male colleagues Sergio Aguiló (PS), arguably the most consistent male proponent of feminist legislation in the Congress, and Fernando Meza (PRSD).

The posttransition history of the Senate Labor Committee reflects similar challenges. The first posttranstion committee included PPD senator Laura Soto, the only representative to introduce feminist legislation in the Senate between 1990 and 1994. Despite her membership on the committee, Soto was unable to keep the committee from burying her 1992 paternity bill (bill 719). As with the Constitution Committee, after 1994 the Labor Committee became more conservative, reflecting the growing strength of the Center-Right in Congress.[32]

The Family Committee: Feminists Find a Way In

Early in the first administration, feminist representatives in the Chamber of Deputies recognized their fellow representatives' lack of interest in pursuing women's rights legislation, and they also understood that their own ability to push for change in this area was hampered by their exclusion from the most relevant committees, particularly the Constitution Committee. From their position outside the crucial committees, feminist legislators had minimal influence over the modification of bills, and they had no way to prevent the committees from permanently shelving proposed legislation. In 1994, however, feminists found a way to exploit their colleagues' lack of interest in feminist legislation and to use the institutional structure of the Congress to their advantage.

Feminist representatives lobbied the rest of the Chamber to create a new committee to address the concerns of women and the family. While not enthusiastic about this plan, many representatives assumed that it would play a marginal legislative role and would alleviate the need to discuss "women's issues" in the major committees. In 1994 the Chamber voted to create the Family Committee. Tellingly, the committee was originally to be called the

---

32. The Labor Committee included one representative from the PDC, two from the RN, one designated senator, one Socialist (the chair), and no women.

Committee on Women, Family, and Youth, but the Chamber voted to delete the other two terms and call it simply the Family Committee.[33] It was two years before the committee was assigned a permanent meeting room, and Christian Democratic deputy Mariana Aylwin claims that there was a continual campaign to discredit the committee's work.[34]

Feminist representatives lobbied their parties for appointment to the committee. But rather than allow the Chamber to marginalize women's rights by delegating them to this new and unprestigious committee, feminists maneuvered to give the Family Committee a central role in debates on women's rights. When feminists introduced a proposal in the Chamber, members of the committee were first lobbied for sole review of the bill. If the bill was nevertheless sent to other committees, such as Constitution or Labor, the Family Committee would lobby to form a joint review committee or to co-review the legislation separately. (Such a request must be voted on by the full Chamber. In cases where a second committee requests the right to co-review a particular bill, the request must be approved unanimously by all the members present in the Chamber.)

In this way feminist representatives created a mechanism for pressuring other committees to act on these bills. By issuing its own analysis of a bill and bringing it to the floor, the Family Committee can force the main review committee (usually Constitution) to issue its own version of the bill and its own recommendation. In cases where the Family Committee co-reviews a bill with another committee, members of the Family Committee, who by and large support feminist policy proposals, can bring enough votes to the table to force a committee vote on a bill. This is what happened with the 1995 divorce bill, when the Family and Constitution committees formed a joint committee. As detailed in chapter 5, the addition of members from Family gave the joint committee enough votes in favor of the divorce bill to bring it to the floor for a vote. This was the first time that the legalization of divorce had ever been discussed in Congress, and the subsequent passage

---

33. Feminist representatives point to this as indicative of the "proper scope" the Chamber envisioned for the committee, and the way in which women's issues in Chile are often redefined to focus on the family. Family Committee members, interviews by author, Valparaíso, March–April 1997.

34. Aylwin claimed that because most members of the committee are strongly committed to the bills they review, they tend to spend more time than members of other committees studying and modifying the bills. In the course of the first year, President Frei even publicly complained about the pace of their work, which has rarely happened with other committees. Aylwin, interview by author, Valparaíso, March 12, 1997.

of the bill in the Chamber of Deputies gained the committee considerable respectability.

The existence of the Family Committee has been a contributing factor to the increasing success of congressional bills on women's rights since 1994. In the committee's early years, it co-reviewed the 1993 and 1994 divorce bills, the 1993 sexual assault bill, and the 1993 paternity bill. In addition, it was the primary review committee for the 1994 bill protecting pregnant students from expulsion, the 1994 bill stipulating child support in cases of spousal abandonment, the 1995 marital property rights bill, and the 1995 divorce bill, as well as more recent efforts in 2007 and 2008 to legislate on violence against women. Since 2006 the committee has increased its influence within the Chamber, in some cases winning sole review of feminist legislation (see appendix 4). In 1998 a bill was introduced in the Senate to create a similar committee in that chamber, but this bill has not progressed.

Feminist Leadership in the Congress

In addition to appointment to key committees, feminist influence in Congress depends on feminists' access to positions of leadership. Here again, the low number of feminists in Congress (and the low position of women within the parties) has been reflected in the relative absence of women—especially feminists—in leadership posts. Feminists have gained ground in this area in recent years, however; three feminists have been elected to top leadership posts in the Chamber of Deputies. In 1997 María Antonieta Saa (PPD) was elected vice president of the Chamber, a position she held until 1998 (a one-year term is standard). In 2002 PPD deputy Adriana Muñoz was elected president of the Chamber, and she was followed in 2003 by PS deputy Isabel Allende. These success stories suggest that feminists are gaining the confidence of their male colleagues and are increasingly seen as belonging to the mainstream of their parties.

Policymaking in the Senate

Policymaking in the Senate exhibits its own dynamic, owing to its more conservative character relative to the Chamber and to the overall closer relationship the Senate enjoys with the executive branch. The more conservative wings of both the Christian Democrats and the Far Right parties dominate their parties' caucuses in the Senate. Furthermore, prior to the constitutional reforms of 2005, the existence of nine "designated" (unelected) senators gave conservatives additional weight in the upper house. All of these factors have posed obstacles to feminist legislation. The designated senators represented a predominantly conservative force, which worked with the Right to block feminist initiatives. In addition, because of the transversal nature of feminist policy issues and the complicated position of Sernam within the executive branch, feminists have not been able to take advantage of the close working relationship that exists between senators and the executive on other policy issues.

The Designated Senators

In addition to the thirty-eight elected senators, prior to a series of constitutional reforms in 2005, there were nine unelected senators in the upper house. While no longer a relevant factor, the designated senators were in place during the period when most of the bills examined here were under consideration in Congress. A brief overview of their character and their legislative role will clarify the particular challenges feminists faced in pushing progressive proposals through the Senate.

Like elected senators, the designated senators served eight-year terms. The institution of designated senators went hand in hand with the reform of the electoral law, as part of the institutional reforms of the 1980 constitution. The official justification for designated senators was the need to create a group of legislators who would stand above the ideological conflicts that divided political parties and thus contribute to consensual policymaking in the Senate. That the designated senators were chosen from predominantly conservative institutions makes it clear that the real motive behind their appointment was the strengthening of conservative forces in the upper house.[35] Although they rarely initiated legislative proposals, most designated senators allied themselves with the Far Right to block policy initiatives from the Concertación. Particularly in the case of constitutional reform, which required a larger percentage of votes than a simple majority, the unified opposition of

---

35. The designated senators were chosen from the following institutions: two former Supreme Court justices (chosen by the Supreme Court); one former comptroller-general of the Republic (also chosen by the Supreme Court); one ex-commander from each of the three branches of the armed forces (army, navy, and air force), and one former director-general of the police, all chosen by the National Security Council; one ex-rector of a state university (chosen by the president); and one ex-minister of state (also chosen by the president).

the designated senators played a critical role in blocking legislation.[36] The president appointed only two of the senators, making the overall appointment of progressive senators difficult.

The combination of the d'Hondt voting system, which disproportionately favors the Right, and the designated senators resulted in a Senate that was significantly more conservative than the Chamber of Deputies. Feminist proposals that passed the lower house with relative ease were routinely stalled in the Senate as a result. In most cases these were not particularly controversial bills. For example, the designated senators opposed bills that dealt with the education rights of pregnant students, child support for abandoned spouses, and child care for working mothers. Eventually these bills passed the Senate after additional modifications were made to appease Senate conservatives.

Informal Mechanisms of Senate Influence

Research on Chilean political institutions has long argued that Congress, particularly the Senate, has more policy influence than is apparent from a consideration of formal powers alone (see, for example, Agor 1971). More recently, Ferraro (2006) has argued that the Senate exercises informal oversight over the executive in three main ways: by suggesting candidates for positions in public administration, by linking Senate committees to specific executive ministries, and by encouraging parties to specialize in particular policy areas. Unfortunately, each of these informal mechanisms is weaker when it comes to women's rights legislation, not only because of the dearth of feminist senators but because of the way feminist policy transcends traditional issue areas.

Because of the absence of feminist senators (and women senators in general), the Senate has not lobbied as strongly for candidates to head Sernam as it has for other ministerial posts. The head of Sernam has rotated among the parties of the Concertación, with the minister from one party and the vice minister from another, as is the case across the cabinet. Because most of the top leaders have been chosen without wide consultation with the feminist community, the government has appointed primarily women who built their careers through the political parties rather than the women's movement

---

36. Under the 1980 constitution, certain types of legislation, most notably constitutional reform, must get three-fifths or two-thirds (depending on the particular bill) of the vote in each chamber to pass.

(this lack of linkage to the movement is one reason why feminist organizations and feminists in Congress have been wary of Sernam).

The structure of the Senate committee system parallels that of the executive cabinet ministries. It allows each congressional committee to form a close link to the relevant executive ministry, which facilitates cooperative policymaking between the branches of government. Weekly meetings between committee members and members of the relevant ministry encourage cooperative policymaking. Ferraro (2006, 4) has found that senators networked regularly with an average of ten to forty public officials.

In trying to replicate this process, Sernam and congressional feminists face some specific challenges. First, as mentioned above, Sernam suffers from a relatively low status within the bureaucracy. Although its mandate allows it to introduce its own legislation, it is also supposed to monitor the policy developments of other ministries. Sernam's attempts to coordinate with other ministries through regular meetings have not met with enthusiasm from the rest of the bureaucracy. With some notable exceptions (as when former PDC deputy Mariana Aylwin served as education minister from 2000 to 2003 or Michelle Bachelet was appointed to head the Ministry of Health [2000–2002]), government ministers and lower-level civil servants have not shown much interest in exploring the gender implications of their policies with the head of Sernam.

Second, there is no Senate committee linked directly to Sernam. In the Chamber of Deputies, the Family Committee is a natural ally, but no comparable Senate committee exists. Furthermore, it is evident from the range of feminist legislation introduced since 1990 that women's rights cover a multitude of issues that might be handled by other ministries and reviewed by any number of congressional committees, such as Health, Education, Constitution, Foreign Relations, or Labor. In fact, even in the Chamber of Deputies, the Family Committee usually does not review a bill on its own; it is much more likely to participate in a co-review of a bill with another committee, such as Health (appendix 4). That feminist policy proposals are reviewed by different congressional committees makes it impossible for a Senate committee to specialize in women's rights issues and to develop a mutually supportive policy relationship with a particular executive ministry.

Finally, Ferraro (drawing on Laver and Shepsle 1996) argues that when political parties specialize in particular policy areas, their policy expertise gives them added influence within their coalition; their policy proposals carry more weight in the Congress as well as the executive branch. "The association of parties with an area of public policy is established not only by means of a concentration of resources (information, specialized personnel and networks of contacts)," he explains, "but also by the association of certain public policy proposals with 'symbolic and ideological values' sustained by the party" (2006, 9). Because of the cross-issue nature of women's rights, there is less party specialization here than in other policy areas. In recent years, however, the PPD has decided to make women's rights one of its policy specializations. Ferraro concludes that the "PPD represents in Chile a particularly interesting case of party specialization because of its evident *post-materialist* orientation. . . . Under the name of 'civic agenda,' the questions included are the defense of consumers, divorce, contraception, the fight against AIDS, the defense of indigenous minorities and the protection of the environment" (11). Despite this, and even with the abolition of the designated senators, feminist legislation faces significant obstacles when it reaches the Senate.

Staffing and Legislative Assistance

Finally, a challenge policymakers face in both chambers involves the inadequate staff of most legislators. The lack of legislative staff and resources hampers representatives' ability to craft successful legislation. Legislative staff is usually minimal, and the vast majority of a legislator's budget is spent on election activists, not legislative assistants. As a result, legislators must depend on technical experts in government to assist with the writing of bills. The largest legislative staffs are found in the offices of right-wing representatives, a number of whom have the personal funds to employ a larger staff. The Left feels the lack of legislative assistance most keenly, and since the Left introduces most of the congressional bills on women's rights, this disadvantage is particularly onerous when it comes to efforts to draft competitive congressional bills on these issues. As we shall see in the following chapter, one of the key weaknesses of congressional bills on women's rights has been their technical inferiority relative to the bills introduced by Sernam. Congressional committees also lack an independent budget, and this affects their ability to get technical advice on the bills being debated. Committees can invite outside experts to testify, and each committee has a secretary who is a lawyer, but committees cannot count on consistent access to technical expertise when drafting and modifying legislation (see Franceschet 2005; Haas 2000; Siavelis 2000).[37]

These formal and informal political institutions shape the behavior of feminist representatives, members of Sernam, and the political opposition as they attempt to affect policymaking on women's rights issues. But this institutional structure also helps determine the role that outside actors will play in the policy process. The two most important actors outside the state are the Catholic Church and the Chilean women's movement (particularly the feminist community). Although progressive on issues of poverty and human rights, the church has opposed many of the feminist proposals on women's rights. The church's political and cultural influence in Chile creates a powerful counterweight to feminists who pressure the state for reform.

The Influence of the Catholic Church

The Catholic Church exerts significant influence over posttransition politics, particularly on contentious issues of social reform. The role that progressive sectors of the church played in supporting human rights during the dictatorship gave the church as a whole renewed moral authority following the transition.[38] On such issues as women's rights, the church is the most influential extragovernmental actor in the opposition. As noted above, church opposition causes particular conflict for the Christian Democrats, whose liberal wing often supports legal reforms on women's rights but whose historic ties with the church make it difficult for the party to vote in opposition to official church teaching. Since the transition to democracy, right-wing politicians, particularly from the UDI, have made common cause with the church in opposing a number of feminist proposals. While public opinion appears to be liberalizing on many social issues (Blofield 2006), which suggests that official church positions may be less politically salient in the future, the church still exerts a significant political influence over the development of policy proposals from both the Concertación and the Right.[39]

---

37. The lack of adequate legislative assistance was also a common complaint in my interviews with members of Congress.

38. I argue in Haas 1999 that this increased political influence benefited even those members of the clergy who were sympathetic to the military regime.

39. For a more detailed discussion of the church's role in Chilean politics, see Fleet and Smith 1997; Haas 1999; Blofield and Haas 2005.

Although the Catholic Church has long played a role in Chilean politics, its current political incarnation owes much to the role it played during the military regime. Under the dictatorship, progressive sectors within the Catholic Church in Chile played an important role in defending human rights and speaking out against the economic policies of the military government. This gave the church as a whole great moral authority among progressives and helped it gain a prominent role in posttransition politics. The church has emerged as a conservative political force since the transition, however, thanks to increased public debate and policy proposals on issues of family, sexuality, and gender roles. This change is due in part to the emergence of more conservative leadership, together with the fact that new issues have emerged on which the church has historically held a conservative view (see Fleet and Smith 1997; Haas 1999). With respect to feminist policy proposals, the church will not exert a strong lobbying effort in favor of a bill, but it will lobby hard against a bill it strongly opposes. In other words, church opposition may be an influential factor in the fate of a bill on women's rights, but active church support is not a relevant factor in the successful passage of feminist legislation.

In the cases discussed here, only the issues of divorce and abortion have aroused consistent, strong church opposition. In the case of abortion, the church speaks out generally against legalization, and concern about church reaction contributes to representatives' reluctance to sponsor a bill. The 1991 Muñoz bill that would have legalized therapeutic abortion died in committee (see chapter 4), and a later bill drafted by women's organizations was rejected for lack of sponsorship.[40] The church has rejected calls for public debate on abortion and would strongly oppose any bill debated in Congress. Indeed, the expectation of church opposition—and the effect it would have on the Concertación as well as on the Right—is a main reason why representatives who favor the decriminalization of abortion will not support a bill, even one that merely restores the pre-1989 abortion law.[41] In addition, despite the

---

40. Therapeutic abortion is defined as an abortion performed when a pregnancy poses a danger to a woman's life or health. A therapeutic abortion law was in effect in Chile from 1931 to 1989.

41. Lidia Casas, a law student who drafted a bill on abortion for a coalition of NGOs involved with issues of reproductive rights, explained that no congressional representative—not even those who favored legalizing abortion—would agree to introduce the bill in Congress. The feminist representatives felt that if efforts to legalize divorce had failed, there was no hope for abortion, and that sponsoring such a bill would be political suicide. Casas, interview by author, April 1997. See chapter 4.

high rate of illegal abortions in Chile and some survey evidence of public support for limited decriminalization, abortion remains a cultural taboo, and there is a lack of open public support for policy reform.[42] Given the resistance to legalization from the Catholic Church, the Christian Democrats, and the Right, considerable public mobilization would be needed if such a bill were to have any hope of passing.

By contrast, the legalization of divorce enjoyed wide public support for years before the passage of the divorce law.[43] Numerous bills on the topic had been introduced in the past, beginning as far back as the turn of the century, and they had increased in frequency since the transition to democracy. The last bill to legalize divorce, introduced in 1995, was the first to make it out of committee and be debated by the Chamber of Deputies, where it passed in September 1997. The bill passed the Senate in 2004, instituting civil divorce for the first time in Chile's history. In this case, the church launched an aggressive lobbying campaign against the bill but was ultimately unsuccessful in preventing its passage (see chapter 5).

The Catholic Church exerts a low but consistent level of influence on legislation through such means as pastoral letters and public sermons, as well as through personal ties with specific representatives. This influence contributes to keeping the most controversial issues, such as abortion, off the political agenda. If a controversial bill is nevertheless introduced, the church exerts a tremendous effort to influence legislators, but, as the divorce law demonstrates, church opposition alone cannot ensure a bill's defeat.

Representatives feel the legislative influence of the Catholic Church at two levels: first, and most directly, the parties of the Right and especially the Christian Democrats have close ties to the church, and representatives from the church are often invited to speak before congressional committees on particular bills. When the church hierarchy is fairly united with regard to a specific proposal, such as on the issue of legalizing divorce, church influence is naturally greater than in cases where church opinion is divided, as was the case with a paternity reform bill and a bill protecting pregnant students from expulsion. Because the Catholic Church remains an influential moral voice

---

42. Despite its illegality, it has been estimated that as many as one in three pregnancies ends in abortion (Cáceres et al. 1993, 7–8). The survey evidence in favor of decriminalization is reviewed in Blofield 2001.

43. According to public opinion polls cited by the Center for Research on Women, 85 percent of Chileans favored legal divorce in 1996. Centro de Estudios de la Mujer 1996b, 4; see also chapter 5.

in Chilean politics, representatives often try to gain the support of some member of the church hierarchy. On a number of the women's rights bills, conservative committee members invited conservative clergy to testify, while liberal members invited more progressive members of the church to testify. On topics where there is conflicting church testimony, the influence of the church is obviously diminished. Some representatives from these parties believe that their personal faith as Catholics means that they should not promote legislation that conflicts with church teaching. Other representatives feel pressured by their party to reflect church teaching in their positions on legislation, or at least not to oppose it.

At a second level, related to this last point, there is concern among legislators that the church's public statements on these issues could have negative electoral implications for legislators in their constituencies.[44] It is important to distinguish here between the church's institutional connections to parties and individual representatives and the degree of religiosity of the population. Blofield (2006, 21) cites World Values Survey results on church attendance to argue that the Catholic Church enjoys political influence disproportionate to the strength of religious affiliation of most of the population. In 1990, for example, as debates over women's rights issues were heating up in Congress and society, surveys showed that more than half of Chilean adults (53.4 percent) attended church rarely (i.e., only on holidays) or never. Only 27.7 percent attended once a week or more.

Yet the close institutional relationship between the Catholic Church and the Center-Right in Chile affords it disproportionate influence over public policy. This is particularly the case with women's rights issues, where public opinion data suggest that public adherence to church teachings is relatively low on issues such as contraception, sex outside marriage, abortion, and divorce. Blofield (2006) reviews existing data on both public opinion and public behavior (including, for example, abortion rates, per capita rates of births to single mothers, and rates of marital dissolution) to demonstrate convincingly that public opinion is significantly more liberal than the official Catholic position on these issues (see chapter 4). Nevertheless, Blofield argues that, through its extensive media ownership, the church plays an influential role in shaping public discourse on women's rights. The powerful cultural presence of the church and its media spokespersons suppresses public debate on

---

44. For example, during the debate on the 1995 divorce bill, several bishops exhorted their parishioners not to vote for representatives who supported the bill. Medina 1995, 2; Fuenzalida 1997, 10; Haas 1999.

contentious social issues and obscures the significant gap between public discourse and public practice in Chile.

The lack of open public debate and the relative paucity of survey data on public opinion on these issues mean that it is often difficult for representatives to gauge the impact that a concerted church campaign may have on voters in their districts. This is particularly the case when church leaders target specific representatives, as in the case of therapeutic abortion and divorce. As a result, despite the level of public support that may exist in favor of policy reform, representatives still fear the negative repercussions of openly defying the church. This concern was evident during the debates on the 1995 divorce bill, when a visible group of clergymen was among the visitors present in the Chamber to observe the debate. In response to such pressures, those representatives on the right who supported the divorce bill attempted to arrange for a secret vote on the bill, but this motion was voted down on the floor.[45]

The Influence of the Women's Movement over Policymaking

Organized, sustained counterpressure from the women's movement could mitigate each of these obstacles to feminist policymaking. The Chilean women's movement, and the feminist movement in particular, was the formative influence in the development of a political agenda to reform laws on women's rights. Yet, in the two decades since the transition, the movement has mobilized only sporadically in support of particular legislative proposals, and its participation in the legislative process overall has been marginal and largely indirect. When the movement has mobilized to influence the legislative process, as was the case with domestic violence and, to a lesser degree, divorce legislation, the movement has had an impact on the policy process. However, there are multiple obstacles to more effective participation by the women's movement. Once the transition to democracy had taken place, and after the issue of violence against women had been addressed by the first democratic administration, individual organizations began to focus more narrowly on particular political concerns, complicating movementwide action. The organizations within the women's movement faced severe funding cuts following the transition, which put financing for an ongoing lobbying

---

45. Committee members, interviews by author, Valparaíso, January 1997.

effort out of reach.[46] Within the movement, deep divisions emerged over the utility of formal political participation. Sernam exacerbates this ambivalence by privileging professional NGOs over grassroots organizations.

The cycle of activity in the Chilean women's movement conforms to many of the patterns identified in the comparative literature on social movements. A particular advantage in the Chilean case was that women were able to form a broad-based, cross-class movement in opposition to authoritarian rule, and this provided a diverse and powerful base from which to pressure for women's rights during the transition period.[47] Following the transition, the movement remained largely united behind its first major policy goal: the passing of domestic violence legislation. The Intrafamily Violence Law was passed in 1994 (see chapter 3), and after this success the movement disintegrated into various suborganizations, many explicitly feminist, focusing on a wide range of issues (see Valdés 1998; Valenzuela 1998; Waylen 1997, 2000). Women's organizations were particularly challenged by the sharp decrease in international funding after the transition. Research by Fisher (1993), Fitzsimmons (2000), and Hipsher (1996) charts the rise and fall of movement activism, with particular emphasis on working-class women, who had organized self-help organizations in the shantytowns. Additional work charts the early interactions of the women's movement with the democratic government, including political parties and Sernam (Baldez 2001; Cáceres et al. 1993; Mlynarz and Muñoz 2003; Valenzuela 1998; Waylen 1997). Like other Latin American women's movements, the movement in Chile has struggled to transform a politics of protest against an authoritarian regime into a politics of engagement with a democratic state. And like social movements in general, after decades of activism it confronts battle fatigue, loss of leadership, and lack of generational replacement, all made more challenging by ongoing conservative opposition to political change. The results for feminists in civil society have been low public visibility and relatively little influence over policy development. Maruja Barrig (1997, 12) concludes, "The movement (women/feminist) does not move much, renews itself little, and congregates in the streets even less" (quoted in Ríos Tobar 2003).

---

46. Most of the funding for movement activities came from abroad, particularly from the European Union. Most of this funding evaporated once the dictatorship ended. See Baldez 2001; Francheschet 2003, 2005.

47. For a detailed history of the Chilean women's movement, see Baldez 2002; Chuchryk 1994; Fisher 1993; Frohmann and Valdés 1993.

A number of analyses trace the current ineffectiveness of Chile's feminist movement to its disintegration after the transition to democratic government in 1990. Baldez, however, argues that the subdivision of the Chilean women's movement into smaller, more focused feminist organizations is not necessarily a bad thing for feminist influence over policymaking:

> The inevitable dissolution of women's movements may appear as grim news—but only if sustained unity is perceived to be the desired outcome.... Studies of women's movements frequently conclude with a call to consolidate women's mobilization, but that recommendation may prove self-defeating when it comes to meeting women's particular demands.... The natural next step [in research] focuses on which strategies lead to the most significant and sustained policy gains for women. It is far from self-evident that unified organizing among women is the best way to pursue their (our) collective interests. (2002, 207–8)

The more relevant question, then, is how the subdivision of the women's movement, together with other posttransition political changes, has affected the ability of feminist organizations to lobby effectively for policy reform.

The global trend toward the "NGOization" of women's movements has hit Chile particularly hard. This is particularly evident in the evolving relationship between Sernam and the women's movement. The creation of Sernam was a direct result of pressure on the traditional political parties from the women's movement and feminists in the parties (Matear 1997; Valdés 1998), but feminists accuse the ministry of neglecting to incorporate the movement into its political activity. Sernam has focused on building relationships with feminist NGOs, which can assist it with technical expertise and legislative assistance, but has excluded "popular" grassroots organizations. The shift from grassroots organizations to professional NGOs has created a clear hierarchy among feminist organizations that seek to participate in politics. Franceschet (2005) notes the class bias in granting professional (that is, middle-class) NGOs more access to the state. Richards (2004) concludes that there is an ethnic bias here as well, as the system marginalizes indigenous women (and their policy concerns). In both cases, it is not only the policy concerns of poor and indigenous women that are left off the policy agenda; the system systematically excludes these constituencies of women from political participation. Franceschet explains that Sernam "has been able to devise mechanisms for improving women's movements' access to arenas of policymaking. To date, however, access exists for organized women in the NGOs, but not for grassroots activists, further fragmenting an already divided women's movement" (2005, 135).

Moreover, it is not simply the NGOization of the movement that is problematic. Among NGOs themselves, competition for funding from the state causes division and conflict. Waylen (2000) argues that Sernam "beheaded" the women's movement, as money that had gone to feminist NGOs was shifted to the state, where NGOs were forced to bid for contract work. The result of this process is that Sernam taps the same NGOs repeatedly for future work. One clear effect of this trend is that moderate NGOs, which are less critical of the state, are granted more access. Waylen (2000) and Schild (1998) argue that this system rewards moderate groups over more critical—and more autonomous—organizations. Teresa Valdés, a founding member of Chile's feminist movement, asserts, "If NGOs had their own resources, the discussions around autonomy would be totally different than when you have to go presenting bids to Sernam" (quoted in Franceschet 2005, 156). Waylen (2000) concludes that the paradox of Sernam is that its strength depends on the autonomous movement outside it and the pressure of that movement on the parties and government, yet that very strength undermines the influence and strength of the independent movement. The women's movement continues to struggle with its relationship to Sernam in an effort to balance political participation and influence against the need for independence from state control.

To a large degree, these tensions were inevitable, as the return to democracy in Chile meant the reemergence of traditional political actors, particularly the political parties. Sociologist María Elena Valenzuela, a member of the women's movement who worked in Sernam during the first democratic administration, explains, "So much political space is occupied by the parties that it doesn't leave a lot of space for those outside it. This is largely responsible for the exit from the scene of the women's movement. The parties grant you legitimacy to negotiate."[48] Other feminists echo the complaint that the rigidity of political institutions makes access nearly impossible. Verónica Matus, of the feminist NGO La Morada, asserts that unlike feminists in other countries, the Chilean feminist community has failed to create a feminist constituency that can make proposals "above this institutionality." The

---

48. María Elena Valenzuela, interview by author, Santiago, January 9, 1997.

women's movement, she says, is caught "in the shadow of these institutions, and if you want to get out from under it, you have to travel so far [in discourse and proposals] that no one even sees you anymore."[49]

The movement of many feminist leaders into the state and political parties has contradictory effects in this respect. On the one hand, the incorporation of feminists into the state has the potential to build critical networks between the state and feminist organizations in civil society. On the other hand, this same process depletes the leadership of feminist organizations. Ríos Tobar (2003) explains that even when feminists in the parties or government are able to maintain their connections to the movement, their position within the state compromises their independence and makes it difficult for them to disagree publicly with party or state policy.

The larger context of posttransition politics also affects the ability of feminist groups to agitate for broader policy reforms. As mentioned above, research on Chilean political culture notes the dominance of conservative discourse in the public sphere (Blofield 2006; Fleet and Smith 1997; Franceschet 2005; Guzmán, Hola, and Ríos 1999; Haas 1999). Blofield (2006) details the consequences for public discourse of conservative (and specifically church) control of the media. Franceschet (2005) concurs that the Right has effectively redefined political issues through the lens of traditional morality. This discourse overwhelms competing political frames based on equality or democracy. Thus feminists must continually defend even modest proposals for reform against charges that they are antifamily, foreign, even antinationalist (Haas 1999).

Finally, Chilean political culture has historically been very statist, with political demands channeled almost exclusively through the political parties. As a consequence, interest group politics is a relatively recent development. When such groups do form, their tendency is to try to work individually with the state rather than coordinate with one another. Ríos Tobar (2003, 259, drawing on Guzmán, Hola, and Ríos 1999) points to a study by the Centro de Estudios de la Mujer that found that "most of the social actors interviewed expected the Government to promote their political participation and organization; women's groups favoured establishing links with the state and political parties rather than with other organization within civil society."

As with feminist movements globally, the question of movement influence in Chile is difficult to define. As Ríos Tobar (2003) argues persuasively,

---

49. Verónica Matus, interview by author, Santiago, April 2, 1997.

Chilean feminists have succeeded in influencing the broader culture by increasing the visibility of women's rights issues and working to demystify feminism in the public mind. Changes within political parties, academia, and popular culture reflect a growing familiarity with feminist issues. Nevertheless, it is clear that a number of obstacles inhibit greater movement impact on policy. Divisions and disagreements within Chile's feminist community, exacerbated by chronic funding crises, limit the ability of feminist organizations to lobby effectively for feminist policy. Sernam's preference for working with professional feminist NGOs has narrowed the opportunities for political participation by poor and working-class, as well as indigenous, women. Finally, self-censorship, which is often the price of participation for middle-class groups, limits the extent to which these groups can bring a broader political critique to their work with the state.

All of these factors have diminished the feminist movement's ability to mobilize around a set of policy priorities. PPD deputy Adriana Muñoz, the most active representative on women's rights issues in the first democratic Congress (1990–94), introduced fewer feminist bills in later years. She explains that the lack of a clear policy agenda from the feminist community left her without a clear mandate for reform: "I have not proposed any bills [on these issues] because I don't have [a] clear [idea] what is important for women today. . . . I know that the question I have to ask myself is, 'For which group of women do I want to legislate?'" (quoted in Franceschet 2005, 103).

Conflict and Cooperation in the Struggle for Policy Reform

As Isabel Duque of ISIS International has said, "It's hard to insert the issue of gender into public debate. Sernam has had a difficult time legitimizing these issues to the rest of the government. If Sernam is marginalized, imagine the degree of marginalization of civil society."[50] The comparative literature on feminist policymaking concludes that the creation of policy networks among feminists in the political parties, national women's agencies, and civil society offers the best hope for achieving progressive policy reform. To date, however, there has been relatively little research on the complex nature of these strategic alliances, in particular on the potential conflict that may

---

50. Isabel Duque, of ISIS International, interview by author, April 9, 1997.

emerge among these various actors and the disincentives that may exist to closer cooperation. The relationship between feminist representatives and Sernam, and the access both provide to the women's movement, will shape the types of issues that are adopted by the government, the framing of those issues, and the ultimate success or failure of the proposals. My research suggests that feminist policymaking depends on the successful negotiation of often competing loyalties among feminists at all levels of the process, including party and constituency issues for congressional representatives, interbranch conflict between feminists in Congress and Sernam, and debates about autonomy versus participation within the women's movement. Building cooperative policy networks among all these actors is critical if feminists are to combat effectively the opposition to women's rights legislation. Across the state and within civil society, the more feminists are able to develop a shared vision for policy change, the more pressure they will bring to the process, and the fewer compromises will need to be made to the political opposition.

In this respect, the history of feminist policymaking since the transition to democracy reveals several important trends. Feminist representatives introduced a number of women's rights bills in the first democratic administration (1990–94), but only one of these bills (the Intrafamily Violence Law) was enacted into law. These early congressional bills were introduced almost exclusively by feminist legislators on the left. The failure of most of these bills is especially striking when compared to the relative success of Sernam-sponsored legislation in the same period (appendix 1). As a result of these failures, beginning in the second democratic administration, feminist legislators began to seek legislative alliances with their counterparts in the Christian Democratic Party and the moderate Right. These alliances led to greater success for congressional bills after 1994, but they often required that feminists negotiate with conservatives on the bills' scope and content in order to gain cross-party support.

Particularly in the absence of executive institutional support for a congressional bill, the alliance of Right and Left is often critical to a bill's success. As the case studies illustrate, party unity has been difficult to achieve on the issues examined here, for the Center-Right more than for the Left. For this reason, the supporting coalition on most of these bills has not been an alliance of parties but a coalition of the leftist parties and individuals from the Christian Democrats and the Right. It is quite common for a significant sector of the Christian Democrats to unite with the majority of the Left in support of these bills, and some sectors of the Right have demonstrated an increasing willingness to vote in favor of expanding women's rights as well.

There now exists a predictable cohort of male support within the Left, not only for supporting bills after their introduction but for drafting feminist legislation. While support among Christian Democrats remains low at the drafting stage, feminists have also expanded their support within this party for feminist proposals that make it to the floor. Most surprisingly, right-wing legislators—men as well as women—have increased their support for feminist policy. Although relatively few representatives on the right are consistent supporters, they have voted in favor of some of the most controversial recent bills, covering gender quotas, reproductive rights, and sexual assault.

Such broad political alliances come at a price, however, and feminists both inside and outside government struggle over how much to compromise with conservatives in order to win support for feminist proposals. I argue that the limited public visibility of the feminist movement in Chile contributes to a policymaking dynamic that necessitates significant compromise. The strength of political opposition from the Center-Right parties and the Catholic Church fundamentally affects the choice of issues for debate. But these factors also shape the strategies of the actors who draft feminist policy. Feminists have taken various approaches to building support, from limiting the scope of their bills to defending their proposals with "pro-family" rhetoric that mirrors the language of political conservatives. These strategies are passionately debated within feminist circles. Feminism seems to be gaining ground both culturally and politically in Chile. At the same time, opposition to reform runs high, and many feminists question the wisdom of passing inadequate legislation that may undermine future attempts at reform.

The case studies that follow illustrate these dynamics. In each of the policy areas examined here—domestic violence, abortion, and divorce—feminists continue to debate how best to achieve legal reform. Each of these cases reveals the significant obstacles that continue to inhibit feminist policymaking. More important, the case studies demonstrate that feminists have learned how to achieve impressive policy gains even on the most contentious issues of women's rights.

3

SUCCESS AT A PRICE:
PASSING DOMESTIC VIOLENCE LEGISLATION

> What we're talking about are precisely those cases in which women are being tortured by their husbands, being beaten all over by them, and in which women are in a state of psychosis as a result of the violence they've suffered. And the visible bruises are a minor indication of what's happening internally.

The passage of the Intrafamily Violence (Violencia Intrafamiliar, or VIF) law in 1994 counts as one of Chile's most significant legislative successes on women's rights.[1] As one of the earliest feminist proposals to follow the transition to democracy, the law has also come to symbolize the challenges to cooperation between Sernam and congressional feminists and the obstacles feminist organizations face in their efforts to participate in policymaking. Competition between the minister of Sernam and congressional representatives over ownership of domestic violence legislation led to poor institutional cooperation on the bill. Congressional representatives and members of the feminist movement blamed the ministry for weaknesses in the resulting law. Cultural opposition to domestic violence legislation was lower than in the case of the other proposals examined here, but it was still a factor in the final shape of the legislation, which lacked the necessary funding for implementation and was weak on victim protection and on punishment for abusers. In this case, moderate institutional cooperation and

---

1. The epigraph that opens this chapter is from Paulina Weber, director of the Movement for the Emancipation of the Chilean Woman (MEMCH), interview by author, Santiago, March 25, 1997.

moderate strategic framing led to only moderate success—the bill passed, but in a form that was widely criticized on content. A decade after the passage of the law, an improved institutional relationship between the leadership of Sernam and congressional feminists led to a successful effort to improve the VIF law. But the participation of feminist organizations in policymaking debates has yet to return to the levels seen during the fight for domestic violence legislation.

The VIF law illustrates feminist learning at several levels. Despite the law's passage, many feminists in civil society concluded that cooperation with the state on women's rights policy was not possible without unacceptable compromises. Feminist legislators learned to distrust Sernam, which they felt had commandeered the effort to pass domestic violence legislation and had forced through changes to the bill over their opposition. The longer-term repercussions for feminist learning have been more positive. The failure to decriminalize therapeutic abortion (the subject of chapter 4) and the struggle to legalize divorce (see chapter 5) convinced feminists inside and outside government of the need to build stronger policymaking networks if they were to surmount opposition to reform. In recent years feminists and their supporters have returned to the subject of violence against women, and their latest legislative efforts illustrate their increased political sophistication. As we shall see below, later legislative proposals in this area took a multifaceted approach and enjoyed a broader base of support within the Congress. Several of these later bills received strong support from Sernam. Finally, feminists in civil society have reengaged with the policy process with renewed confidence and have simultaneously strengthened their efforts to educate the public on these issues.

The Significance of the Bill

The political dynamic that emerged over domestic violence legislation illustrates the dominance of the executive branch in policymaking on women's rights. Eager to prove its mettle in the first democratic administrations, Sernam pursued an ambitious legislative agenda, introducing bills on a wide range of topics, including paternity, sexual assault, property rights for married women, the rights of domestic workers, and antidiscrimination. In each of these cases Sernam's initiatives met with greater success than did those of feminist representatives (appendix 1). Sernam's executive powers, which give it greater legislative breadth than the Congress possessed, access to all committees during legislative debate, and the right to prioritize its legislative initiatives during most of the year, combined with the ministry's superior resources and staff to give it much greater power than Congress to write viable bills. These advantages can greatly facilitate legislative efforts, but the policymaking dynamic that results exacerbates interbranch tensions and plays into the fears many feminist organizations bring to cooperation with the state.

Debates over domestic violence legislation took place within the context of early posttransition politics. The introduction of the VIF bill in 1991 coincided with the return of party politics, the creation of Sernam, and the crisis within the broader women's movement caused by the evaporation of external funding and conflicts over the "double militancy" of its members. As a result, domestic violence legislation took on tremendous symbolic importance in terms of the character of Sernam, the effectiveness of congressional feminists, and the influence of the women's movement in formal democratic politics.

The framing of the issue of domestic violence and the negotiation of the VIF bill's content proved critical to its ultimate success. The manner in which these decisions were made, however, was as important for long-term feminist policymaking as the decisions themselves. Sernam's assertion of a dominant role for itself in the development of the congressional bill angered both the bill's congressional supporters and feminist organizations that sought to influence the legislation. Because of Sernam's high profile in the controversial negotiations on the bill, many feminists have blamed Sernam for the weaknesses of the resulting law. Anger about the process itself made it impossible for many feminists to see Sernam's strategic compromises as anything more than a reflection of its inherent conservatism. In subsequent years, however, as congressional feminists attempted to legislate without the ministry's support, they found reason to make their own strategic concessions to congressional conservatives. Debates over the wisdom of watering down feminist proposals to assure passage in Congress continue to divide feminists inside and outside government. In the case of domestic violence legislation, these compromises, together with the perception that Sernam forced the changes through over the protests of congressional feminists, have had long-term repercussions for feminist policymaking.

Institutional Cooperation

Violence against women was a central policy issue for the Chilean women's movement. Feminists succeeded in calling attention to the issue and in connecting it with the broader issues of human rights and the violence of the military regime. Mobilizations against domestic violence were frequent in the last years of the military government, and after the transition the movement focused on the need for legal reform in this area. The influence of the women's movement during the transition period resulted in a commitment by Christian Democrat Patricio Aylwin, the first posttransition president, to making the issue of violence against women a priority in his program of legislative reforms. Following the transition to democracy, both the newly created Sernam and feminist representatives undertook the development of legislative proposals on the issue of domestic violence.

Feminist organizations were in a particularly good position to participate in the development of such initiatives, given their expertise on the issue of violence against women. During the nearly four years that the Congress debated the VIF bill, feminist organizations supported the legislation in various ways. ISIS International (an international feminist organization with a branch office in Santiago), the Network Against Violence (a collective of Chilean feminist organizations focusing on violence against women), and other NGOs provided information on the issue for legislators. Feminist organizations also submitted information on violence against women to the congressional committees that reviewed the bill, and members of key organizations testified before the committees. Feminist NGOs held public demonstrations in Santiago and Valparaíso (site of the Congress) in support of the bill, and they collected signatures and letters of support as part of their effort to lobby representatives. The VIF law is a rare instance of feminists undertaking an organized and concerted lobbying effort in favor of a bill, and they targeted both supporters and opponents in Congress. The involvement of the women's movement in efforts to legislate on domestic violence represents the most significant posttransition mobilization of the movement to date. Feminists' experience with this issue shaped the movement's later perceptions about the utility of participation in formal politics.

Socialist Deputies Introduce a Domestic Violence Bill

Efforts to develop domestic violence legislation were undertaken early in the first democratic administration and were concentrated on the political left, particularly in the efforts of feminist deputies. At a theoretical level, the idea of legally punishing violence against women, particularly domestic violence, was relatively uncontroversial, and representatives across the political spectrum voiced informal support for developing some kind of legislative initiative.

Socialist deputies Adriana Muñoz and Sergio Aguiló introduced a domestic violence bill in September 1990 (bill 157).[2] While the bill included all family members in its definition of domestic violence, it focused specifically on the physical and psychological abuse of women by their husbands or partners, which made up the majority of cases of family violence. The bill cited research calculating that while 1 percent of women abuse their husbands or partners, and in 23 percent of cases there is mutual abuse, without one person clearly being dominated by the other, fully 76 percent of abuse is committed by men against women.[3] "This demonstrates," the bill concluded, "that in general the most assaulted adult is the woman in a stable relationship with a man, generating a chronic syndrome of violence that is unidirectional: it always goes from the man to the women."[4]

The only sanction in force at the time required nonfamily witnesses and physical evidence of injury in order for action to be taken against the aggressor. The existing law also failed to provide for the immediate removal of the accused aggressor from the home once a complaint had been filed. The question of how much protection the law needed to give victims of abuse was complicated by the fact that there were virtually no shelters for abused women in Chile. Muñoz and Aguiló argued that the wide cultural acceptance of this type of violence, and the lack of obligatory mechanisms for denunciation by health personnel, teachers, family members, or victims themselves, made a comprehensive effort to impose legal sanctions impossible. Their bill allowed for anyone with direct knowledge of abuse to file a complaint, allowed for the removal of the aggressor from the home, effected a restraining order for workplace or school, and set up a system of family

---

2. Bill 157. Cámara de Diputados, *Redacción de sesiones* (Valparaíso: Biblioteca del Congreso Nacional de Chile, 1990), legislative session 320/35, September 13. Although not explicitly part of the original congressional bill, during the first round of committee review progressive representatives defined marital rape as a type of domestic abuse. As discussed below, a later version of the bill deleted this provision.

3. These figures are taken from "La Mujer Maltratada," cited in Cámara de Diputados, *Redacción de sesiones* (Valparaíso: Biblioteca del Congreso Nacional de Chile, 1992), legislative session 322/30a, December 15, p. 2626. Most research concludes that roughly 25 percent of Chilean women suffer some form of domestic abuse.

4. Ibid.

support for the period in which the aggressor was away from the home. The bill specified that therapy for the aggressor would be a mandatory component of any rehabilitation program, together with options for prison sentences, fines, and community service work for the municipality.[5]

The bill noted that Sernam, which was developing a comprehensive program of public education on the issue, would be an ideal institution to undertake the therapy component of an offender's punishment. Finally, the bill recommended the establishment of family courts, with judges specially trained to handle cases of domestic violence. Since the creation of family courts would require executive action, the bill specified that in the meantime, existing civil courts would handle cases of domestic abuse.[6]

The Initial Failure of Institutional Cooperation

The domestic violence bill entered the Chamber of Deputies in September 1990. The start of the extraordinary legislative session forced Muñoz and Aguiló to seek executive sponsorship for the bill from Sernam, which was already involved in a number of different projects aimed at addressing the issue of violence against women.[7] At the same time, unsure whether the ministry would agree to sponsor the bill, the representatives sought to attract media attention and to raise public awareness of the issue of domestic violence. "We want to advance as rapidly as possible," Muñoz explained, "but if [executive sponsorship] is not to be, we want to take advantage of the time [before the ordinary legislative session] so that society might debate the bill" (quoted in *La Época* [Santiago], November 5, 1990). Organizations from the

---

5. The bill's recommendation of community service was meant to serve as a form of public sanction for the offender and to focus community attention on the issue of domestic violence, in an effort to counter the wide cultural acceptance of violence against women. This aspect of the bill was rejected in the final version, as a number of representatives found the measure unnecessarily humiliating for the offender and thought it presented potential legal problems for the municipality (for example, if the offender was hurt on the job, would the government be responsible for paying worker's compensation?).

6. The legal changes the bill proposed would be covered under a reformed civil code, as opposed to the penal code, which would allow judges more flexibility in dealing with the problem of domestic abuse.

7. Sernam had undertaken an extensive survey to gauge the extent of domestic abuse in Santiago households. In addition, it had begun what would become a wide-ranging municipal-level program focusing on education and training on the issue of family violence for municipal employees, judges, social workers, and hospital personnel. Finally, Sernam was developing a public awareness campaign to combat cultural tolerance of and misconceptions about family abuse.

women's movement were following the development of the bill and requested meetings with Muñoz and Aguiló to hear the specifics of the bill and offer feedback.

A series of meetings with Sernam followed in November 1990. Sernam had begun work on its own domestic violence bill, and the deputies hoped that by incorporating Sernam's suggestions into the congressional bill, it would get the executive sponsorship it needed to be taken up by the Congress during that legislative session. The specifics of the joint bill were discussed, and the deputies left the meetings with the understanding that Sernam would sponsor the congressional bill and would ask the president to declare the bill "urgent" and include it in the extraordinary session. In January 1991, however, Sernam introduced a bill on domestic violence as an executive proposal. Sernam's bill on "intrafamily violence" closely resembled the joint proposal that had been negotiated between the ministry and Deputies Muñoz and Aguiló.

Muñoz and Aguiló responded with anger, publicly denouncing Sernam for usurping Congress's legislative efforts. The restrictions established by the 1980 constitution already severely constrained the possibilities for congressional policymaking, and 80 percent of congressional bills introduced up to that point (one year into the first democratic government) had been rejected as unconstitutional. Muñoz and Aguiló argued that this institutional imbalance would only worsen if the executive insisted on submitting its own version of bills that Congress had already introduced, reducing Congress's role to reviewing executive bills (*El Fortín*, January 19, 1991).

That the extraordinary session covered most of the year[8] meant that even when congressional proposals were well crafted and enjoyed support, they needed the sponsorship of the executive to be debated in Congress, and this made congressional proposals vulnerable to being amended or, in the case of the VIF bill, adopted by the executive. The Office of the Secretary General of the Presidency was called in to mediate a solution between Sernam and the representatives. Sernam agreed to withdraw its bill in favor of the original congressional proposal, but it insisted on playing an active role in the amendment process.

While some of the bill's supporters resented Sernam's deep involvement in the shaping of the legislation, this executive sponsorship brought with it

---

8. As noted in chapter 2, this aspect of the legislative calendar was changed with the constitutional revisions of 2005.

clear political advantages. None of the bill's congressional sponsors sat on the committees that would debate the bill, but Sernam minister Soledad Alvear had permanent access to the committees and invited Deputies Muñoz and Aguiló to accompany the ministry's legal team to the hearings on the bill, in both the Chamber of Deputies and later in the joint committees that would resolve differences between the Chamber and Senate versions of the bill. In addition, Sernam invited members of key feminist organizations working on violence against women to testify before the committees and submit data on the issue for the committee reports. For both feminist representatives and members of the women's movement, Sernam's involvement with the bill thus created crucial opportunities to participate in the policy process. Throughout the bill's three-year progress through the Congress, the executive included it in the extraordinary legislative sessions and declared it urgent at key moments.

Strategic Framing and Negotiation

The bill entered the Chamber of Deputies during the 1991–92 extraordinary legislative session. In order to overcome conservative congressional opposition to the bill, Sernam's minister agreed to a number of content changes that had the cumulative effect of shifting its focus to the maintenance of family unity rather than the protection of victims of abuse. Both the Human Rights and Constitution committees independently reviewed the Muñoz-Aguiló bill, which was now renamed the "intrafamily violence bill," Sernam's preferred title. Sernam submitted extensive background information on domestic violence to the committee, some of it the result of the ministry's own research on the issue and some the work of feminist organizations.

Tension between the ministry and the bill's authors did not end with the bill's introduction. Having agreed to withdraw its own bill, Sernam became intensely involved in the amendment process. Sernam submitted a separate report to each committee to which the bill was sent, urging major content changes. These suggested amendments were developed without consultation with Deputies Muñoz and Aguiló and constituted, to their minds, another attempt by Sernam to replace their bill with one that reflected the ministry's more conservative thinking. The Human Rights Committee, in issuing its first report on the VIF bill in September 1992, noted the breakdown of coordination between Sernam and the bill's congressional supporters: "The executive, together with including the project in the extraordinary legislative session of 1991–1992, sent a report with amendments referring to almost the entire bill. [The committee] indicated that for the elaboration of the bill the authors of the bill should coordinate with Sernam, to facilitate a joint project and obtain a common result."[9] Minister Alvear, together with a team of three Sernam lawyers, became a constant presence at committee hearings on the bill. Sernam invited Deputies Muñoz and Aguiló, who were not members of either review committee, to participate in the review of the bill in order to facilitate the development of a bill that would satisfy both the deputies and Sernam.

In stark contrast to the review process for other bills on women's rights, various members of the most important women's organizations, such as ISIS, the Network Against Violence, the Women's Institute of Santiago, the Casa de la Mujer of Valparaíso, and the Women's Collective of La Florida, a Santiago women's group, also testified before the committees and submitted data on the issue of domestic violence, which the committees incorporated into their reports.[10]

While the statistics on family violence cited by the committee focused primarily on the abuse of women, from this point forward in the bill's process, content changes shifted attention to other types of violence, such as child abuse and abuse of the elderly. In practical political terms, this change in emphasis slowed the progress of the VIF bill as it came into conflict with other bills already being processed on child abuse. More significantly, this change of focus raised alarms for the feminist community, which felt that even on an issue in which the vast majority of victims were women, women were once again being considered not in terms of their rights as individuals but in terms of their role within the family.

Other changes to the bill made in committee focused on the scope of activities that legally constituted abuse. The committee broadened the definition of abuse to include "mistreatment in word or deed to a person forming

---

9. Cámara de Diputados, *Redacción de sesiones* (1992), legislative session 322/30a, December 15, p. 2640.

10. For example, the following statistics from the Network Against Violence are cited in the first committee reports: A woman is beaten in one in four Chilean families. In one in three she is psychologically assaulted. Fifty-six percent of children are beaten by mother, father, or both, and 62 percent of abusive men were abused as children. Eighty-three percent of abused women don't go to the police, and only 26 percent get medical attention; the reasons for not reporting are fear, shame, protection of the abuser, and not knowing how to get help. This perpetuates the cycle of abuse. Experts from the Chilean Criminology and Sexology Society further testified that there is an even greater instance of domestic abuse in rural areas, and that the law should take into consideration a history of abuse and the lack of shelters and other institutional supports when prosecuting a woman for killing her partner. Ibid., 2626.

part of the family unit, even when such mistreatment does not leave scars or bruises." Sernam attempted to include abuse by omission (i.e., neglect), but this was rejected as too abstract. Despite the committees' willingness to consider verbal threats as constituting abuse, the idea of marital rape was rejected. It was argued that the concept of marital rape was controversial and that the issue was more logically covered under sexual assault laws (the reform of which would come later). Attempts to define what level of child discipline constituted abuse were also rejected, the committee preferring not to distinguish between those activities that would be considered abusive to a child versus an adult.[11]

Sernam's revisions to the bill, approved by the committees, increased the original bill's emphasis on nonincarceration options for dealing with abusers, including community service work and therapy. In support of mandatory community service work for offenders, the Human Rights Committee explained in its report that, "more than penalize, [the bill] seeks to educate in such a way that the aggressor becomes aware of the community's censure and the damage to his reputation, by forcing him to submit to sanctions that expose his quarrelsome behavior within his family."[12] The committee's report concluded that the goal of developing legal guidelines for dealing with domestic violence should be to end the domestic abuse while maintaining the unity of the family. The right of judges to order the immediate removal of the accused aggressor from the home withstood a constitutional challenge and was retained in the bill, but the final version gave judges discretion over when, and whether, to remove the aggressor from the home.[13] Feminists insisted at the hearings that women would not denounce abuse if the abuser remained in the home following the filing of charges, but Sernam's legal team argued that developing nonincarceration measures for responding to domestic violence would make it less likely that women would later drop the charges rather than see their partners sent to jail. Members of the feminist community criticized these changes to the original bill, arguing that the lack of victim protection under the new law would increase the danger to women who reported abuse.

---

11. Ibid., 2626, 2635.

12. Ibid., 2650. As noted above, this provision was later rejected.

13. The debate on the constitutionality of these protective measures centered on whether "the constitutional rights of the victim to physical protection are superior to the aggressor's right to property" (i.e., access to the home). Cámara de Diputados, *Redacción de sesiones* (Valparaíso: Biblioteca del Congreso Nacional de Chile, 1993), legislative session 324/42a, January 19, p. 3434.

Sernam's high level of participation in all stages of the bill's progress was amply evident in the floor debate. Normally, questions regarding a bill's content are addressed to the president of the Chamber, who may refer when necessary to a member of the review committee for clarification. In this case, however, the minister of Sernam interrupted the debate a number of times to correct representatives or to expand upon some particular aspect of the bill's content.

The bill passed the Chamber of Deputies in April 1993 with almost unanimous cross-party support. The broad support for the bill did not, however, imply comprehension of the scope and causes of domestic violence or agreement with the explicitly feminist framing of the issue by representatives like Adriana Muñoz. Misperceptions are evident in the discourse of many representatives as to the roots of the problem, including a tendency to blame domestic violence on the process of "modernity" and the stress resulting from changing gender roles, as well as a strong focus on the family unit as the beneficiary of the proposed legislation. RN deputy María Angélica Cristi claimed that family violence had reached epidemic levels in Chile in part because of the "loss of traditional values." UDI deputy Andrés Chadwick justified his vote for the bill by explaining, "When Deputy Muñoz made her speech, she expressed very clearly that this bill was especially important and transformative for women. I share this opinion but want to add that this bill, more than referring to some aspect that affects women, has great relevance for the family."[14]

Such discourse was not limited to conservatives. For example, Socialist deputy Jorge Molina declared that family violence legislation was necessary to ensure the equal rights of women, but he also explained that women experience this violence in part because men become insecure when women attempt to break out of traditionally assigned gender roles.[15] Comments such as these, from across the political spectrum, illustrate the obstacles to framing women's rights legislation in explicitly feminist terms. The pro-family framing adopted by Sernam in the VIF bill, and later by congressional feminists on other bills, is an attempt to undermine the first and most obvious opposition they will face to their legislative reforms.

14. Ibid., 3455, 3465.
15. Ibid., 3441.

The Senate's Modification of the VIF

Although the bill moved more quickly through the Senate, there was noticeably less enthusiasm for the VIF bill in the upper house (in this case, the quick four-month review was an indication that not many representatives were interested in going over the bill in detail). The bill was sent to the Senate Constitution Committee, which was dominated by conservatives, but it passed the first review fairly easily.[16] Minister Alvear addressed the floor of the Senate in November 1993, when the bill came up for the first-round general vote, and she gave a detailed exposition of the causes and consequences of family violence and outlined the development of the VIF in the Chamber of Deputies. While many senators welcomed the talk, others were visibly impatient with the length of Alvear's speech. Senators interrupted her more than once to address other legislative business.

The Senate enacted major modifications to the bill. In the definition of family violence, the Senate committee voted to insert the word "significant" before "abuse."[17] Most critically, the Senate committee changed the provision that allowed for the immediate removal of the aggressor from the home. Instead, judges were prevented from removing an alleged aggressor from the home for ten days after the complaint was filed, to see whether the denunciation of abuse would hold or whether the couple would "reconcile."[18] Minister Alvear and other members of Sernam were present at these committee meetings and protested these changes, but they failed to dissuade the majority of committee members.

Both Deputy Muñoz and Minister Alvear subsequently participated in a joint committee tasked with negotiating these changes. The joint committee agreed to remove the word "significant" from the definition of abuse. Furthermore, in the matter of removing an aggressor from the home at the time of the complaint, the joint committee agreed on a compromise version in

---

16. The most progressive member of the committee was the chair, Socialist Hernán Vodanovic. The other members included RN senator Sergio Diez, designated senators Carlos Letelier and Sergio Fernández, and Christian Democrat Máximo Pacheco.

17. Designated senator Sergio Fernández defended the change by explaining that "any kind of abuse whatsoever is not included in this situation, but only those which have some grade of importance and significance." Otherwise, he reasoned, the courts would be flooded with all kinds of complaints, and real abuse would not get attention, resulting in a weak law. Senado, *Redacción de sesiones* (Valparaíso: Biblioteca del Congreso Nacional de Chile, 1993), legislative session 327/18, December 14, p. 2748.

18. Ibid.

which the judge would be neither forced to remove the aggressor immediately nor prevented from doing so, but rather would have discretion to remove the aggressor when it was deemed appropriate.[19] The bill passed the joint committee at the end of January 1994.

Passage of the Intrafamily Violence Law

Before the VIF bill was signed into law, a cross-party group of deputies and senators, many newly elected, successfully petitioned the president to agree to veto the bill unless a few last-minute changes could be made. Among this group were two of the newly elected women representatives from the Concertación, PPD deputy Martita Wörner and Independent (formerly Socialist) deputy Fanny Pollarolo. The proposed amendments did not alter the spirit of the bill but sought to clarify a number of legal points, particularly those regarding the processing of complaints. This move to petition for a veto is noteworthy, however, for two reasons. First, it brings up the power of the executive to influence the process at all stages and reaffirms the benefits of having executive support for a bill. Second, it indicates the interest of a politically broad group of representatives in an issue of women's rights, and their intention to involve themselves in the policymaking process.

When the bill returned to the Congress for a final vote on the president's modifications, a number of newly elected representatives used the opportunity to voice their strong support for the protection of women's rights. For example, Christian Democrat Mariana Aylwin committed herself to pursuing the institution of family courts, so that the application of the VIF law would be handled by judges trained in family law.[20] PPD deputy María Antonieta Saa, a longtime member of the feminist movement, reminded the Congress that efforts to reform existing law on family violence had begun with the women's movement, and that the movement continued to play a critical role in promoting education and public awareness on the topic. "There is much more to do," she concluded, "because [violence against women] . . . is a consequence of a culture. But it's necessary that we, as representatives of the people, be capable of seeing these problems and not

---

19. Senado, *Redacción de sesiones* (Valparaíso: Biblioteca del Congreso Nacional de Chile, 1994), legislative session 328/9a, April 20, p. 940.
20. The law creating family tribunals finally passed the Congress in 2005, after Deputy Aylwin had left office.

shutting our eyes, and of making inroads toward a democratic society, deep and real, where men and women have equal opportunities, and the inequality of women is confronted from a wide-ranging perspective, recognizing that there exists an authoritarian culture that we must destroy in order to construct a human, civilized, and democratic society."[21]

The bill passed the Chamber of Deputies on May 5, 1994, and the Senate on May 31. The VIF bill was signed into law by President Frei in July 1994.

Feminist Response to the VIF

When asked to discuss the biggest advances in women's rights in Chile since the transition to democracy, members of the women's movement invariably mention the passage of the VIF. But the law, focused as it was on the chief area of concern for the women's movement, also came, for many in the movement, to symbolize the disadvantages of working within the formal political arena, particularly with Sernam. Common criticisms of the VIF law include the broad family focus of the resulting law and its technical weaknesses. Many feminists view these problems as the result of their exclusion from negotiations on the bill.

The movement's perceived marginalization in the case of the VIF law is a common complaint, despite the high level of participation of the movement on the VIF law relative to all other legislation on women's rights. Because the movement was highly mobilized for the VIF law and actively sought to participate in the debate, members of the movement keenly felt the ways in which they were sidelined. While most of their frustration was focused on Sernam, feminists also complained that congressional representatives ignored them as well. For example, members of the organizations that testified before the Chamber committees felt that committee members had treated them poorly. One member of the Network Against Violence stated that the committee had treated them "like little girls," had ignored them, speaking among themselves instead, and had cut them off when they did speak, claiming that time had run out. One member of a feminist organization that had tried to participate in the process alleged that even the progressive members of the committee accused the women's movement of trying to involve the state inappropriately in intimate family matters.[22]

---

21. Senado, *Redacción de sesiones* (1994), legislative session 328/25a, May 19, p. 2014.
22. Verónica Matus, member of La Morada (Santiago), interview by author, April 2, 1997.

Early in the process, feminists were alarmed by the change in the title of the bill from "domestic" to "family" violence. They interpreted this change as a reflection of Sernam's willingness to capitulate to the political opposition. As a member of La Morada put it, "that action spoke volumes."[23] Feminists protested that shifting the focus from women to the family made family unity, rather than the protection of women from violence, the primary objective of the law. Paulina Weber, a member of MEMCH, one of the oldest and most respected feminist organizations in Chile, felt that protection of the victims of violence had been sacrificed so as to make the bill more politically acceptable. Weber blamed Sernam for making the VIF law

> more educative than disruptive, to the point that if a man hits a woman, the man has to educate himself so that he'll stop beating the woman. It allows him to demonstrate that he won't continue to beat the woman; he's forced to submit to therapy so that he won't continue to abuse, but in no way should this imply that the couple ceases to function as a couple. In other words, the concept behind it is that the couple cannot be split apart, and it's recommended that the man be good and not beat the woman, and to the woman it's recommended that she have a lot of patience with the man, and this is where the justice system ends—it ends with the judge calling the parties together and giving the man a slap on the wrist and saying "behave yourself" to him and saying "have patience" to the woman.[24]

In Weber's view, the VIF law enshrined the "ludicrous" idea that an abused woman must defend her marriage over her own life.

A further criticism is that even the "toothless" version enacted into law lacks the funding for proper implementation. Although Sernam is officially in charge of implementing the VIF law, the legislation failed to allocate the resources necessary to build shelters and provide medical training to help victims, neglected to give the courts the resources to hire and train more personnel to assist with these cases, and did not establish family courts to try the cases. As María Elena Valenzuela, a sociologist and longtime member of the women's movement who later worked at Sernam, put it, "The law is in force, but it is crippled for lack of resources."[25]

---

23. Ibid.
24. Weber, interview.
25. María Elena Valenzuela, interview by author, January 9, 1997.

Yet feminists' disillusionment with the policy process goes beyond the specifics of the VIF law to focus on how the very idea of negotiation plays out in formal politics in Chile. Chilean feminists complain that the idea of consensus does not imply a negotiation of political differences or an active attempt to convert the opposition to one's cause but rather the avoidance of divisive issues at all costs. "In practice," Valenzuela explains, "'consensus' means that we're going to behave as though we have no differences. We're not going to negotiate our differences, what doesn't unite. We're going to make agreements based on what we agree upon, and as for the other things, we'll almost act as if they don't exist. And [women's rights] is an issue that divides. So we're going to work out an agreement on this issue as if we didn't think so differently. So for this reason you'll often encounter situations that really don't satisfy anyone, instead of arriving at something that is the fruit of all of us."[26]

Feminist Learning in the Wake of the VIF Law

Careful! Machismo kills!

In reviewing the history of the VIF law, it is clear that Sernam's sponsorship of the initiative enhanced the bill's chance of passage.[27] Deputies Muñoz and Aguiló originally appealed to Sernam for help so that their bill could be included in the extraordinary legislative session. After Sernam agreed to sponsor it, the bill was included in the extraordinary legislative session every year, and it was also declared urgent at key moments in his path through the Congress.[28] In addition, President Frei was willing, at the request of representatives in both houses, to use the presidential veto to modify specific aspects of the bill after it had already passed the Congress. In addition to the use of such formal executive powers, the constant presence of members of Sernam, including the minister herself, at committee hearings and floor

---

26. Ibid.
27. The epigraph to this section is a slogan of the Chilean Network Against Domestic and Sexual Violence, used during an eighteen-month campaign against violence against women that began in July 2007. The campaign included demonstrations in cities across Chile, among them Santiago, Valparaíso, Concepción, and Puerto Montt.
28. The bill was declared urgent in January 1993, so as to get it out of Chamber committee and onto the floor for the first round of debate, and in May 1994, in the Senate, to encourage a final floor vote on the executive's modifications.

debates at each stage of the bill's passage through Congress was a critical factor in negotiating modifications to the bill and keeping it alive in committee. In these respects, feminist members of Congress and the women's movement recognize Sernam's valuable contribution to the VIF bill. Nevertheless, the legislative process created long-term problems for Sernam's relationship with feminist legislators and policy-minded feminist NGOs. Feminist representatives became acutely aware that executive support would come at a cost. And feminists' perception that the government had marginalized them further divided the feminist movement over the merits of participating in formal politics.

It is important to understand what executive strength implies for other political actors, particularly the Congress and policy-focused organizations within the women's movement. In the early posttransition years, Sernam's executive power over the legislative process seemed to come at the expense of congressional influence. This is clearest in the greater success of Sernam's bills compared with congressional proposals on the same issues. Yet the relationship between Sernam and feminist representatives is complex, as feminist legislators both appreciate and resent Sernam's legislative strength. They recognize that Sernam can overcome the conservative opposition to women's rights legislation more easily than they can, because they lack the resources, technical expertise, and access to review committees that executive ministries may employ. Yet feminist representatives recognize in Sernam's success their own legislative limitations. This is particularly evident on issues like abortion and divorce, where representatives could not count on executive support for their bills.[29]

Despite its considerable formal and informal powers, Sernam's dominance of the policy process on women's rights issues also negatively affects the long-term institutional health and policy influence of the ministry itself. The ability of actors inside and outside government to participate in the policymaking process determines the possibility of forming long-term policy networks on women's rights legislation. Should a conservative party head the government in the future, stable policy networks will be needed to overcome ideological changes in Sernam's leadership, which would have a large impact on the ministry's willingness to pursue legislative reforms. Thus the particular legislative dynamics that govern the development of

---

29. This changed after 2000, with the election of Socialist Ricardo Lagos as president (see chapter 5).

feminist proposals have critical implications for the long-term viability of feminist policymaking.

The perception that Sernam deliberately avoids cooperating with feminist members of Congress is bolstered by the comments of Socialist Paulina Veloso, who was subdirector of Sernam during the second democratic administration. Veloso concurs that the ministry tried to establish ownership of the VIF bill, but she argues that the legislative and legal inexperience of feminist representatives undermines the development of viable bills.

> The executive ministers and their subsecretaries worry about the ideological content, and they have a bunch of little "elves" that draft the actual bills and put in whatever is necessary technically to create an adequate bill. If one then brings this to the Congress and meets up with [the supporters of the bill], then they begin to say, hey, why don't we change this word to this one, which fits better? It's enough to give you fits, because with this change of wording they're destroying it, so for this reason the relationship isn't easy. That's where you've got to negotiate effectively, but it's complicated, and in that sense I understand why you don't want to have to get together with the female representatives to discuss this foolishness. Yet the other thing is, at the same time, if you make an appointment with them to go over the technical aspects [of a bill], they don't go, because it bores them. So it's a complicated relationship. But I believe that the criticism of Sernam or some other ministry is more than anything a criticism of the system, and that's not going to improve as long as [representatives] don't have technical assistance.[30]

Sernam's legislative success reflects not only the formal institutional powers of the executive branch but the legislative weakness of feminist legislators. The dearth of legislative staff and the inexperience of legislators—disadvantages that continue to plague the Congress—were particularly acute during the first democratic administration. Even legislators with congressional experience before the 1973 coup had not practiced legislative politics for seventeen years, and almost all of the women legislators were serving in Congress for the first time. In addition, as explained in chapter 2, the 1980 constitution substantially skewed legislative power in favor of the executive,

---

30. Paulina Veloso, interview by author, Santiago, May 7, 1997.

and legislators had to learn to adjust to and strategize within this more restricted legislative arena. With regard to feminist legislators in particular, none of the feminist representatives elected to either the Chamber of Deputies or the Senate were lawyers. Their history of participation in the women's movement, in academia, or as party militants had given them a clear sense of the issues they wished to pursue in the Congress, but they lacked both adequate staff and technical knowledge about developing legislative proposals. This complicated their ability to draft viable legislation that could withstand congressional opposition. Deputy Adriana Muñoz lamented that the lack of staff and resources available to representatives hits representatives on the left particularly hard, as representatives on the right are often able to supplement their stipends from their own money or through support from right-wing interest groups.

> We only have two and a half million pesos a year, and for legislative assistance that's nothing. What do I do with that? Commissioning a study to begin to think through the idea of a proposal costs me a million and a half, and a good professional will charge me three million. Even a young student assistant charged me a million and a half, and there goes the entire fund. . . . So the laws that are drafted are of terrible quality, and that hits projects in the most vulnerable political areas particularly hard—family, women, employment—areas that don't have high visibility for the government. . . . It's hard to find people in the government willing to help you on these issues.[31]

The lack of legislative assistance available to members of Congress constitutes a serious impediment to their ability to write viable bills, especially in complex legal areas. For example, the congressional bills on paternity (bills 374 and 719) and marital property rights (bills 1707 and 1719) were technically too simplistic and failed to address many of the social and legal implications of the proposed changes to existing law. When broad congressional support for a bill is lacking, a committee will usually kill the bill rather than undertake the time-consuming task of substantially modifying it. Because of the technical and financial resources available to Sernam, its bills, by contrast, tend to be technically sound and legally complete, and thus harder for the committees to ignore. In recent years the executive branch has earmarked

---

31. Adriana Muñoz, interview by author, Valparaíso, June 5, 2001.

additional funding for the development of legislative assistance for congressional representatives, but funding remains well below the levels that would place congressional bills on an equal footing with executive proposals.

The Legacy of the VIF Law

Feminists learned both short- and long-term lessons from their experience in passing the VIF law. The short-term lessons were largely negative, as feminists concluded that Sernam would not be a strong advocate for feminist policymaking and would attempt to legislate without the participation of feminists, both members of Congress and NGOs. The short-term response of feminist legislators was to attempt to legislate as independently of Sernam as possible. Many feminists outside government likewise learned that it was not possible to cooperate productively with the government on policymaking. Adriana Muñoz's proposal to decriminalize therapeutic abortion, detailed in the next chapter, reflects both of these trends.

The longer-term consequences of the VIF law for feminist learning have been more positive. With time, feminists inside and outside government learned that cooperation with one another on policy development was a critical prerequisite for engagement with the political opposition. In subsequent years, and particularly after Bachelet's election, supporters of women's equality returned to the issue of violence against women and introduced a number of legislative proposals in this area. As discussed below, these more recent attempts illustrate feminist learning in a variety of ways. Within the state, Sernam and feminist representatives forged a much more cooperative and productive relationship, which has facilitated policy development in this area. Both Sernam and congressional representatives have also strengthened their links with feminist NGOs. Outside the government, feminists have learned to develop clearer and more united arguments in support of reform, and they have learned to use public protest as well as newer public forums (like YouTube) to raise public awareness of the issue of violence against women.

The VIF law is a particularly useful example of feminist policymaking because it suggests that even ostensibly successful policymaking can have contradictory effects on future feminist efforts. On the one hand, the passage of any feminist reform creates a law that both legitimizes a particular women's rights issue and gives feminists a legal precedent they can use to push for broader reform. On the other hand, the strained interactions among Sernam, congressional representatives, and feminist NGOs sapped the motivation of many feminists in civil society. Over the long term, the VIF law has set an important precedent for ongoing legislative efforts to combat violence against women. But in the short term it has reduced participation by the feminist movement and strained relations between Congress and Sernam.

The VIF law marks the low point of congressional-executive cooperation on women's rights legislation. Congressional representatives and members of the feminist movement consistently cite it as a defining moment in their relationship with Sernam. Since the passage of the VIF law, relations among the ministry, congressional representatives, and feminist NGOs have improved, but the ripple effects of the process can still be felt in multiple ways, from ongoing efforts to address violence against women, to the internal politics of the women's movement, to the strategies feminist legislators employ in other policy areas.

Despite the weaknesses of the VIF law, it laid the groundwork for later attempts to improve the law. In 1999 two feminist deputies, Adriana Muñoz (who had joined the PPD) and fellow party member María Antonieta Saa, introduced a motion to strengthen protection for victims of domestic abuse and increase funding for the law (Law 20.066). This bill, which passed the Congress in 2005, explicitly criminalizes domestic violence and allow for the rapid removal of the aggressor from the home. Together with the new family tribunals (created in 2005), the new law should allow for a more rapid processing of abuse complaints and a higher rate of convictions (Ross 2004). Sernam minister Cecilia Pérez lobbied heavily in favor of the bill before Congress, the bill was included in the extraordinary legislative session, and it received numerous urgency labels in both the Chamber and the Senate. The dynamics surrounding this bill represented a stark contrast to the struggle over the VIF law, and it bolstered the confidence of both feminist representatives and feminist organizations working to combat violence against women.

Following her election to the presidency in 2006, Michelle Bachelet made violence against women a focus of the government's social policy. Most significantly, Bachelet increased Sernam's budget by 30 percent specifically to expand the network of support for victims of violence, through the construction of domestic violence shelters and the expansion of legal assistance for victims of violence. Representatives responded to this increase in executive support by introducing a series of new bills addressing violence against women. Of the sixteen bills on women's rights introduced since Bachelet assumed office, nine address some aspect of violence against women. Recent bills in this area have addressed domestic violence (bills 4106, 5200, 5235, and 5569), as well as more controversial areas of sexual violence against women, including bills on incest (bill 5726) and marital rape (5727).

These renewed policy networks are particularly visible in a 2007 congressional bill to criminalize femicide (bill 4937). The bill itself was introduced by women and men from across the Concertación, and it has received strong support from both Sernam minister Albornoz and President Bachelet. Most encouraging, however, has been the close coordination between the sponsoring representatives, the executive branch, and feminist organizations. The Chilean Network Against Domestic and Sexual Violence, a national coalition of feminist groups focusing on violence against women, undertook an extensive campaign to raise awareness of the issue of femicide. Beginning in July 2007, demonstrations against violence against women were held throughout Chile. A wide range of women's organizations participated, and the protests drew wide media coverage. The network has also built an Internet presence to publicize its work. In addition to its own Web site, the network is reaching out to young Chileans by posting videos of its demonstrations on YouTube and linking to popular networking sites like MySpace.[32] These developments serve as an optimistic reminder of the potential of feminists inside and outside government to create effective political alliances.

These positive advances aside, recent progress should not lead us to overlook the more immediate destructive impact that the VIF law had on larger feminist policymaking dynamics. In the short term, feminists' participation in the development of domestic violence legislation shaped their expectations about future cooperation with Sernam. Feminist organizations, already beset by external and internal pressures, decreased their public presence in the wake of the passage of the VIF law. Feminist representatives in Congress, stung by the public battle with Sernam over ownership of the bill and recognizing the ministry's resistance to more controversial feminist issues, such as abortion and divorce, resigned themselves to the need to legislate independently of executive support. Congressional feminists' attempts to decriminalize therapeutic abortion, the first test of this strategy, are the subject of the next chapter.

---

32. More information about the Network Against Domestic and Sexual Violence (La Red) can be found at http://www.nomasviolenciacontramujeres.cl/.

4

THE LIMITS OF FRAMING: LEGISLATING ABORTION RIGHTS

> In Chile, anyone who talks about abortion is considered an abortionist.

Attempts to reform Chile's abortion law, which criminalizes abortion even when it would save the life of a pregnant woman, have been, at first glance, unmitigated failures.[1] In 1991 Socialist deputy Adriana Muñoz introduced a bill to decriminalize therapeutic abortion, but the bill died in committee without debate. In 1994 an alliance of feminist organizations, the Open Forum on Health and Sexual and Reproductive Rights, developed a second proposal, but no congressional representative would sponsor the bill, and it was never introduced in Congress.[2] Since 2000, progressive representatives have introduced a spate of bills on abortion and reproductive rights, but to date none has been debated in committee. The fate of legislative initiatives to decriminalize abortion suggests the limits of feminist policy reform. Indeed, given the controversial nature of the issue, the general conservatism of much of Chilean political culture, and the entrenched political power of the opposition, the failure of these policy efforts seems overdetermined.

Yet the shifting political strategies and alliances that shaped the fate of these proposals reveal a policy process in which alternative outcomes are

---

1. The epigraph to this chapter is from a member of Sernam's legal team, interview by author, Santiago, January 9, 1997.
2. El Foro Abierto de Salud y Derechos Sexuales y Reproductivos is an alliance of feminist organizations focusing on reproductive rights. More information on the organization is available at http://www.forosalud.cl/forosalud/index.asp (accessed June 22, 2003).

possible. Feminist representatives and their political allies learned critical lessons from the failure of efforts to reform public policy on abortion. Muñoz introduced the first therapeutic abortion bill in the midst of the conflict with Sernam over the intrafamily violence bill. Sernam adamantly refused to support a bill to decriminalize abortion, and the ultimate failures of both the Muñoz bill and the subsequent effort by the Open Forum on Health and Sexual and Reproductive Rights illustrate the challenges of legislating policy reform in the absence of executive support. The struggle within the Forum to agree on a framework for its bill, and the group's ambivalence about supporting publicly Muñoz's efforts, taught feminists that without some degree of unified public mobilization in favor of reform, congressional efforts on controversial issues are unlikely to bear fruit. At the same time, feminist representatives learned that organized feminist groups in civil society expected to be participants in policymaking, not simply cheerleaders for the government's proposals. In terms of legislative strategies, both feminists within the Forum and congressional supporters of abortion reform learned that with careful framing of their proposals and a willingness to lobby the opposition, they could build support for reproductive rights beyond the Left.

Finally, in the wake of the legalization of divorce (discussed in chapter 5), feminists learned that policy reform is possible even on Chile's most contentious social issues. Bolstered by the success of divorce legislation and the elections of Socialist presidents Ricardo Lagos and then Michelle Bachelet, supporters of reproductive rights have renewed their efforts to fight for policy reform in this area. In 2000 Lagos appointed Bachelet minister of health, and one of her first major initiatives was to legalize emergency contraception. Representatives have responded to this improving political environment by introducing multiple bills on reproductive rights, focusing not only on therapeutic abortion but on sex education and women's right to reproductive health care, including contraception.

The bills on abortion analyzed here thus illustrate a number of general policymaking dynamics on women's rights as well as important moments of feminist learning. Legislative efforts in this area illuminate congressional feminists' desire to mount a legislative agenda independent of Sernam, the difficulty of doing so successfully, and the ongoing debates among feminists inside and outside government over the limits of framing and political compromise. An analysis of the decisions about institutional cooperation and issue framing made in the development of the first two abortion bills, together with a consideration of more recent efforts, can help us gauge where feminist strategy could yield more positive results.

Stifled Discourse, Hidden Practice: Abortion in Chile

Abortion is arguably the most difficult issue to debate publicly in Chile today. As one of its last acts of public policy, the military government outlawed abortion in all circumstances. Most of the nation's media, politicians, and social actors declare themselves opposed to the legalization of abortion, and public debate on the subject is taboo. Yet from 1931 until 1989 therapeutic abortion, defined as an abortion performed when a pregnancy is deemed a threat to a woman's life or health, was legal in Chile.[3] Despite the absence of widespread mobilization in favor of legalization, surveys indicate that a majority of Chileans support the limited decriminalization of abortion.[4] In fact, support for abortion rights has increased significantly in recent years (see tables 1 and 2).

Table 1 Question: Under which conditions would you approve of abortion?

When...	Approval (%)
The mother's health is at risk	75.3
The fetus is handicapped	40.8
The mother is unmarried	36.5
The couple does not want a child	13.9

SOURCE: Blofield 2001, 18, citing World Values Survey, 1990 (published 1994).

Table 2 Question: In which cases should abortion be permitted?

When...	Agreeing in 1996 (%)	Agreeing in 2000 (%)
The mother's life is in danger	58.7	77.9
The pregnancy is the result of rape	47.7	55.1
The fetus is deformed	32.6	54.4
The family cannot afford the child	8.4	—
The woman does not want more children	10.7	—

SOURCE: Blofield 2001, 19.

---

3. For a history of public policy on abortion in Chile, see Htun 2003.

4. A 1989 CERC survey had found that 75.8 percent of respondents "believe that the interruption of a pregnancy should be legally permitted when the mother's life is at risk or the child would be born deformed." Similar survey results were found by APROFA-CERC (1989, 1990), DIAGNOS (1984), and Flacso (1988). Cited in Cámara de Diputados, *Redacción de sesiones* (Valparaíso: Biblioteca del Congreso Nacional de Chile, 1991), legislative session 41a, September 17, p. 4089.

Public opinion on the issue appears to reflect public behavior: Chile is considered to have one of the highest abortion rates in Latin America, with an estimated one-third of all pregnancies ending in abortion (Guttmacher Institute 1996; Requena-Bichet 1990). The high incidence of abortion in practice and the public health crisis resulting from its illegality, particularly for the poor, make abortion, and reproductive rights more broadly, an important focus for Chilean feminists. Casas (1996) notes the class bias at work in the current system. The overwhelming majority of women prosecuted for abortion are poor because they are the ones most often hospitalized for abortion complications. Blofield argues that the social effects stemming from the approximately 120,000 to 175,000 abortions annually "constitutes one of the most urgent public health problems in Chile."[5]

Yet the political opportunities for reform are few. The Christian Democratic Party and the parties of the Right have an official policy position against any liberalization of abortion laws. While the Left is more sympathetic to reproductive rights, politicians on the left are ambivalent about pursuing legislation likely to engender enormous opposition with little chance of success. Furthermore, the first attempts to legislate reform of abortion laws took place within the particularly inauspicious context of early posttransition politics. The failure of these early attempts discouraged feminists from pursuing further reform.

In the first democratic administration, the Christian Democrats were the largest party in the Congress and therefore the biggest player in the Concertación coalition. The PDC controlled the presidency, and a Christian Democrat, Soledad Alvear, was picked to head Sernam. Alvear made it clear to congressional feminists that the ministry would not enter a public debate on abortion or support legislative efforts for reform. Within the Left, the combination of coalition pressure and church opposition meant that the parties would not take an official position in favor of decriminalization. Prior to the transition to democracy, the women's movement had consciously downplayed the issue of abortion (Baldez 2002; Franceschet 2005), and feminist organizations continued to debate the timing and shape of possible proposals for reform. Nevertheless, despite the clear obstacles a proposal on abortion would face, there was sufficient political will within the Left, among congressional feminists, and within feminist circles outside government to pursue the issue.

---

5. For example, Blofield 2006 estimates that in 1995 more than thirty-three thousand women were hospitalized for abortion complications. Only 10 percent of these cases were estimated to be "spontaneous" abortions, i.e., miscarriages.

The first bill to decriminalize abortion was introduced as negotiations on the intrafamily violence (VIF) bill were already under way, following the conflict with Sernam over ownership of the bill (chapter 3). The 1991 therapeutic abortion bill was introduced by Adriana Muñoz, who was simultaneously involved in the push for the VIF bill. The competitive dynamic that emerged over ownership of the VIF bill convinced congressional feminists that Sernam would be a complicated ally, even on issues where there was broad policy agreement with congressional feminists and the larger feminist community. On particularly controversial issues, such as abortion and divorce, congressional feminists understood that they would receive no institutional support from Sernam. The therapeutic abortion bill is evidence of congressional feminists' desire to develop a legislative agenda independent of Sernam, and it represents a critical step in feminists' learning curve on policy development.

On both of the main explanatory variables for feminist policy success, a supportive institutional context and strategic framing of proposals, the issue of abortion presents daunting challenges. In the absence of institutional support from Sernam, building support for bills early within Congress as well as with feminist organizations outside the state becomes critical. Furthermore, the bill's supporters must prioritize the strategic framing of the proposal to anticipate and deflect political opposition. The history of the congressional bill on therapeutic abortion as well as the subsequent proposal developed by a feminist NGO reveals that supporters of policy reform struggled in each of these areas. As with the VIF bill, feminist organizations felt excluded from political debate on the congressional proposal. In this sense, the therapeutic abortion proposals illustrate even more dramatically than the VIF bill the difficulty congressional feminists have had coordinating policymaking with feminist NGOs. The bills also illustrate not only the potential limits of framing controversial feminist issues but why the very idea of framing and political compromise is a matter of debate among feminists.

Framing the Debate: The Political Discourse on Abortion

In her analysis of public policy on abortion and divorce in Chile, Argentina, and Brazil, Htun (2003) argues that legislative reform becomes difficult when an area of public policy is successfully framed as a "moral" issue. For decades, abortion in Chile was largely uncontroversial and was bureaucratically regulated through the civil code. The criminalization of abortion by the military government was made possible because policy reform was not subject to democratic debate. That abortion has not been decriminalized since the return of democracy owes much to the successful reframing of the issue by political conservatives. Once the military government outlawed abortion on moral grounds, this became the default political frame for the issue. The challenge that feminists face is to reframe abortion as an issue of public health, women's equality, and human rights.

Following the 1973 coup, the group of military leaders and conservative scholars who convened to write a new constitution considered drafting a "right-to-life" amendment that would outlaw abortion.[6] Grau et al. (1997) argue that this position in favor of a complete prohibition on abortion was part of a larger "pro-natalist" discourse of the military government, which also discouraged contraception and encouraged women to have large families for the "fatherland."[7] Yet despite the cultural regression on women's rights during the military government, when the members of the committee first met in 1974, most of the members of the constitutional convention favored maintaining the status quo of legalized therapeutic abortion. That even these appointees of the military regime favored the status quo reflects the lack of controversy surrounding the law at the time.[8]

However, the issue was revisited following the defeat of the military government in the 1988 plebiscite. Facing the loss of power after seventeen years of military rule, the government attempted to link the issue of abortion to a broader threat of cultural change from the democratic opposition. In the election campaigns that followed the plebiscite, members of the feminist community called for public debate on abortion and divorce, and a number of politicians on the left began promoting broader liberalization of existing

---

6. The best-known member of the committee was Jaime Guzmán, a constitutional lawyer from Catholic University and longtime conservative political activist. Guzmán was active in the opposition to Allende. Prior to the transition to democracy, he founded the UDI. Guzmán was assassinated in 1991 by a member of the Manuel Rodriguez Patriotic Front.

7. For example, international efforts to distribute information on contraception, such as those by Planned Parenthood International, were characterized by the military government (and by some conservative members of the Catholic Church) as part of a larger imperialist offensive by the United States to weaken the Chilean nation (Grau et al. 1997, 307). For more on the gendered discourse of the military government and its internal contradictions, see Valenzuela 1987.

8. For a transcript of these discussions, see *Actas oficiales de la Comisión Constituyente* (Santiago: Talleres Gráficos Gendarmeria de Chile, 1976), session 87a, November 14, 1974, p. 14.

abortion laws, together with the legalization of divorce. The possibility that a future democratic government might liberalize social policy on such contentious "moral" issues produced tremendous political tension for conservative sectors within the military government and the Catholic Church (Grau et al. 1997, 307; Haas 1999). The legal status of therapeutic abortion came to be seen as a dangerous opening through which left-wing political sectors could legislate a complete liberalization of abortion laws. In 1989 the military government responded by outlawing abortion completely, even in cases where a woman's life is at stake.[9] Since that time, political and social sectors opposed to abortion have vociferously resisted efforts to overturn the 1989 law or to promote public debate on the topic.

The Right: Moral Order and National Security

Discourse on abortion in Chile runs to extremes, and three distinct currents of thought are evident in the statements of major social and political actors. The discourse of the Right rejects abortion as an attack on the family and a threat to fundamental national values. This discourse emphasizes motherhood as the core of a woman's identity. In the lead-up to the 1989 elections and during the first democratic administration, Sara Navas, a lawyer for the RN, was a primary spokesperson for this view.[10] In interviews with the Chilean press, Navas insisted that the essential difference between women and men was a biological fact and that women who refused to have children denied their very identities and the "essence" of their femininity. Linking the private behavior of women to the security of the nation, Navas argued that countries that legalized abortion were forced to "confront the loss of feminine values and the masculinization of women, which puts in grave danger the sexual morality of humanity. . . . Maternity is the primordial and undeniable mission toward which women have been directed since the beginning of time" (quoted in Grau et al. 1997, 317). In this view, because abortion threatens the very identity of women, it threatens by extension the family and ultimately the nation itself. Thus the liberalization of abortion laws and the reevaluation of traditional gender roles that such liberalization

---

9. Interestingly, even as it outlawed abortion on "pro-life" grounds, the committee reinstituted capital punishment.

10. Baldez 2002 notes that Navas first became politically active in the women's movement against Allende. See also Power 2002.

implies become inextricably linked to the moral structure and the security of Chilean society.

At its most extreme, the logic of this perspective extends so far as to prohibit abortion even in cases where a woman's life is at stake. Jaime Guzmán, a constitutional lawyer from Catholic University, spearheaded the development of the 1980 constitution. As a member of the military government's original constitutional committee, he argued in 1974 for a complete constitutional ban on abortion, explaining that sometimes a person finds himself in situations where he must choose between death and moral compromise. In such cases, that person "must opt for heroism, or martyrdom, or whatever. . . . The grave consequences or the tragedy which follows from the observance of a moral law can never be invoked as a reason to excuse someone from their obligation to fulfill that law. For this reason the prohibition on abortion must be absolute, because . . . the moral order is equally so."[11] Most Chilean citizens and politicians would reject this extreme position; indeed, in internal discussions during the 1974 constitutional convention, most members of the convention rejected it. Yet this perspective is currently enshrined in Chilean law. The difficulty in challenging the law arises because of the great fear on the part of conservatives that debate on the justifications for abortion could lead to legalization beyond the strict case of threats to the mother's life. Any effort to debate abortion is thus characterized as "pro-abortion."

To avoid having to argue that women should die rather than resort to abortion, most members of the political Right focus on advances in medical technology, which they argue have nearly eliminated situations in which a physician must perform an abortion to save a woman's life.[12] Conservatives argue that no other reason for abortion takes precedence over the more basic right of an unborn child to life. The practice of illegal abortion is sufficiently widespread in Chile that most conservatives support strict legal sanctions, including incarceration, to deter women from having abortions and to punish abortion providers. In addition, since the transition to democracy the Right has introduced a number of bills to increase further the existing sanctions both for women who have abortions and for abortion providers. These bills are timed to counteract proposals aimed at liberalizing abortion law. Among the recent bills are two authored by UDI deputy Marisol Turres,

---

11. *Actas oficiales de la Comisión Constituyente*, session 87a, November 14, 1974, p. 14.

12. As noted below, the Chilean Medical Association has argued that abortion should be left to individual conscience.

who was elected in 2006 and is a member of the Constitution Committee. In 2006 Turres co-sponsored a bill that would require a constitutional amendment to decriminalize abortion (bill 4122) and another to increase the penalty for having an abortion (bill 4121).

The Left: Abortion Rights as Pragmatic Politics

The emphasis of most of the political Left and the feminist community is on the inevitability of abortion and the need to regulate its practice to protect the lives and health of women. While they support efforts to prevent unwanted pregnancies, these groups see legal abortion as a necessary part of larger preventive efforts. A number of politicians on the left have called directly for public recognition of the widespread practice of illegal abortion in Chile. For example, Green Party deputy Laura Rodríguez declared, "The Party takes on the problem of abortion with the motto 'forward in truth, enough of the hypocrisy'" (quoted in Grau et al. 1997, 309). PPD deputy María Antonieta Saa declared herself "absolutely in agreement with therapeutic abortion" (interview in *La Nación*, May 23, 1993, 5). Socialist deputy Adriana Muñoz explained, "The fact that we debate [abortion] doesn't mean that abortions will increase in Chile or that we are against life. What we are doing is recognizing a fact of reality and preventing legislation from becoming outmoded, as it is now, when there exists a law which penalizes abortion and more than 150,000 women abort every year" (interview in *La Nación*, June 27, 1991). This view closely resembles that of the feminist community. While insisting that they are not "pro-abortion," feminists explain that abortion is a social fact that needs to be recognized, and that the cultural myths and stereotypes that contribute to the high rate of unwanted pregnancies need to be exposed as false. Feminists have sought to expose the destructive cultural beliefs that persist in economically vulnerable sectors of the population, beliefs that portray women as "less feminine" if they use contraception and question a man's virility if he does not impregnate a woman (Grau et al. 1997, 311). Feminists argue that solutions to high abortion rates will come from promoting public debate on the issue, which would force public recognition of men's contribution to the problem of unwanted pregnancies and the larger cultural forces at work in promoting myths and stereotypes about sexuality. In addition, much of the feminist movement and the political Left focus on abortion as an economic problem, "related to the grave economic problems which women heads of household in 'popular' homes have to confront" (Casas 1996, 5). In 1985 the Open Forum on Health and Sexual and Reproductive Rights, an alliance of NGOs, was formed to focus attention on the issue of abortion and to coordinate movement action in this area. But given the strength of social and political forces opposing the decriminalization of abortion laws, it has been extremely difficult to promote public debate on the issue, and abortion has not been a focal point of the women's movement.

The Center: Sympathy for Women "Victimized" by Abortion

The centrist position, advocated by Christian Democrats and Sernam, is to view women who have abortions as victims of unwanted pregnancies. The emphasis here, as Hector Salazar put it in *La Epoca,* is that "a woman arrives at the point of abortion forced by circumstances that escape her control" (quoted in Grau et al. 1997, 318). These groups oppose both abortion and legal sanctions against women who abort, focusing instead on the prevention of unwanted pregnancies. In the opinion of more liberal centrist politicians, preventive efforts should include sex education and better availability of contraception. This reflects the position of Sernam, and, beginning with Minister Josefina Bilbao (1994–98), Sernam's ministers have argued strongly against incarcerating women for having abortions.[13] Sernam has also come into conflict with the church and political conservatives over its efforts to promote a national program of sex education in Chilean schools. Promoting sex education and contraceptive use is much less problematic for the parties of the Left, who do not have the Christian Democrats' and, less formally, the Right's historical and ideological links to the Catholic Church.

The Catholic Church: Unqualified Opposition to Abortion

The policy positions of the Catholic Church defy easy categorization as "Right" or "Left." The church takes a progressive stand on many social issues, such as human rights, workers' rights, and economic inequality, and on these subjects the church's position overlaps with that of the political Center-Left. The church's position on abortion, however, most closely resembles that of the Right, because the church rejects as immoral both abortion and

---

13. Bilbao elaborated this position in a number of interviews with the press. See, for example, "Me molesta la gente intolerante," *La Epoca* (Santiago), June 30, 1995, 6.

efforts to prevent abortion such as sex education and contraception. Furthermore, the Catholic Church's official statements on abortion are devoid of references to the larger social context in which abortions occur, the class bias inherent in abortion practices in Chile, or any reference to women as victims, forced by circumstances to resort to abortion. With the transition to democracy, the Chilean church began to reiterate strongly an absolute prohibition on abortion. In response to public statements by some politicians on the left and by members of the women's movement in favor of liberalizing abortion laws, the National Episcopal Conference issued the following statement: "Thank God there is no talk in Chile today of authorizing, much less promoting, abortion. To the contrary, a law has just been passed which prohibits abortion in any circumstance, for which we are grateful to the past government. But the country must know that, in the case of danger, the church will defend human life, from the moment of conception to the last breath."[14] The church's renewed moral authority following the transition and its consequent political influence in democratic politics meant that the church would be a major player in any debate on the reform of abortion laws.

Congressional Representatives Address Abortion

Socialist deputy Adriana Muñoz was among a group of representatives from the political Left who had been calling for the liberalization of abortion laws since before the transition to democracy. In 1991, following her election to the Chamber of Deputies, she introduced a bill to restore legal therapeutic abortion. Four fellow party members, Armando Arancibia, Carlos Smok, Juan Pablo Letelier, and Carlos Montes, co-signed the bill, and the following month Humanist/Green Party deputy Laura Rodríguez added her name to the proposal. The text of the bill itself was a mere two sentences: "Only toward therapeutic ends may a pregnancy be interrupted. To undertake this intervention the documented opinion of two medical surgeons is required."[15]

---

14. Conferencia Episcopal de Chile 1989, 18–19. The Episcopal Conferences are national-level assemblies of Catholic bishops that coordinate the church's programs and policies in that country. The Episcopal Conferences issue "pastoral letters" (often published in major newspapers) outlining the church's position on various issues.

15. Bill 499-7, p. 1. Legislative proposals consist of the bill itself and an introduction outlining the justification for it, necessary background and data on the policy issue, and reference to influential groups or individuals supporting the bill.

As Muñoz described it, the therapeutic abortion bill aimed merely to return to the pre-1989 statute, which allowed for abortion in extreme cases—specifically, when continuing the pregnancy would constitute a threat to the woman's life or health. The introduction to the bill was carefully framed to try to address the expected opposition to the proposal. The bill referred to the position of the Chilean Medical Association in support of decriminalization and to evidence of public opinion in favor of reform. The bill also mentioned other Catholic countries that had decriminalized abortion. Finally, an attempt was made to place the entire proposal in a "pro-family" frame by arguing that abortion rights are necessary to support healthy families.

While the proposed law mentioned only therapeutic abortion, the precise limits of what would be considered a legal abortion were not defined. Indeed, the preamble presented justifications for abortion that went beyond a strictly defined threat to a woman's life or health, including, for example, a woman's mental health, fetal deformity, pregnancy resulting from rape or incest, and cases in which a pregnant woman wished to abort because she was infected with HIV. The lack of clarity in the definition of therapeutic abortion weakened support for the bill among potential supporters and provided ammunition for the opposition.

Although, prior to the bill's introduction, there was no significant mobilization by the women's movement in support of the decriminalization of abortion, pro-choice organizations, especially the Women's Institute in Santiago, served as a resource for Muñoz as she wrote the bill.[16] Anticipating the arguments they would face, Muñoz and members of the Women's Institute played down references to individual rights as a defense of decriminalization.[17] Taking the existence of abortion as a given, the preamble to the bill concentrated on the harm done to the family as a result of the complete ban on abortion, namely:

> the numerous psycho-social consequences for children and for the family in general, which result from the loss of the life or health of the

---

16. El Instituto de la Mujer in Santiago is a feminist NGO founded in 1987. It focuses both on women's political participation and on a number of specific policy issues, including reproductive rights. More information is available on the institute's Web site, http://www.insmujer.cl/.

17. The use of arguments on individual rights to support abortion rights, the primary argument of proponents of legal abortion in the United States, is often interpreted by conservatives in Latin America as evidence of a self-centered perspective among feminists, who are seen as being antifamily or antichildren. A community- or family-focused defense of abortion is similar to the framing of the issue in European law.

mother, which not only destroys a marriage but also traumatizes the
children, who will suffer a lack of affection because a person fundamental to their formative development (in the sense of transmitting
values, knowledge, etc.) has disappeared. The gravity of the situation
of small children due to the absence of the mother, [because she is]
poor and/or single or deceased, leads to [the children's] probable "in-
ternment" in a Children's Home . . . homelessness, or in the majority
of cases, life in foster homes.[18]

In a critical strategic move, the bill's authors thus defined the average
woman seeking an abortion as *already a mother*. By framing abortion rights
as a necessary resource for mothers who are struggling to take care of existing
children, the bill's authors offered a compelling counterimage to the stereo-
type promoted by the Right—that of a woman who rejects family, children,
and her very biology. As framed in the therapeutic abortion bill, women who
seek abortions are trying to be good mothers (and wives). By presenting
supporters of abortion rights as "pro-family," the bill's authors aimed to undermine the opposition's primary line of attack.

Recognizing the social and political influence of the Chilean Catholic
Church, the bill's sponsors tried to preempt the church's opposition by noting that other Catholic countries, such as Italy, Spain, and Portugal, had
decriminalized abortion, and that within Latin America only Chile, the
Dominican Republic, and Haiti had illegalized abortion completely.[19] By
noting that most Catholic countries make some legal allowance for abortion,
the bill's authors argued that the Catholic Church can coexist with a secular,
democratic government that provides reproductive rights to its citizens.

In an implicit challenge to arguments that abortions are medically unnec-
essary, the proposal cited the opinion of the Chilean Medical Association
that therapeutic abortion is "a question of conviction and of individual conscience that must be respected." The official position of the Chilean Medical
Association, as written in article 26 of the association's code of ethics, is that

---

18. Cámara de Diputados, *Redacción de sesiones* (1991), legislative session 322/41a, September 17, p. 4087.

19. Ibid., 4089. Since this bill was written, a complete ban on abortion has also been instituted in Nicaragua and El Salvador (2006). Abortion rights have been expanded in Mexico City
(2007) and Colombia (2006). Cuba has the fewest restrictions on access to abortion in Latin
America. See the Web site of Mujeres Latinoamericanas en Cifras at http://www.eurosur.org/
flacso/mujeres/.

three conditions must be met before an abortion can be performed: the abortion must be considered therapeutic in the opinion of the doctor; at least two appropriate medical specialists must give written consent; and the abortion must be performed by a specialist trained in the procedure. The association has stated that in cases where a particular doctor is opposed to abortion, the law cannot obligate that doctor to perform it, but he or she must find a doctor who is willing to perform the procedure, thereby guaranteeing the woman qualified medical care.[20] The bill's sponsors used the existence of such protocol, in place for many years before the 1989 law was passed, to argue that while specific individuals within the medical profession may be opposed to abortion under any circumstances, the profession as a whole recognizes the medical and ethical legitimacy of abortion in some situations and aims both to define those circumstances and to ensure the proper care of women who have abortions.

The preamble to the bill also cited recent public opinion surveys, noted above, that indicated that a clear majority of Chileans favor the decriminalization of abortion in a narrowly defined set of circumstances. Finally, the proposal made a case for decriminalization on constitutional grounds, noting that article 19 of the constitution, which "ensures all people the right to life," has been interpreted in other situations to allow for one person to end the life of another, be it through self-defense or, in some cases, in defense of one's property. Indeed, the bill noted that the framers of the 1980 constitution recognized such limitations on the right to life. Even as they outlawed abortion, they reaffirmed the legality of the death penalty.[21]

The bill entered the Chamber of Deputies in 1991 and was sent to the Constitution Committee, but no further action was taken. The public support Muñoz expected from the women's movement was slow to materialize. The issue of abortion divided the women's movement, which was struggling to redefine itself, its policy priorities, and its relationship to the state following the transition to democracy. Unlike violence against women, a core issue for the women's movement, abortion was not the type of issue likely to unite the women's movement or garner public demonstrations of support. With the exception of her work with the Women's Institute, Muñoz had not contacted other feminist organizations when drafting her bill and had assumed

---

20. Cámara de Diputados, *Redacción de sesiones* (1991), legislative session 322/41a, September 17, p. 4088.

21. *Actas oficiales de la Comisión Constituyente,* session 87a, November 14, 1974.

that movement support would materialize after the bill's introduction. Organizations that focused on reproductive rights resented the introduction of a bill that had not sought their input.[22] Nevertheless, a year after the bill was introduced, and as it languished in committee, the Open Forum on Health and Sexual and Reproductive Rights held a symposium in Santiago to debate therapeutic abortion and mobilize public support for the bill. But this belated support was not enough to overcome the obstacles the bill faced within Congress and the Socialist Party.

Attempts to frame the proposal strategically could not compensate for the institutional obstacles, which went beyond a lack of explicit support from Sernam. Conservative political forces dominated the Constitution Committee. The committee chair was conservative Christian Democrat Hernán Bosselin, who spearheaded efforts to introduce a number of socially conservative bills (among them a proposal aimed at counteracting efforts to legalize divorce, introduced in January 1991). Bosselin strongly opposed debating the bill and found support among the majority of committee members, who included four other Christian Democrats, five members of the right-wing opposition, and three members of the PPD. No women and no Socialists served on the committee, and the three PPD members, who might have supported the bill had there been greater support from other sectors, constituted a small minority. Without the backing of the executive, the bill's sponsors had no access to the committee.

Despite the Socialist Party's backing of decriminalization, there was no party-level support for the bill. Beyond the party's weak presence on the review committee, many in the party resisted involvement in such a controversial issue so soon after the transition to democracy. Socialists felt that identifying with such a bill early on would hurt their future electoral chances, especially at the presidential level. The party thus kept silent when Muñoz was vilified in the press, and when she ran for re-election in 1994, the Socialists offered her no support in her district. Muñoz blamed her electoral loss on the lack of party support, which she attributed to her introducing the therapeutic abortion bill against the wishes of the party leadership.[23] Muñoz

---

22. Members of the Open Forum on Health and Sexual and Reproductive Rights, interviews by author, Santiago, January 1997.
23. Some members of the feminist community agree with this assessment, while others do not. For example, Alicia Frohmann of Flacso considers the party's abandonment of Muñoz an example of the low standing women have within the parties, even those on the left. Others have attributed the problem to personality conflicts between Muñoz and the party leadership.

feels that she was singled out for punishment because she led the effort to introduce the bill. By contrast, the male representatives who co-signed the bill retained party support in their districts, and all but one were reelected. As a result of this lack of party support, Muñoz switched her party affiliation to the PPD and was reelected to the Chamber of Deputies in 1998.

In the end, despite the earlier legality of therapeutic abortion, the high abortion rate, and public opinion in favor of reform, the 1991 bill failed to be debated in committee and was formally archived in 1997. The experience of this first posttransition abortion bill illustrates the difficulty of coordinating support for policy proposals, particularly in the face of organized opposition. Diffuse public opinion in favor of reform could not be expected to gel on its own into a visible and effective source of legislative support, and feminist organizations were slow to rally behind a proposal developed without their participation. In the future, the Left will have to balance party support for the issue in general against the more immediate electoral concerns of party members. Representatives will need to develop bills in consultation with interested sectors, and they will need to mobilize broader political support before a bill's introduction in Congress. The "pro-family" framing of the bill could be an effective defense against the opposition, but a successful bill will need its supporters to define therapeutic abortion more clearly, so as to avoid confusion or purposeful misinterpretation of the bill's aims.

Feminist NGOs Draft an Abortion Bill

Following Muñoz's electoral defeat at the end of 1993, the feminist NGO Open Forum on Health and Sexual and Reproductive Rights drafted another bill to decriminalize abortion. Given the failure of the congressional bill, what accounts for the Forum's timing? The impetus to develop a new bill on abortion did not originate with the Forum itself but with an international agency focused on reproductive rights. In 1993 the International Women's Health Coalition offered the Forum a grant to write a bill decriminalizing abortion, and the members of the Forum decided to take advantage of this funding opportunity.[24] The process exposed the internal divisions within the organization over the proper scope of a legislative proposal on

---

24. The International Women's Health Coalition works on a variety of feminist issues, but its main focus is in the areas of sexual and reproductive rights. More information can be found on its Web site, http://www.iwhc.org/.

abortion and the utility of compromise with the opposition. Members were also sharply divided over whether, and how, to lobby representatives over the bill.

None of the Forum's members were lawyers, and the grant from the IWHC would not cover the cost of hiring one to write the bill. Therefore, the Forum contracted Lidia Casas, a law student at the University of Chile, to assist in drafting the proposal. Casas had published a book on the state of reproductive rights in Chile, emphasizing the class bias in the existing law (Casas 1996). The Forum that believed Casas's expertise on the social repercussions of the ban on abortion would help them write a persuasive proposal.

In the course of drafting the bill, divisions emerged within the Forum over the scope of the proposal. Although all the members of the Forum referred to the proposal as a therapeutic abortion bill, there was no agreement on what that meant. Most members preferred to propose a law that liberalized abortion laws beyond overturning the 1989 law and that went significantly beyond the Muñoz proposal. After two years of working on the bill, there was still no consensus on exactly what type of bill the Forum was proposing. The problems were twofold. Part of the difficulty was that the Forum as such met irregularly, and different representatives from the member organizations would often attend from meeting to meeting. Once a particular vision of the bill was decided by those present, it would often need to be reworked completely at the next meeting.

More significantly, there was ideological disagreement among many members, who were reluctant to compromise, for purposes of political expediency, on the type of abortion law they sought. Some members wanted a radical proposal, arguing that any bill would be watered down in the course of congressional debate and that the more radical the original proposal, the more sweeping the final version of the bill would be. For example, some versions made no mention of term limits for abortion. Supporters of this approach were highly critical of the tone of the Muñoz proposal, which they felt ceded critical ideological ground to the opposition. Members argued that the Muñoz bill's conservative framing, particularly its portrayal of women as mothers driven to abortion out of concern for their existing children, played into conservative stereotypes that defined maternity as women's primary identity. These members preferred to assert an individual-rights approach to reproductive rights. According to this perspective, any move to alter existing gender relations would be met with fierce opposition from conservatives, and therefore the feminist community might as well craft a proposal worth battling for. In the words of one member of La Morada, a feminist NGO that participated in the Forum, "I don't believe that something is better than nothing. I thought so at one time, when I believed that political compromise was necessary, but now I believe that one can go on fighting for what one believes in, because you're going to encounter resistance either way. . . . The discourse of the Right will be the same, whether we keep quiet or declare our differences. The discourse of the Right is the discourse of the traditional Catholic Church, and it's not only the Right, I think there are also a lot of progressive groups that employ the same discourse."[25] This activist argued that the feminist community worried too much about rocking the boat and antagonizing the social and political establishment. As a result, she believed, feminists engaged in a kind of "self-censorship" that ceded too much ground to more established institutions, such as Sernam or the parties of the Left.

Another faction within the Forum argued that, given the conservative nature of Chilean society and politics, a radical proposal would be rejected immediately. The best strategy would thus be to propose nothing beyond a return to the pre-1989 law, and then later attempt to expand on that law. This faction argued that a broader proposal would not survive long enough in Congress for support to be mobilized. Witnessing these internal disagreements over the course of two years, Casas observed, "If the Forum still did not know what it wanted, if the debate was not settled at the Forum, how would it be settled elsewhere?"[26]

Disagreements over whether and how to lobby congressional representatives began as the details of the bill were still being debated. The lobbying process itself was not afforded high priority; a few individuals from the Forum were assigned the task of lobbying, in addition to their numerous other responsibilities, and they found it difficult to make time to travel to Valparaíso.[27] In addition, Forum members lobbied only the few feminist representatives they felt certain would support the bill, with the expectation that

---

25. Verónica Matus, interview by author, Santiago, April 2, 1997.
26. Lidia Casas, interview by author, Santiago, January 8, 1997.
27. As mentioned in chapter 2, prior to the transition to democracy, the military government built a new congressional building in Valparaíso, a two-hour drive from Santiago. The physical division of the different branches of government between the two cities forced representatives to set up multiple offices: one in Valparaíso, one in Santiago, and one in the home district. This arrangement complicates not only the business of government but communication between the government and the public, including lobbyists.

these representatives would then build a broader alliance with their congressional colleagues. The Forum concentrated most of its lobbying efforts on PPD deputy María Antonieta Saa and Left-Independent deputy Fanny Pollarolo (later a member of the Socialist Party), but both women refused to sponsor the bill. Their rejection was not based on their position on the issue, for in the recent past both had publicly declared their support for the legalization of therapeutic abortion. Instead, they argued that abortion reform was a lost cause, and that Adriana Muñoz's electoral loss was a clear indication of the risks involved in supporting such a bill. Saa argued that in a country like Chile, where it was impossible even to legalize divorce,[28] advocating legal abortion amounted to political suicide. She further argued that no representative would take such a political risk unless the women's movement had already mobilized in support of the decriminalization of abortion. Although Pollarolo had criticized "the failure of the State to provide couples the means to carry out their reproductive rights" (quoted in Grau et al. 1997, 301), she made a similar argument for not sponsoring the bill.

Forum members saw no point in lobbying the opposition. Casas explained that within the Forum there was no sense that one needed to talk to the opposition, to show them that "you're not Satan," and to "put a normal, human face on the feminist movement."[29] Casas took it upon herself to lobby Christian Democrat Mariana Aylwin, a decision that the Forum later criticized as a waste of time. Casas considered Aylwin a potential ally because she had braved the opposition of both the Catholic Church and her party's leadership in introducing legislation to legalize divorce (discussed in chapter 5). But she was opposed to abortion, and she was also extremely reluctant to become involved in another controversial policy issue. Casas related that in the course of their discussions, however, Aylwin became sensitized to the class bias inherent in the current system of prosecuting women who had abortions. Casas explained that Aylwin "realized that although she was against abortion, she would not necessarily be in support of women being prosecuted. . . . Of course she's a Christian Democrat, and she doesn't believe in putting an end to a life, whether it's an embryo or whatever. So her

---

28. Divorce was not legalized in Chile until 2004.
29. Casas, interview. As discussed in chapter 2, the lack of sophisticated lobbying has historical roots. For seventeen years under General Pinochet, there was no lobbying of any kind. Prior to that, there were no lobbying organizations independent of the parties. The women's movement finds its closest ideological allies in the parties of the Left. For this reason the Forum did not understand why Casas would suggest lobbying the opposition.

stance is strongly on prevention of unwanted pregnancy, which is fine, but you don't have her as an 'enemy.' There is common ground . . . so that's the road we paved."[30] Evidence of Aylwin's changing perspective on reproductive rights is seen in her subsequent participation in efforts to develop a reproductive rights bill, which outlined means of prevention of unwanted pregnancy, primarily through sex education for teenagers.[31] In 2000, President Lagos appointed Aylwin minister of health, and she continued to pursue issues of reproductive health and sex education from her position within the executive branch. (An interparty group of representatives introduced a reproductive rights bill [2608] in November 2000 that reflected many of Aywlin's earlier efforts.) Such efforts signal an evolution in thinking on the part of a member of the PDC, which underscores the importance of focusing lobbying efforts on opposition and undecided members of Congress. In the end, the Forum's therapeutic abortion proposal was never reviewed by any members of Congress, and it was never debated within the women's movement outside the group of NGOs that made up the Forum.

Feminist Learning from the Failure of Abortion Reform

> The best way for the world to thrive is to ensure that its women have the freedom, power, and knowledge to make decisions affecting their own lives and those of their families and communities.
> —Former UN Secretary-General Kofi Annan

The posttransition efforts to decriminalize abortion illustrate the enduring challenge of tackling controversial policy issues in the absence of executive support and in the face of entrenched cultural opposition. Sernam refused to support congressional efforts to decriminalize therapeutic abortion, and congressional representatives alone lacked the institutional strength and political support to overcome widespread opposition to the bill from the Right, conservative Christian Democrats, and the Catholic Church. In the case of the congressional bill on therapeutic abortion, attempts to frame the legislation as "pro-family" failed to appeal to political moderates and could not

---

30. Ibid.
31. Aylwin discussed her work on this project in our interview, Valparaíso, March 12, 1997.

overcome the almost complete lack of institutional support for the bill. Following the bill's burial in congressional committee, a feminist NGO developed a new proposal, only to find that no member of Congress would agree to sponsor it.

The failed attempts to legislate on abortion point not only to the strength of cultural and political opposition to abortion in general but to the particular weakness of the two posttransition bills that sought to liberalize abortion laws. The isolated efforts of both the feminist representative who introduced the first bill and the NGO collective that drafted the second weakened both proposals from the start. Deputy Muñoz believed that the women's movement and representatives on the left would rally to support her bill. Similarly, the Open Forum on Health and Sexual and Reproductive Rights thought that feminist representatives who had not been involved in their bill's development would be willing to sponsor it in Congress. Neither Muñoz nor the Forum anticipated the strength of opponents of legalized abortion, and neither sought to preempt the opposition by negotiating a bill with broader political support from the start. In addition, both failed to define clearly the limits of their bills (precisely what was meant by "therapeutic abortion"?), which made it difficult to rebut inaccurate claims about the bill's implications.

It is clear that a lack of institutional support from Sernam has critical implications for congressional bills. Feminists inside and outside government have criticized Sernam's unwillingness to take on the most controversial feminist policy issues. Sernam has countered that feminists expect the ministry to achieve things that the women's movement itself has been unable to accomplish. For example, Verónica Baez, who worked in Sernam's Health Division in the first two democratic administrations, argues that the movement is hypocritical to criticize Sernam for taking over the movement's agenda yet at the same time chastise the ministry for not "leading the charge" in areas like abortion and reproductive rights.[32] Baez insists that it is the movement's responsibility to familiarize society with these issues; only then, with clear demonstrations of popular support, could Sernam begin to speak publicly in favor of an issue as controversial as abortion.

Arguably, in the absence of institutional support from the executive, a controversial policy proposal could succeed only by carefully building support within Congress before a bill is introduced, by framing the proposal in such

---

32. Verónica Baez, interview by author, Santiago, March 1997.

a way as to head off opposition, and by mobilizing support and pressure outside government. Mariana Aylwin's evolution on the issue of reproductive rights also demonstrates that political alliances can be built with the opposition if supporters of reform are willing to take the long view and make the necessary compromises. Recent bills on abortion and reproductive rights show that representatives have made significant progress since the failure of the Muñoz bill.

A particular challenge in the case of abortion, however, is that opposition to reform is much stronger, and much better organized, than on any other feminist policy issue. In addition to opposing bills that seek to liberalize abortion laws, conservative representatives have introduced numerous bills seeking to block liberalization. In 1994 several UDI deputies, including María Angélica Cristi, introduced a bill that would have increased the penalties for having an abortion, including incarceration for women and their doctors.[33] Cristi added an amendment to the bill allowing women to avoid punishment if they turned in their doctors. After 2000, when efforts to enact reform increased, conservatives introduced a new round of antiabortion legislation. UDI representatives introduced two bills that sought to increase the penalties for abortion (2978 [2002] and 4447 [2006]) along the lines of the 1994 bill. In addition, conservative Christian Democrats teamed up with members of the Right to introduce two bills banning the use of ultrasound technology as part of an abortion (3449 [2004] and 4307 [2006]). Two more bills sought to make liberalization more difficult by mandating a constitutional amendment to change laws on abortion (4121 and 4122 [both in 2006]). Two additional bills were more symbolic in nature, seeking to erect monuments to the "innocent unborn victims" of abortion (3608 [2004] and 4818 [2007]). To date, none of these bills has made it out of committee. In addition, sixty members of the Chamber of Deputies have formed the Frente Parlamentario por la Vida (Parliamentary Front for Life), which is committed to blocking legislative attempts to decriminalize abortion.[34] Outside the government, the efforts of the Catholic Church are bolstered by conservative lobbying groups like Acción Familia (Family Action), which monitors congressional actions on conservative issues.

---

33. Although not part of this study, the full text of this bill (1298) and other conservative counterproposals can be found on the Web site of the Chilean Senate, http://www.senado.cl/ (under "Tramite de Proyectos").

34. The Frente is composed of twelve representatives from the PDC, one Independent, two members of the PRSD, fourteen RN representatives, and thirty-one members of the UDI. No representatives from the Socialist Party or the PPD have joined the group.

The Legacy of Attempts to Decriminalize Abortion

In the years immediately following the failure of the Muñoz and NGO bills on abortion, representatives made no further attempts to legislate policy reform on abortion. Since 2000, however, representatives have introduced six bills seeking to expand women's reproductive rights, and a growing number of politicians on the left, both male and female, have publicly declared themselves in favor of a return to the pre-1989 law. Most significantly, beginning in 2003 a number of representatives from the RN have added their voices to the calls for reform of abortion laws (appendix 1).

The election of Socialist Ricardo Lagos as president in 2000 no doubt increased the hopes of reformers. During his presidential campaign, Lagos had declared himself in support of therapeutic abortion (although he later backtracked in the face of church opposition). A more important boost came from Michelle Bachelet, who was appointed minister of health in 2000, as noted above. In her efforts in that position to make emergency contraception available by prescription, she weathered enormous political opposition from the Right, conservative Christian Democrats, and the church.[35]

While none of these bills has been debated in committee to date, it is clear that the political alliance in favor of reform is growing. The six pro-reform bills address reproductive rights from a variety of angles and reflect different legislative strategies. Some of them are narrow in scope, attempting to minimize the controversial nature of the legislation by strictly defining the limits of the proposed law. Bills 3197 (introduced in 2003) and 4751 (introduced in 2006) seek to decriminalize therapeutic abortion only, but both provide a fairly broad definition of "therapeutic" (including protection of the mental and physical health of the woman as well as the health of the fetus). Bill 3197 was co-sponsored by men and women from both sides of the political spectrum. (Interestingly, very few Christian Democrats have sponsored these recent bills, suggesting that reproductive rights continue to divide the party.) Bill 4751 was introduced by a single representative, Nelson Ávila. But because Ávila is a senator and a member of the centrist PRSD, his proposal reflects increased interest in the issue in the upper house of Congress and

---

35. In 2001 emergency contraception became available by prescription. After Bachelet was elected president, she extended the law to provide emergency contraception in public clinics. The law took effect in 2006. In the face of vociferous opposition from the Right and pressure from the Vatican, Chile's constitutional court outlawed the distribution of emergency contraception in 2008.

among centrist representatives. Bill 4845 (introduced in 2007) represents a slightly different strategy. It too would decriminalize therapeutic abortion, but only to protect the life of the woman. This bill was co-sponsored by a group of male and female representatives on the left.

Another series of legislative proposals attempt to legitimize the concept of reproductive rights in the hope that future reforms will broaden the scope of these rights. These three bills, 2608 (2000), 3702 (2004), and 4277 (2006), do not mention abortion. Rather, they link the concept of reproductive rights to human rights and to women's overall right to health care. These bills also argue that individual sexual liberty deserves legal protection. These bills, too, reflect growing support for reform. Male representatives on the left wrote bills 3702 and 4277, which suggests an unexpected level of interest and initiative among male representatives, who are now doing more than simply supporting bills introduced by their feminist colleagues.[36] It is evident from the content of all of these bills that representatives are trying to apply the lessons of earlier legislative failures to their efforts.

Of particular note in this respect is bill 2608, which focuses on "sexual and reproductive rights." Introduced in 2000, this bill was co-sponsored by men and women from across the political spectrum, including Christian Democrats. Of the six most recent bills, 2608 is the most expansive in scope. Its purpose is to establish that reproductive rights are human rights and to argue that women's equality is fundamental to a democratic society (the bill makes multiple references to UN declarations and other international agreements). The bill outlines a series of steps needed to help eradicate sexism in Chilean society, from reform of the education system to better access to sex education and contraception. It addresses the many forms of sexual violence endemic in Chilean society. While it does not advocate the decriminalization of abortion, it does assert that fear of prosecution under the current law results in many deaths from complications of illegal abortions. The bill's authors argue that the health-care system should treat women who have abortions as patients in need of medical care, not as criminals. The bill also argues for the liberty of all adults to exercise their sexuality and to choose

---

36. In discussing the phenomenon of growing male support, some feminist legislators and members of feminist organizations expressed anger that male representatives would develop and introduce these types of bills without trying to coordinate their efforts with congressional feminists. But feminists also acknowledged that the broadening of interest in these issues beyond a small cohort of feminists is a positive sign. Interviews with various feminists by author, Santiago, November 2006.

their sexual partners, and it explicitly extends these rights to gays and lesbians.

Outside Congress, there are signs that feminists are becoming increasingly active in defense of reproductive rights. In addition to the Open Forum on Health and Sexual and Reproductive Rights, other feminist organizations are focusing on sexual and reproductive health. Widespread protests greeted the court decision to ban emergency contraception in 2008. In addition to protest marches and e-mail and letter campaigns, the feminist NGO Mujeres Públicas launched a "massive apostasy." In opposition to Vatican pressure on the Chilean court to institute the ban, almost a thousand women publicly renounced their Catholicism. While public activism in favor of reform is not widespread, such protests signal a significant shift in Chilean political culture. Despite the lack of legal reform on reproductive rights to date, the growing movement in favor of reform, both inside and outside government, is creating new possibilities for feminist policy networks. The increasing cultural acceptance of the concept of reproductive rights augurs well for future reform efforts.

Abortion is without question the most challenging political issue for feminists in Chile. In the first two democratic administrations, feminists often cited abortion and divorce as the two women's rights issues on which reform was impossible. It was in many ways an apt comparison: Sernam refused to support the efforts of feminist representatives on either issue, and, like abortion, divorce was an issue that elicited a great deal of opposition from the political Right and the Catholic Church. Yet the fate of divorce legislation represents an optimistic counterpoint to the failed bills on abortion. While several posttransition divorce bills suffered the same fate as the abortion bills, the 1995 bill to legalize divorce eventually passed the Congress in 2004 (Law 19.947). Many of the factors missing from the abortion efforts—including executive support and a broad coalition of support within Congress—were initially lacking for the divorce proposals as well. How proponents of divorce reform were able to prevail in spite of formidable opposition is the subject of the next chapter.

5

WINNING THE GAME:
THE LEGALIZATION OF DIVORCE

> If marriage falls, it is my conviction that so too falls the family. And next will come marriages of homosexuals and lesbians.
> —UDI representative Hernán Larraín

The legalization of divorce in Chile in 2004 was arguably the greatest legislative victory for feminists since the transition to democracy.[1] The passage of the divorce law represents the culmination of political learning by congressional feminists and signals a positive shift in representatives' relationship with Sernam. This success invigorated the feminist movement and forced public debate on women's rights, and it suggests that feminists can achieve fundamental policy reform even on controversial issues if they can successfully strategize around institutional constraints and cultural opposition.

The New Civil Marriage Law was introduced as a bill in 1995 and became law nine years later. One can identify two phases of the policymaking dynamic on this legislation. In the first phase, the absence of institutional cooperation necessitated significant compromises on the bill's content. In the second phase, strong executive support allowed representatives to renegotiate more fundamental policy reform. Compared with earlier divorce bills, which were liberal in content and narrow in their base of support, representatives approached the 1995 divorce bill much more strategically, negotiating with the conservative opposition early on. Major concessions on content, together

---

1. The epigraph by Larraín is quoted in Castillo and Meléndez 1994, 27.

with a conscious effort to frame the topic within a pro-family discourse, allowed feminist representatives to exploit ideological divisions within the Christian Democratic Party and build PDC support for the bill early in the legislative process. This was a key factor in the bill's passage in the Chamber of Deputies in 1997. Executive support after 2000 reactivated the bill in the Senate and, most important, allowed legislators to renegotiate and pass a more progressive version of the bill.

The example of divorce legislation is particularly useful, as it allows us to gauge how changing conditions over time affected efforts to legalize divorce. As proponents of legal divorce evolved more sophisticated legislative strategies, public support for divorce was increasing. The initial absence of executive support for legalization was reversed following the election of a Socialist administration. Finally, party alliances shifted in Congress as support for legal divorce increased within the PDC and the Right. Each of these factors increased the political opportunities for reform.

A Pressing Need for Policy Reform

With the legalization of divorce in Ireland in 1996, Chile became the only nation to lack some type of legal divorce. Although the Catholic Church grants marriage annulments in specific circumstances, until 2004 there was no legal way to receive a civil divorce. Divorce *a la Chilena* referred to the one method of obtaining a civil annulment: committing perjury before the civil registrar by claiming that one had lied on some aspect of the original marriage license, thereby voiding the contract.[2] Efforts to legalize divorce focused on the widespread use of perjury to gain civil annulments and argued that the government should replace this informal system with a set of logical and equitable legal guidelines to regulate the dissolution of marriage.

Pursuing a civil annulment is expensive. One must hire a lawyer as well as two witnesses to testify that the original marriage contract contains a falsehood. Proponents of legal divorce focused on the class bias at work in the granting of annulments: if one has the financial means, getting a marriage annulled is quite easy; if one does not have the resources, it is impossible. In addition, prior to 2004, the lack of formal divorce made the establishment

---

2. Couples must marry at the civil registrar in the home district of the man or woman. The easiest way to void the marriage contract is to have witnesses testify that at the time of the marriage neither party actually lived in the district where they registered.

of alimony and child-support payments extremely difficult. This difficulty was aggravated by the fact that, until the reform of paternity laws in 1998 (Law 19.585), Chilean children born outside marriage had less right to parental financial support and inheritance than children born within marriage.[3] In 1995, 40 percent of Chilean children were born outside marriage, many of them to parents who had previously been married and so were unable to remarry (Centro de Estudios de la Mujer 1996b, 3). Advocates of legal divorce thus argued that the lack of civil divorce unfairly penalized women and children.[4]

Both the Right and the Left recognized Chile's high rate of marital separation and the frequent use of perjury to gain annulment, but their proposed solutions differed greatly. Conservative Christian Democrats and the political Right looked for ways to end the practice of perjured annulments without legalizing divorce, while progressive Christian Democrats and the political Left argued for a more pragmatic legal reform that would allow divorce under specific circumstances. Following the transition to democracy, both sides concluded that some sort of legislative reform of Chile's marital law was necessary; to that end, both introduced bills on the issue. Chronologically, the conservative bills, which sought to preserve the indissolubility of marriage, were timed to compete with and derail the bills introduced by the Center-Left.

Feminist representatives and their allies on the left began a legislative campaign to legalize divorce immediately after the resumption of democratic politics. These efforts coincided with congressional attempts to reform abortion laws, and at first glance divorce legislation faced similar challenges. The political will to legalize divorce appeared to be isolated within the Left, while the Right, bolstered by an aggressive antidivorce campaign by the Catholic Church, positioned itself strongly in opposition. Yet important differences in the political alliances and larger context of public opinion surrounding divorce created a more auspicious political context in which to pursue policy reform.

On the issue of divorce, the position of the Christian Democrats was deeply divided, and therefore politically more dynamic, than in the case of either domestic violence or abortion. The issue of domestic violence was uncontroversial for the overwhelming majority of Christian Democrats

---

3. For a discussion of the reform of Chile's paternity laws, see Haas 2000.
4. Opponents of legal divorce make the opposite claim, insisting that legal divorce has a detrimental economic effect on women and children (see, for example, Larraín 1996).

(which is not to imply party unity over the details of proposed reforms), whereas liberalization of abortion laws was anathema. By contrast, the issue of divorce revealed two distinct camps among PDC representatives—those who favored a reform of marriage law that would allow for some form of divorce, and those who were staunchly opposed to any liberalization of existing law. Given the party breakdown in the Congress, it was clear from the start that roughly half the PDC representatives in the Chamber of Deputies would have to be brought on board in support of a divorce bill (appendix 2). The Senate posed a greater challenge, but representatives strategized that passing a bill through the lower house would force the issue into public debate and thereby increase pressure on conservatives in the Senate.

Despite early acknowledgment of the need for Christian Democratic support, feminist representatives initially focused their lobbying efforts on solidifying political support among their male colleagues on the left but neglected to seek PDC participation in the development of the proposals. These early bills failed to progress in congressional committee. The successive divorce bills introduced between 1991 and 1995 illustrate the increasing success of feminist representatives in broadening the base of support for divorce legislation. Coordination with Christian Democrats, and even with moderate members of the RN, at the drafting stage, and a willingness to negotiate the content of the proposals were critical to the eventual development of a bill that could withstand congressional and church opposition. Advocates of legal divorce learned to use the committee system more effectively to keep their bills from being buried, and they marshaled the force of public opinion to help counter conservative opposition. By so doing they were able to keep divorce legislation alive in Congress for years in the absence of executive support.

Proposals and Counterproposals: Confronting Divorce in the First Congress (1990–1994)

Humanist/Green Party deputy Laura Rodríguez introduced the first posttransition bill on divorce in 1991 (bill 355), and Socialist Adriana Muñoz and three male Socialists co-sponsored it. This bill sought to legalize divorce in cases of "the prolonged rupture of the harmony of the couple, permanent and irreversible, which is grave enough that it will not permit the couple to re-initiate communal life."[5] Among other requirements for divorce that a judge would have to consider were the express declaration by both parties that they wished to divorce, the fact of separation of domicile for more than one year, adultery by either party, or the presence of physical or mental abuse in the relationship. The bill was careful to assert that divorce would not relieve either party of responsibilities toward the children. If a judge rejected a petition for divorce, the parties could reapply after three years. Once enacted, a divorce would be permanent.

Following its introduction in Congress, the bill aroused strong reaction from the Catholic Church but little support from representatives outside the Left. The bill was sent to the Constitution Committee in the Chamber of Deputies, where conservatives dominated; conservative Christian Democrat Hernán Bosselin was the chair. Bosselin was at the forefront of efforts to block efforts to legalize divorce and was instrumental in blocking the bill from debate in committee. Although the bill died in the Constitution Committee, its introduction provoked a strong counterresponse from conservatives, who characterized the Rodríguez bill as an attack on the family. Both the Catholic Church and representatives from the political Center-Right portrayed the legalization of divorce as the first step in an inexorable moral disintegration of Chilean society.

When the Rodríguez bill died in committee, feminist representatives began planning to draft another bill. Bosselin used his position as chair to preempt these efforts by introducing his own bill in 1991 (bill 264). The Bosselin bill was co-sponsored by four other Christian Democrats but was rejected by moderate Christian Democrats and the Left. Its purpose was to protect the institution of marriage by making it more difficult for couples to perjure their way to an annulment. To this end, the bill mandated a number of legal sanctions, including incarceration for married couples, lawyers, witnesses, or Civil Registry officials who knowingly participated in fraudulent annulment proceedings.

But even this conservative bill caused conflict with the Catholic Church. The bill's supporters faced the complicated legal question of determining the legal status of marriages that had been annulled by the church. They reasoned that if the church had declared a marriage invalid, civil law should allow the couple to dissolve their union. But what consequences would such

---

5. Programa de Asesoría Legislativa, "Boletín 355: Divorcio," *Bitácora Legislativa* no. 116, May 9–13, 1994, 15.

a law have for non-Catholics, who, not having been married in a Catholic ceremony, would have no basis for receiving an annulment from the church? The bill's supporters made a rather torturous attempt to reconcile religious mandates with civil law by outlining a set of circumstances for civil annulment that mirrored the Catholic Church's requirements for annulment but did not require a church annulment a priori. The Bosselin bill failed to win support from other political sectors or from the church itself. Bosselin was thus unable to use his chairmanship to force debate on the bill. Like the Rodríguez bill before it, the Bosselin proposal died in the Constitution Committee.

Two years later a third divorce bill was introduced, this one drafted by Socialist deputy Adriana Muñoz and co-sponsored by three male colleagues, Socialists Mario Devaud, Juan Pablo Letelier, and Carlos Montes (bill 1090). This third bill reflected a significant degree of political learning on the part of representatives, and major concessions had been made compared with the earlier Rodríguez proposal. The Muñoz bill tried to pacify the opposition by distinguishing between annulment, separation, and divorce and requiring different conditions for each. Annulment covered situations in which the original marriage was not contracted freely by one or both partners, and anyone related to the couple could initiate annulment proceedings. Legal separation was possible by judicial consent if both parties had maintained separate residences for at least six months, if one spouse had abandoned the home, or in cases of adultery, alcoholism, drug abuse, or situations of physical or psychological abuse. Separation would give legal recognition to the cessation of communal life and would specify the terms of child care but would not legally dissolve the marriage itself. Finally, divorce could be solicited by both parties by mutual consent, or by one party if certain conditions were met, among them the definitive and permanent establishment of separate domiciles or personal endangerment (specifically, attempts by one spouse to take the life of the other spouse or other members of the family). A crucial concession was that divorce would be temporary and could be rescinded by mutual consent. As with the previous bill, the Muñoz divorce bill was sent for review to the Constitution Committee. The presence of multiple and competing divorce bills in the same committee, coupled with the fact that the committee chair was the primary author of one of the bills, made it extremely difficult for any of the bills to be placed on the table for debate. After the failure of the Muñoz bill, no further bills on divorce were introduced until the second posttransition Congress.

Feminist Representatives Renew Efforts to Legalize Divorce (1994–1998)

With the election of a new Congress in 1994, progressive representatives renewed their efforts to legalize divorce. The possibilities for institutional cooperation on divorce reform improved as the Concertación increased its representation in both houses, and the number of women representatives increased slightly as well (see appendices 2 and 3). The most prominent feminist representatives of the first Congress did not return: Adriana Muñoz lost her bid for re-election, and Laura Rodríguez died in 1993. Three new feminist representatives entered the Congress, however, each from a different party within the Concertación: Socialist Fanny Pollarolo, PPD deputy María Antonieta Saa, and Christian Democrat Mariana Aylwin. The presence of feminists in different parties presented new opportunities for the development of interparty alliances. There was also growing interest among male representatives from the Concertación and among some female representatives from the RN in women's rights issues.

The election of Mariana Aylwin was especially significant in that it broadened the possibilities for building support for women's rights legislation within the Christian Democratic Party, which remained the head of the governing coalition as well as the largest party in the Congress.[6] In fact, Aylwin (along with two male colleagues, Christian Democrats Ignacio Walker and Sergio Elgueta) spearheaded the drafting of the next two bills. The emergence of Christian Democratic leadership in favor of reform challenged the framing of divorce as a "leftist" issue at odds with family values and had an enormous impact on the dynamics of the debate in Congress.

In 1994 Aylwin, Walker, and Elgueta drafted a bill that was very limited in scope, focusing primarily on reforming the practice of fraudulent annulments (bill 1370). Aylwin and Walker were simultaneously writing a book promoting the legalization of divorce (Aylwin and Walker 1995), the substance of which would form the basis of the 1995 divorce bill. But the logic behind this first bill was to address the one aspect of the current situation on

---

6. Given Mariana Aylwin's opposition to abortion, some might question my classification of her as a feminist. In her interview with me, Aylwin identified herself as a feminist. Beyond the issue of self-identification, I would argue that Aylwin's support for the women's rights legislation introduced during her tenure in office (with the exception of the therapeutic abortion bill) qualifies her as a feminist. Particularly on the issue of divorce, she braved the opposition of her party's leadership to introduce feminist legislation. Abortion is arguably a particularly difficult policy issue, even for those who support women's equality, and I would therefore argue against using it as a litmus test.

which all parties seemed to agree—the unacceptability of the unregulated nature of marital annulments. Once that bill passed, the sponsoring deputies hoped that it would force debate on the need for a more fundamental reform of marital law. Like the various bills on divorce introduced in the first Congress, this bill was sponsored by a few individuals within one political party, and it did not garner broader support after its introduction.

Nevertheless, one critical aspect of the bill's processing in the Congress differentiated it from its predecessors. The Family Committee, created the same year, asked to co-review the bill with the Constitution Committee. Such a request must receive the unanimous support of all those present in the chamber, and in this case representatives granted permission for the joint review. While there was support for the Aylwin-Walker bill within the Family Committee, the bill was tabled and died in the Constitution Committee. Because both committees did not agree to debate the bill, it did not make it to the floor for debate. Still, it established the informal precedent of the Family Committee's right to review bills of this sort. This would prove to be a critical factor in the subsequent, and ultimately successful, 1995 divorce bill.

The first Christian Democratic bill in 1994 was narrowly defined and uninspiring, but it encouraged debate on the subject of divorce within the PDC and renewed the interest of the Left in drafting another bill. Most important, supporters of legal divorce had become convinced that without significant support from the Christian Democrats and some support from the Right, a divorce bill would not withstand opposition and would never make it out of committee. In an effort to craft a bill that would enjoy broader political support, supporters undertook intense lobbying efforts that focused on conservative Christian Democrats and the more moderate wing of the RN.

A Second Conservative Counterproposal

As lobbying efforts increasingly targeted wavering Christian Democrats, a conservative faction within the PDC wrote a counterproposal. This competing bill was drafted by ten Christian Democrats, led by Deputy Carlos Dupré. It was strictly a Christian Democratic bill, as no outside political support had been sought in the course of its development. The Dupré bill illustrates the struggle within the PDC to find a compromise bill on divorce that would pacify both conservatives and reformers. The bill reflects a common Christian Democratic frame on social policy, as it attempts to strike a balance between the often stark and punitive rhetoric of the Right, which betrays little sympathy for individuals who violate traditional social norms, and what the PDC views as the excessive pragmatism of the Left. In the case of divorce, this meant an attempt to address the social stigma and economic vulnerability of "extramarital" families, yet one that stopped short of advocating the legalization of divorce.

The Dupré bill went significantly further than the earlier Bosselin proposal in recognizing the concerns of those who supported the legalization of divorce. Whereas the Bosselin bill had insisted on the inviolability of the marriage contract and had sought to close the loopholes in existing law, the Dupré bill sought to address the prevalence of extramarital unions and the needs of partners and children in these situations. It attempted to maintain the indissolubility of marriage while offering legal acknowledgment to stable extramarital relationships. The bill created the concept of the "recognized family," defined as a "stable relationship between a man and a woman, who were legally prohibited from marrying and who had children in common, with whom they formed a common household."[7] The proposal allowed for common property ownership between the partners and a limited right to benefits on the part of a surviving partner, and mandated the obligations of both partners to their children. Conservative opponents of the bill characterized it as a divorce bill in disguise, while proponents of legal divorce accused the bill's sponsors of eschewing a coherent proposal for legalized divorce in favor of a system of "legal concubinage."[8]

After the bill was submitted to the Constitution Committee for review, the Family Committee again sought to participate in the debate. Concerned that the Constitution Committee would again bury the divorce bill, the Family Committee again asked to co-review the bill with the Constitution Committee. The influence of the Family Committee is increased substantially if it becomes part of a joint review committee. When the Family Committee acts as a second independent review committee, as it did for the first Aylwin-sponsored divorce bill, it can pressure the main review committee to debate the bill by sending its own report to the floor. But, as seen in the case

---

7. Bill 1517, cited in Programa de Asesoría Legislativa, "Projecto de ley que sustituye la ley de matrimonio civil, de 10 de enero de 1884, y sus modificaciones," *Ficha Legislativa* no. 504, March 6–10, 1995.

8. María Elena Valenzuela, interview by author, Santiago, January 9, 1997.

of the earlier divorce bill, this action alone cannot force the main review committee to debate the bill, and no floor vote can be taken until all the review committees have issued their reports. By contrast, when the Family Committee joins with another committee to co-review a bill, the joint committee must vote as a whole on whether to debate the bill and whether to pass it on to the floor. Because the Family Committee is generally more progressive than other committees on women's issues, the median vote of the joint committee shifts to the left. If Family Committee members on the joint committee vote as a united bloc, the additional support of only one member of the other committee is enough to place the bill on the table for debate. The Family Committee's request to form a joint committee with the Constitution Committee was granted, but before the joint committee could debate the Dupré bill, yet another divorce bill was introduced in the Congress: the 1995 new civil marriage bill. Eventually, the joint Family-Constitution Committee would debate both these bills simultaneously.

"It's Not a Divorce Bill": The New Civil Marriage Bill

The 1995 divorce bill was qualitatively different from its predecessors in content and thus in the breadth of its political support. Introduced by two Christian Democratic deputies with broad support from the Left and even a few representatives from the RN, the new civil marriage bill made major concessions to conservatives on content and also reframed the bill to be more "pro-family." Supporters of divorce legislation recognized that the only way to gain the necessary political support on an issue that faced strong church opposition was to move away from justifications for divorce based on individual rights.

The new bill argued for legal divorce within a broader framework that nevertheless prioritized the preservation of family unity. For example, the bill included a mandatory five-year waiting period for a divorce, and judges were given broad powers to deny requests for divorce. Combined with the closing of the annulment loophole, the 1995 bill in effect made divorce much more difficult to come by than under the current system, and this allowed Christian Democrats and members of the Right to argue that in fact the bill would strengthen the family. The very title of the 1995 bill reflected an effort to avoid even the word "divorce." As Christian Democrat Ignacio Walker, one of the bill's sponsors, put it, "It's not a divorce bill. It's a marriage bill."[9] Walker explicitly rejected the idea of individual rights as justification for legal divorce.

Many of the bill's amendments reflected the earlier Muñoz bill, including its distinction between annulment, separation, and divorce. In this bill, unlike the Muñoz bill, however, divorce meant the permanent dissolution of the marriage contract. The bill also incorporated some aspects of the Bosselin bill: it closed the loopholes being used to procure annulments, and it incorporated parts of the Catholic Church's canon law into the prerequisites for annulment. The bill contemplated divorce in cases where two years had passed since the granting of an official declaration of separation or more than five years of de facto separation had occurred. In other circumstances the requirements were more vague and therefore left more to the judge's discretion. For example, other grounds for divorce included finding "one spouse in a situation or acquiring a conduct which contradicts the goals of marriage, or makes it impossible to fulfill those goals" (article 54), and "one spouse charging the other with committing acts or failing to commit acts that constitute a grave and repeated violation of spousal obligations" (article 55). The bill also empowered judges to refuse to grant a divorce in cases where "due to the advanced ages of the spouses or other similar circumstances," the judge believed that a divorce would cause greater harm to the individuals than it alleviated (article 56).[10]

Increasing Institutional Support

The new civil marriage bill was introduced in November 1995 and received support from representatives from all the major parties except the UDI. The bill was sent to the joint Family-Constitution Committee, which was simultaneously reviewing the Dupré bill. There was significant support for both proposals in the joint committee. While the Dupré bill was not highly regarded on its own merits, as pressure to bring a divorce bill to the floor mounted, some opponents came to see some sort of reform as inevitable and

---

9. Ignacio Walker, interview by author, Valparaíso, March 1997. A number of Christian Democrats and members of the RN insisted on referring to the bill as "a civil marriage bill," but most representatives and the public at large referred to the bill as "the divorce bill."

10. Citations of bill 1759 (which became Law 19.947), are taken from Cámara de Diputados, *Redacción de sesiones* (Valparaíso: Biblioteca del Congreso Nacional de Chile, 1997), legislative session 334/41a, January 21, p. 148.

the Dupré proposal as the lesser of two evils. For more than a year members of the joint committee debated both bills, and initial attempts to create a single combination bill failed.[11]

Within the joint committee, nearly half the members (eleven of twenty-six) declared themselves willing to vote in favor of the new civil marriage bill.[12] PPD deputy María Antonieta Saa, a member of the Family Committee, echoed the feeling of the bill's supporters that they were on the brink of a historical moment. Although bills on divorce had been introduced in the previous Congress, the introduction of the 1995 bill signaled something qualitatively different. While more conservative in content than past bills, the 1995 bill had achieved unprecedented levels of interparty support. Feminist representatives recognized the strategic tradeoffs necessary to propel the bill through the Congress. Saa explained,

> The political desire [to debate this bill] is not an isolated thing, prophetic, from one person, but rather a much broader issue, more consensual. . . . It has broader political support, it's not a bill from one deputy or two deputies from the same party, but rather, this proposal reflects a process of negotiation in the construction of the bill with deputies from all the parties except the UDI. . . . And in this regard I had to set aside my own desire to draft a bill which would allow divorce in cases of mutual consent, but I did it thinking that if we gained this alliance, we would, at the very least, begin a historical process in the country, a law, which was the fundamental thing. We've worked almost a year in the development of the proposal.[13]

Supporters pressed for a committee vote, but the conservative Christian Democrats on the committee petitioned twice to postpone it.[14] Supporters finally threatened to hold a press conference to denounce these attempts to stop the vote, and the vote went forward. The committee vote was 12–12, and the proposal went on to the floor. Two RN members of the Constitution Committee, Andrés Allamand and Alberto Espina, abstained. At the time

---

11. Committee members, interviews by author, Valparaíso, January–March 1997.

12. Progressive Christian Democrat Sergio Elgueta was a member of both the Constitution and Family committees and so could cast two votes.

13. María Antonieta Saa, interview by author, Valparaíso, January 15, 1997.

14. Many opponents preferred to postpone public debate on the bill until after the 1997 municipal elections.

both were considering running for the Senate (Espina was also contemplating a presidential run in 2000), and they did not want to take a public position on such a divisive issue. Interestingly, these representatives did vote in favor of the Dupré bill, and as a result both bills went to the floor. On the floor of the Chamber, the Dupré bill was rejected 53–32.[15] It is worth noting that of the female RN representatives, one (Marina Prochelle) voted against the bill, and one (María Angélica Cristi) abstained. Immediately following the vote, debate moved on to the divorce bill.

The Floor Debate: Divorce and the "Sanctity of the Family"

The floor debates on divorce in the Chamber of Deputies provide a clear example of the efforts of the Left, the Right, and the Christian Democrats to frame the issue of divorce to their advantage. As with political discussions of abortion, the arguments for and against the new civil marriage bill reflect three distinct ideological perspectives. The parties presented contrasting visions of the likely consequences of divorce, the place of the traditional family in Chilean society, and the rights of individuals whose marriages have failed. Yet despite their opposing positions on the legislation, it is striking that all the parties attempted to frame their positions in "pro-family" language and to argue that the right to divorce—or the prohibition against it—would strengthen Chilean families. In a tacit acknowledgment of the influence of the Catholic Church, even representatives on the left made explicit reference to "Christian ethics" in explaining their support for the bill.

Most of the Right opposed the legislation as an attack on the family and expressed fears that legalization would lead to other social "liberalizations," such as the legalization of abortion. RN deputy Luis Ferrada asserted, "The central point is that . . . by its very nature, the concept of divorce introduces into law a temporary marriage, that you try on and can discard. . . . Divorce always generates and has generated—historically for two thousand years—well recognized social ills." Ferrada argued that the legalization of divorce

---

15. The Left was united in its opposition to the Dupré bill (and in favor of the Aylwin/Walker bill). The other parties were divided. The breakdown by party was as follows: in favor of the Dupré bill: 0 PPD, 0 PS, 14 PDC, 9 RN, 9 UDI, 0 Other. Against the bill: 8 PPD, 13 PS, 11 PDC, 10 RN, 4 UDI, 4 right-leaning Independents, 3 Concertación-affiliated Independents. Abstentions: 2 PDC, 2 RN.

would lead to social disintegration and that Chile's "community-based" society would become "individualist, irresponsible, [and] atomized."[16] In response to feminist arguments for legalization, a number of congressional opponents argued that divorce would have a detrimental effect on "average" women and children, who would lose the protection that marriage provided them. For instance, Deputy Cristi argued that legal divorce would make it easier for spouses to abandon the home.[17]

Much as they had argued in defense of therapeutic abortion, representatives on the left portrayed divorce legislation as a practical and necessary solution to a glaring social problem. The Left also emphasized the pluralistic nature of Chilean society and the obligation of representatives to legislate for all Chileans, regardless of religion. Yet even as the Left argued for tolerance in a diverse society, it elaborated its own ethically based argument that made reference to Christian values to counter the "pro-family" rhetoric of the Right. There was a clear attempt in leftist discourse to move away from women's rights, and even individual rights, to a focus on the family unit. Framing their support for divorce in terms of the health of the family allowed left-wing supporters to argue that "moral" opposition to divorce was hypocritical because it ignored a profound social crisis. As PPD deputy Luis González observed, "If we continue to avoid our obligation to legislate, we condemn real men and women, of flesh and spirit, to live in bitterness and even in hate, and in danger as well. . . . For these reasons, in the name of Christian love toward real human beings, who suffer religious and social oppression because of a family situation that is irreparably broken, we [the parties of the Left] agree with our votes to approve the present bill." Again struggling to find a coherent policy position between Left and Right, Christian Democrats who supported the bill emphasized their strong support for the traditional family and asserted that the bill would strengthen rather than weaken it. Society must simultaneously promote the ideal of indissoluble marriage, they insisted, and address the social problems that result when people fail to live up to this ideal. Mariana Aylwin explained that representatives' "principal challenge consists in reconciling in our legislation a positive affirmation of marriage, and at the same time a search for the best legal solution possible for irrevocable marital ruptures and new conjugal unions.

---

16. This and the statement below by PPD deputy Luis González are from Cámara de Diputados, *Redacción de sesiones* (1997), legislative sessions 334/44a, January 23.

17. "Dos bellas y audaces: Las protagonistas de la gran disputa del RN," *El Mercurio*, April 27, 1997, D22.

... We don't consider this to be a contradiction, because it confirms as the norm that marriage is for life, admitting, nevertheless, that this norm can have exceptions."[18] The political weight of the Catholic Church is strikingly evident in the floor debates. Most of the arguments against the divorce bill either reflected the reasoning of the Catholic Church against divorce or directly cited church opposition as the reason for their opposition. Christian Democrat Carlos Dupré, for example, exhorted his fellow representatives to vote against the divorce bill, noting that "the Pope indicates that if we Catholics want to be true to our faith, we cannot defend and even less promote a divorce law. . . . There exists clear doctrine with regard to which the Christian cannot resort to the autonomy of his conscience."[19] The Catholic Church was a tremendous force in the debate, both directly through its lobbying efforts and exhortation to Catholics to hold supporters of divorce electorally accountable, and indirectly through the personal conviction of many conservative politicians that one could not vote against the tenets of one's faith. The church's mobilization against divorce represents its most concerted lobbying effort to date, and it is thus worth examining the church's political involvement on the issue of divorce in greater detail.

The Chilean Catholic Church Confronts Divorce

The role of the Catholic Church in Chilean politics has been particularly significant on the issue of divorce.[20] The church's campaigns to block legislative debate on divorce, supported by most of the Right, represent by far the most extensive and aggressive lobbying effort by the church to date. The posttransition period in Chile has been marked by increased church focus on issues of family and sexuality and of church opposition to most feminist policy reform proposals. As noted in chapter 2, however, the church has not pursued a proactive policy agenda but has rather responded in opposition to liberal proposals for policy change. While the church has spoken out strongly against abortion, for example, the church's antiabortion campaign never evolved to the level of its antidivorce campaign, because legislation to liberalize abortion laws did not progress through Congress. The church's strong outcry against divorce is a direct reflection of the level of threat the church

---

18. Cámara de Diputados, *Redacción de sesiones* (1997), legislative session 334/42a, January 22.
19. Ibid.
20. Parts of this section are taken from Haas 1999.

felt from the movement to legalize divorce. While church discourse on divorce has thus been fairly consistent since the 1960s, it has increased in intensity at key moments that coincide with the introduction and debate of divorce bills in Congress.

The arguments employed by the church and the Right emphasize several core themes: that divorce undermines the family as the basis of Chilean society; that legalization of divorce will start Chilean society on a downward slide toward complete social disintegration; that divorce is contrary to natural law and therefore the issue cannot be decided democratically; and that the "imposition" of a divorce law is totalitarian. In terms of lobbying tactics, the church insisted that Catholic legislators could not promote policy that contradicts church teaching, and it maintained a continual lobbying presence in Congress itself and through the press. Although for the most part the Right allied itself with the church's position, some right-wing legislators eventually rebelled against the church's pressure on the Congress.[21]

Church lobbying was particularly strong in response to the 1995 new civil marriage bill, as the bill was the first divorce proposal to leave committee and be debated on the floor. Church lobbying tactics were led by the most influential members of the church hierarchy and included direct pressure on individual representatives and a visible presence in Congress during debates on the bill. Of particular interest is the fact that, in its encounters with representatives of the Left who had been persecuted by the military government, church lobbyists made particular reference to the protection the church had given the democratic opposition during that time. Many representatives characterized this approach as the church's attempt to "collect on the bill" from its work in support of human rights under the dictatorship.[22] In many instances, however, the bishops at the forefront of the divorce debate were not the same bishops who fought for human rights under the dictatorship.[23] In other instances, the same bishops who protected members

---

21. For a more detailed discussion, see ibid.

22. In interviews with the author, members of Congress used this phrase repeatedly to describe the lobbying tactics of the church.

23. For example, Carlos Camus, of Linares, was appointed bishop before the 1973 coup and was strongly involved in the struggle for human rights (Camus retired in 2003). By contrast, Bishop Orozimbo Fuenzalida (retired in 2003), of San Bernardo, and Cardinal Carlos Oviedo (former bishop of San Bernardo and Orozimbo) were also ordained bishops prior to the coup but do not share Camus's progressive reputation. Cardinal Jorge Medina was ordained most recently, in 1985. Medina is among the most conservative of recent bishops, with a reputation for having sympathized with the military government. (The former bishop of Valparaíso, Medina was appointed to the Vatican in 1996 as pro-prefect of the Congregation for the Divine Cult and Discipline of the Sacraments. He was made a cardinal in 1998 and retired in 2002.)

of the Left now petitioned them personally to vote against divorce. For example, Socialist deputy Fanny Pollarolo explained that Bishop Carlos Camus "is very dear, [and was] very progressive in the fight against the dictatorship. . . . We love him a lot, but on the issue of divorce he is the worst. And he is the one who is pressuring the Socialist deputies."[24]

The increase in church lobbying on the issue of divorce has been widely noted in Chile. A 1994 press report observed that "the issue of divorce, on which the church has focused so strongly these past days, is not an isolated example [of church activity in politics], but it does appear to be the most intense by the church." The article quoted Cristián Caro, then auxiliary bishop of Santiago, who declared that the church "cannot remain silent because the stability of marriage and the family is at stake" (Zilci 1994, 19). Bishop Medina concurred that "the introduction of divorce grants the union of man and woman a provisory status . . . disposable if there are difficulties." He criticized the idea that it would be up to the couple to determine the state of their union (as opposed to the church's decision to grant them an annulment). Legalization of abortion was often cited as the most extreme potential consequence, as the end point of a society that had lost its moral grounding. "Behind these arguments [for divorce]," Bishop Medina reasoned, "is the idea that the Powers of the State base their decisions on arguments relying on statistics, above and even in opposition to principles. This is extremely dangerous. If this criterion is accepted, it will be with great difficulty that a way will be found to avoid legalizing, sooner or later, abortion, genetic manipulation, and euthanasia. This is how it has happened historically: once you open the door to legislate by dispensing with principles, it is almost impossible to detain the avalanche and to resist pressures based on various types of convenience" (Medina 1995, 2). While the church recognized the existence of de facto separations, it insisted that granting them legal recognition would replace an existing evil with a greater one (Betsalel 1994, 29–30).

Beyond its focus on the structure of the family, the Catholic Church's larger opposition to divorce stems from its theological conviction that marriage is a sacrament. The sacrament of marriage, once conferred, becomes a permanent state that cannot be undone at the bidding of those involved. (For this reason, the church is able to grant annulments only by declaring

---

24. Fanny Pollarolo, interview by author, Valparaíso, January 15, 1997.

that a particular union never constituted a true marriage.)[25] Thus, as a matter of faith, the Catholic Church could never agree to the legalization of divorce. In insisting that the prohibition on divorce must extend beyond Catholics to be enshrined in civil law, however, the church defends its position on the basis of natural law. As José Manuel Santos, then the archbishop of Concepción, explained, "We believe marriage is indissoluble, not only for Catholics. Marriage is indissoluble by its inherent nature and not only because it is contrary to the church, as is generally thought."[26] Bishop Carlos Camus reasoned that the mandates of natural law apply also to non-Catholics, because "for non-Christians as well the obligation exists to safeguard the stability of the family as the nucleus of society" (Rojas 1991, 5). And Bishop Fuenzalida proclaimed, "We wouldn't want legislators who believe themselves God, or who in their pluralist relativism believe that man has changed and that now he is god of himself and possessor of his own liberty" (Fuenzalida 1997, 10). Surprisingly, perhaps, the church also rejected a legislative bill introduced by Hernán Bosselin to alter civil law to reflect more closely the teachings of the church. The church opposed the bill on the grounds that it would open the door to broader interpretations (Rojas 1991, 6).

Because the church considers marriage indissoluble by its nature, it puts no stock in references to the high number of separations and illegal civil annulments and considers the opinion of the majority of Chileans irrelevant.[27] To the argument that the large number of separations necessitated legal recognition, Archbishop Oviedo remarked, "as if numbers were the same as values."[28] In Bishop Medina's words, "Morality is not based on statistics" (quoted in Betsalel 1994, 30). Like sex education, divorce was considered an issue best protected from the turbulence and unpredictability of the

---

25. The granting of sacramental status to the act of marriage is a specifically Catholic practice. Other religions, including other Christian denominations, view marriage as a solemn contract, one that under certain circumstances can be broken. The differences among Christian denominations with regard to divorce are discussed in Madrid Meza 1996, 36.

26. Delsing 1997, 180. By contrast, Lutheran bishop Ricardo Wagner explained that the problem with reliance on natural law is that its definitions reflect specific social and historical contexts: "To every philosophical or pseudotheological concept of the 'human being' corresponds a specific natural law. For Aristotle, for example, slavery was legitimate and in accordance with natural law. This opinion simply reflected his concept of the human being, according to which only the Greek citizen was fully human. Neither the invocation of 'Christian tradition' nor that of 'natural law' provides solid arguments for rejecting a judicial order that is realistic and in accordance with the needs of existing society; rather [these invocations] arise from clerical interests and ideologies. For this reason, we consider it fully justified that the State legislate on divorce" (ibid., 184).

27. According to public opinion polls cited by the Center for Research on Women, 85 percent of Chileans in 1996 favored legal divorce. Centro de Estudios de la Mujer 1996b, 4.

28. "Arzobispo Oviedo advirtió 'campaña' que prentende disolver a la familia chilena," *La Epoca* (Santiago), June 10, 1991, 11.

democratic process. Despite the evidence of public opinion polls showing a large majority of Chileans in favor of divorce, Bishop Caro declared that "divorce is not a right of the citizens" (ibid.).

As it had done in the past, the church insisted that Catholic legislators could not promote policies that contradicted church teaching. Archbishop Oviedo explained that "a Catholic representative, if he wants to be true to his faith, cannot vote in favor of divorce." Bishop Medina affirmed more forcefully that "a Catholic must not . . . favor any divorce law, defend it or support it. . . . The Catholic cannot claim autonomy regarding material which involves the doctrine of the Church" (Medina 1995, 2). Conservative representatives in the Chamber of Deputies echoed these sentiments.

Finally, the bishops appropriated democratic rhetoric to argue that efforts to legalize divorce were authoritarian. Bishop Fuenzalida urged the Catholics of San Bernardo to tell their representatives that "they have no right to impose this type of divorce law on us" (Fuenzalida 1997, 10) and encouraged his parishioners not to vote for representatives who supported the divorce bill. Francisco Errázuriz, then bishop of Valparaíso, insisted that "no one, including the state, can prevent an engaged couple from having the conviction that marriage, by its very nature, is a union for life—which excludes divorce—and that they make use of their liberty of conscience to contract marriage for life, refusing to contract some other type of union that is not so."[29] The Right had made such declarations for years, and they claimed that the divorce bill being debated in Congress dissolved marriages to such an extent "that it wouldn't permit [couples] to re-initiate their life together" (Instituto Libertad 1991, 6).

Among representatives who favored legalizing divorce, there was strong reaction to the church's pressure. Socialist deputy Isabel Allende denied that the debate was really between those who would protect the family and those who would destroy it, and Deputy José Viera-Gallo asserted, "This bill which introduces divorce was signed . . . by persons who adhere to very distinct beliefs and political positions. Today, we are in a pluralist democracy, which accepts the [UN] Universal Declaration of Human Rights, which respects liberty of conscience and of religion, in which there is neither a confessional State nor official atheism."[30] Progressive Christian Democrat Sergio Elgueta explained that in a pluralist society it is crucial to distinguish

---

29. "Obispo Errázuriz: Divorcio vulnera derecho de pareja," *La Epoca* (Santiago), September 10, 1997, 12.

30. Cámara de Diputados, *Redacción de sesiones* (1997), legislative session 334/43a, January 22, p. 17.

between the political community and the church and between actions undertaken by individual Christians in accordance with their consciences and actions undertaken in the name of the church and in communion with its leaders.[31]

Most significantly, however, by 1997 some members of the Far Right had begun to rebel against church pressure. No member of the political Right had ever supported a divorce bill in the past, but ten of the fifty-eight votes in favor of the 1997 bill came from the Right.[32] RN deputy Arturo Longton claimed that the church could "offer opinions, [but] it cannot undertake actions that go beyond its own competence, especially when it is a religious power that lacks the experience of a mother or father of a family" (Vaccaro 1997, 7). UDI deputy Iván Moreira, a past defender of the church on social issues, called on the church to cease its "religious war" (ibid.) and urged his fellow conservatives to reclaim their legislative independence. In his speech before Congress in support of the divorce bill, he declared, "I am the first to defend the right of all Catholics to marry a single time and not to be legally obligated to get divorced under any circumstances. What doesn't seem right to me is that what is dogma for a minority be imposed on the majority."[33]

The force of the church's lobbying effort on divorce is a dramatic example of the continuing political influence of the Chilean Catholic Church. The church's efforts probably affected the shape of the final divorce legislation. Yet the ultimate success of the divorce bill also illustrates the limits of church influence.

The Divorce Bill Passes the Senate

After the bill passed the Chamber of Deputies in 1997 it was sent to the Senate, where it lay buried in a hostile Justice Committee until 2002. What finally pushed divorce onto the Senate agenda was the creation of a workable policy network between Sernam and congressional representatives, backed by consistent executive pressure. During his presidential campaign, Socialist Ricardo Lagos had promised to push for legal divorce in Chile. After his election in 2000, he gave Sernam a freer hand to help legislate the divorce

---

31. Ibid., legislative session 334/44a, January 23, p. 28.
32. Seventeen of thirty-seven Christian Democrats voted in favor.
33. Cámara de Diputados, *Redacción de sesiones* (1997), legislative session 334/44a, January 23, p. 33.

bill. Sernam ministers Adriana del Piano (2000–2002) and Cecilia Pérez (2003–6) worked with the new justice minister (and former Sernam minister), Soledad Alvear, to update the Chamber version of the divorce bill. Beginning in 2002, the bill was included in the extraordinary legislative session and prodded through the Senate with occasional urgency labels.

This executive support not only forced the Senate to address the bill; it allowed Sernam and the Justice Ministry to undo some of the conservative additions that had been made to the bill in the Chamber of Deputies. The updated version of the bill reinstituted divorce by mutual consent, although couples were still required to be separated for a year before filing for divorce, and judges could take up to an additional three years to complete the filing. Couples also had to submit to mandatory mediation. Minister Pérez staunchly defended these changes before the Senate committee, but Senate conservatives did not yield to executive pressure without a fight. The Senate Justice Committee restored the waiting period for divorce to five years and made this retroactively inapplicable, although it finally approved the bill, by a 3–2 vote, for plenary debate in October 2002. The bill passed the first round of Senate debate, after a long and extremely contentious discussion, in August 2003. To force the bill to a final floor debate, President Lagos declared the bill urgent three times between November 2003 and February 2004, and it passed the second round in February 2004. The modified version was sent back to the Chamber, where it was approved again. A modification to mollify conservatives, as well as executive pressure in the Senate, helped build the interparty support that ultimately succeeded in legalizing divorce in Chile.

Feminist Learning in the Wake of the Divorce Law

The struggle to legalize divorce taught feminist representatives how to prevail even without executive support. After their defeats in 1991 and 1993, feminist representatives on the left finally achieved their goal with the New Civil Marriage Law in 2004. Critical to their eventual success was their ability to reframe the issue of divorce in "pro-family" terms. This necessitated significant compromise on the content of the bill, which included long waiting periods, mandatory mediation, and extensive discretion by judges to deny divorce requests.

While the leadership of Sernam criticized the system of fraudulent annulments and expressed informal support for legal divorce, prior to the Lagos administration Sernam refused to offer formal support for divorce legislation. Despite Sernam's reticence and the vocal opposition of the Right and the Catholic Church, wide support for reform on the left and growing support among factions of the PDC created a more opportune political context for reform than had been the case with abortion. Representatives believed that with enough strategic framing of a proposal and with concerted efforts to reach out to moderates beyond the Left, divorce legislation was possible, even in the absence of executive support.

The 1995 divorce bill offers a clear illustration of the potential for successful congressional legislative policymaking even on the most divisive social issues. In this respect the bill makes for an especially good comparative case study with the abortion bills discussed above. Many of the factors absent in the case of the abortion bills, such as interparty support, a clear understanding of the parameters of the bill, and politicians' recognition of high levels of public support for legalization, were present in the case of divorce. It was also a great advantage that the efforts were led by Christian Democrats rather than left-wing representatives. This gave the proposal a more moderate image that made it easier to broaden support for the bill among conservative Christian Democrats and the Right. In addition, the Family Committee, which had not yet been created when the Muñoz abortion bill was introduced, played a crucial role in forcing the 1995 divorce bill onto the table for debate and in marshaling the needed votes to bring it before the full Chamber. Finally, there was an international dimension of the divorce issue that the abortion initiatives lacked. While abortion remains a controversial topic in many places, Chile was one of the few nations where the basic issue of divorce was still so controversial. Politicians and the public alike felt that the prohibition on divorce ran counter to the image of modernity Chile wanted to project to the world. To a greater extent than with other social legislation, Chile's international image played a role in the minds of many supporters of legalized divorce. These factors helped to overcome the obstacles to divorce legislation, particularly the strong opposition of the Catholic Church and conservatives in Congress.

Sernam's belated support for the divorce bill when it was stalled in the Senate was due in large part to the election of a Socialist president. Without the Christian Democrats' ties to the Catholic Church, the president and Sernam were politically freed to support the bill. Sernam's support for the bill also coincided with the emergence of a more cooperative relationship between the ministry and representatives in Congress.

The Legacy of the Divorce Law

Given the strength of political and cultural opposition to the legalization of divorce, the refusal of the executive branch openly to support legislation in this area during the first two administrations, and given the failure of numerous divorce bills to get out of committee in the past, the eventual passage of the divorce law was a remarkable accomplishment. Nevertheless, the law is far from ideal, and some representatives have pushed for new legislation to liberalize the current law. (Compared to the issues of violence against women and reproductive rights, legislators have made relatively few efforts to improve the divorce law.) The most recent effort is bill 4985, which would eliminate the long waiting period for divorce and would create the possibility of "no-fault" divorce. This bill originated in the Senate and was introduced by male representatives on the left. Both factors are significant. Sponsorship by male representatives is another example of the expansion of interest in this type of legislation beyond a small cohort of feminist representatives. This is especially important given the dearth of female representatives in the Senate. The introduction of a Senate bill also indicates the increasing willingness of representatives in the upper house to introduce progressive, and even controversial, legislation. Given that the Senate has proved an obstacle to much feminist legislation, Senate initiatives in this area a hopeful sign for future feminist policymaking.

The success of the divorce law resonates beyond one particular policy area, however. An equally relevant consequence of the law for feminists is that it demonstrates the possibility for progressive change even on major, controversial policy issues. The increased confidence of legislators in pursuing feminist policy is increasing evident across issue areas, from violence against women to reproductive rights. The cooperative policymaking that characterized the final stages of negotiation on the divorce bill bodes well for future efforts to pass women's rights legislation.

CONCLUSION:
THE FUTURE OF FEMINIST POLICYMAKING

> Feminists should neither dismiss the State as the ultimate mechanism of male social control nor embrace it as the ultimate vehicle for gender-based social change. Rather, under different political regimes and at distinct historical conjunctures, the State is potentially a mechanism either for social change or social control in women's lives.
>
> —Alvarez 1990, 273

The election of Michelle Bachelet to the Chilean presidency in 2006 spawned enormous interest in the impact of a feminist president on the expansion of women's rights. Bachelet's successes and failures in promoting women's rights will have repercussions beyond Chile, as advocates of women's equality look to the Chilean case for lessons in successful feminist policymaking.

Throughout this study I have argued that a country's particular political institutional structure creates specific incentives and disincentives for feminist policymaking. A cadre of committed feminists inside and outside government is fundamental for policy change, but passion for the cause is not enough. Feminists don't act in a vacuum; they must channel their demands for women's equality through a country's existing political institutions, which in every case will grant unequal access to different political constituencies and will prioritize certain political issues over others.

Institutional structures vary from country to country, and feminists in the legislature, the executive branch, and civil society must learn to navigate the institutional setting, anticipating roadblocks and effectively countering the opposition their proposals will inevitably face. This means that feminists both within and outside government must learn to cooperate with one another to develop viable proposals that will be able to weather the legislative process. Complicating this scenario is the fact that these strategies will vary not only across countries but within countries across different policy areas, and even within policy areas over time.

The strategies that feminists employ may themselves be controversial. In Chile, the decision by feminist representatives and the leadership of Sernam to adopt a "pro-family" discourse in defense of their proposals alienated feminists in civil society, who viewed this tactic as a dangerous capitulation to conservative gender ideology. A critical issue that proponents of women's rights have had to confront is the point at which a bill is watered down until it becomes worse than no bill at all. In this highly fluid political context, the success or failure of one bill will affect future policymaking strategies, as each actor weighs the risks and benefits of future efforts.

The case studies analyzed here demonstrate that while institutional structures may remain static for long periods, the larger political environment remains surprisingly dynamic and responsive to political tactics. In other words, politics matters. The most important lesson we can take from the Chilean case is that feminists can learn over time to strategize more effectively to increase the success of their proposals. As noted in the chapters on abortion and particularly divorce, this is true even on a country's most controversial issues.

A Feminist in the Moneda

The election of Michelle Bachelet, an avowed feminist, to the presidency was a watershed in Chilean politics. Feminists in particular viewed her election with great optimism. What impact did she have on the dynamics of feminist policymaking in Chile? President Bachelet's commitment to gender parity in her cabinet and in the appointment of local officials, and her public support of gender quotas for Congress, demonstrated her primary interest in women's rights issues and her willingness to enact controversial political reforms to boost women's political influence. An analysis of the past sixteen years of policymaking on women's rights suggests that this increase in executive support could have a major impact on policy reform efforts.

However, Bachelet's potential to push for reform must be considered within the larger context of Chilean politics, where party strength, interbranch conflicts, tensions within the party coalitions, and the growing opposition of the Right affected her policy options. Differences in institutional structure and in the strength of conservative cultural forces limit the extent to which Chile can replicate the positive gains made in advanced industrial welfare states in the areas of women's participation and progressive policy. Yet the feminist policymaking successes since the transition to democracy demonstrate the potential for progressive reform of women's rights laws even in Chile's relatively constrained political context.

The case studies analyzed here reveal that in addition to the superior formal powers of the executive branch, a number of informal institutional advantages, such as greater staff resources and access to committee debates, are significant factors in the executive's disproportionate weight in policy negotiations. However, the executive's need to maintain the multiparty governing coalition and the increasing political sophistication of congressional representatives have given the Congress an increasingly influential role in policy development. Despite the formal power of the executive in Chile, there is room within the institutional structure for competition over policy between the executive and legislative branches, independent congressional policymaking, and productive cooperation between the branches. In other words, there is ample room for politics in the policymaking process. In no issue area is this more true than in the case of women's rights, where feminist representatives, Sernam, and women's NGOs struggle to cooperate with one another and to unify against the entrenched political resistance to reforming laws on women's rights.

The research presented here thus complicates the picture of executive-legislative relations reflected in much of the literature on feminist policymaking. It is particularly significant that on several of the bills on women's rights, an executive bill proved to be more successful than previous congressional efforts to legislate on the same issue. Bills introduced by Sernam to increase the rights of domestic workers, modernize the laws on rape and sexual assault, abolish distinctions between children born within and outside marriage, and give married women equal control with men over property and salary passed the Congress after earlier congressional bills had died in committee. While this confirms the dominance of the executive, it also illustrates a clear intention by congressional representatives to propose their own policy initiatives. Furthermore, the existence of both executive and congressional bills on the same issues reveals a lack of coordination between the branches and suggests direct competition in the development of policy initiatives. This study allows us to consider the maneuvering room available to political actors within this institutional setting, and to examine attempts by institutionally weaker actors, like the Congress, to strategize for greater influence.

The case studies further demonstrate a number of critical factors in the involvement of the women's movement in policy formation, most significantly the variation in movement activity over time and across issue area and the movement's variable success in influencing policy. They illuminate the internal struggles of the movement and the disagreement over whether, and how, to mount an effective lobbying campaign on feminist policy.

Successful policymaking depends on coordinated cooperation among members of the movement, feminist members of Congress, and Sernam. The case studies analyzed here examine the compromises feminists have made in order to build enough political support for their proposals to pass the Congress. Such compromises are part of the broader strategies feminists have evolved to maneuver more successfully in Chile's challenging political context. The more feminists inside and outside government can cooperate on policy development, the better they will be able to withstand the political opposition to reform. The more they can unite behind a common vision of policy reform, and the more feminists across sectors are able to participate in the policy process, the greater the potential for broad, transformative policy change. In this conclusion I outline the main challenges each actor faces in playing a more effective role in promoting women's rights laws. Finally, I consider Bachelet's impact on feminist policy reform.

Increasing Sernam's Policy Impact

The most obvious conclusion that can be drawn from these case studies is that executive bills are much more successful than congressional bills. Only eleven of the sixty-four bills on women's rights originated in the executive branch, but ten of these bills passed Congress and were enacted into law. By contrast, only nine congressional bills have become law as of this writing. These numbers indicate that Sernam is clearly the stronger legislative player on women's rights. Yet Sernam needs to increase further its independence from the politics of prevailing administrations, its influence and level of cooperation with other ministries, and its relationship with feminists in Congress and in the women's movement.

Sernam has an independent budget, but its funding falls below that of other government ministries. A greater budget would increase Sernam's ability to sponsor (or co-sponsor) feminist legislation, and it would probably increase the ministry's status within the bureaucracy. A more independent ministry would also be more likely to survive future administrations that do not support its feminist policy goals. As noted in chapter 2, many feminists are concerned that future administrations may undermine feminist policy goals by weakening or dismantling Sernam. Stronger links among Sernam, feminist representatives, and the women's movement can help guard against this possibility by ensuring that feminist policymaking can proceed through other channels. An additional challenge Sernam faces is that it is often difficult for the ministry to coordinate policy or to oversee policy implementation with other ministries. On the positive side, the appointment of Sernam's first minister, Soledad Alvear, to head the Justice Ministry under Frei, and President Lagos's appointment of Mariana Aylwin, the most visible feminist Christian Democrat in the Congress, as minister of education, have increased Sernam's influence with two key ministries. As discussed below, Bachelet boosted women's presence further with the appointment of progressive women throughout the cabinet. Yet considerable work remains to be done to build a more permanent place for Sernam in government policy initiatives.

There are multiple reasons for Sernam's often tense relationship with feminist representatives in Congress. Part of the problem, discussed throughout this work, is institutional: both the executive and Congress guard their respective spheres of legislative influence, making cooperation difficult. When intergovernmental competition takes on an ideological component—as when feminist legislators on the left had to work with a women's ministry led by a Christian Democrat—the obstacles to effective policymaking are compounded. Finally, the challenges of better cooperation have a pragmatic element. As Sernam's former subdirector, Paulina Veloso, put it, why seek assistance from feminist representatives if you don't need them? Such a technocratic perspective on feminist policymaking exists at various levels throughout Sernam. This problem is exacerbated by the lack of linkages most ministers have had with the women's movement.

Nevertheless, the lack of coordination, and the occasional competition, between Sernam and congressional feminists that characterized the early posttransition administrations have dissipated over time. Particularly after 2002, under the leadership of Independent Cecilia Pérez, Sernam indicated its willingness to take on more controversial issues by speaking forcefully in favor of the divorce law that had stalled in the Senate. Interestingly, Sernam's position on policy issues, and its overall relationship with both congressional feminists and the larger women's movement, cannot be reduced to party affiliation. When Josefina Bilbao succeeded Soledad Alvear as head of the ministry in 1994, relations with Congress and the women's movement improved dramatically, despite the fact that both ministers were Christian Democrats. With the appointment of Socialist Adriana del Piano in 2000, some analysts predicted that the ministry would take a more explicitly feminist stance on policy issues. Like the ministers before her, however, del Piano rose to political prominence through the party system and did not have strong links to the women's movement. Sernam was not particularly proactive on policy during her tenure. Relations improved with the appointment of Cecilia Pérez (2003–6), and Bachelet's appointment, Christian Democrat Laura Albornoz, has increased the ministry's support for pending congressional legislation.

Sernam's relationship with feminists in civil society remains more problematic. The appointment of ministers with no connection to the women's movement has alienated many feminists and made them suspicious of the ministry's agenda. Particularly in the case of the Sernam's Christian Democratic ministers (Alvear and Bilbao), stronger links to the women's movement might have strengthened the ministry politically in its battles with conservative Christian Democrats. Many feminists note the "conversion" of the Christian Democratic ministers to a more feminist perspective, but this has been a gradual process, and it has slowed the ministry's legislative activity.

Broadening Party Support for Women's Rights Policy

The increasing openness of the PDC and the slow but notable evolution of some members of the political Right to support women's rights suggest an opportunity for feminists to gain ground on these issues beyond the parties of the Left. Although the percentage of women in the Chilean Congress falls far short of the "critical mass" (30 percent) deemed necessary to focus consistent attention on women's rights issues, the modest increase across parties since 1990 is still cause for optimism. It is in this context that bills establishing quotas for women's representation have been introduced by the Chamber, a reform that President Bachelet supported. Quotas are particularly controversial in Chile, where binomial districts already create intense intracoalitional conflicts over candidate placement. Previous congressional bills on the topic remain stalled in committee, and there is still little congressional support for quotas. Nevertheless, Bachelet's public support for a quota bill increased public awareness of women's low political representation and encouraged political parties to adopt quotas at the party level.

The increase in the number of women elected from the Right represents advantages and disadvantages for feminists. To the extent that these women do not support a feminist policy agenda, their opposition complicates the claim that Sernam, the parties of the Left, or the women's movement "speak for" Chilean women. Women representatives from the Right have indeed shown themselves to be more conservative than their feminist counterparts in the other parties. To date, however, they have also shown themselves to be more open to these issues than the rank and file of their parties. RN (and later UDI) representative María Angélica Cristi, for example, has on occasion excoriated her fellow party members for their lack of attention to issues of violence against women. Younger representatives, like the RN's Lily Pérez, have shown greater comfort with issues of women's equality. While conservative women representatives have not supported many of the proposals examined in this study, their increased number and occasional alliances offer some hope for future interparty cooperation. And despite the concerns of some researchers (such as Franceschet 2005) that the younger, more recently elected women on the left are not embracing women's rights issues, some new representatives, such as Socialist Clemira Pacheco, have been active in promoting feminist initiatives.

Thus, despite questions about the political priorities of conservative women, there is evidence of broadening support for feminist policy in the Chilean Congress. Beginning in the second democratic administration, the success rate for congressional bills on women's rights improved significantly (see appendix 1). This increase in success correlates with a marked increase in interparty sponsorship of the legislation. Several interrelated factors are responsible for this positive trend. Many of these early interparty efforts were led by women. In addition to the slight rise in the number of women elected, congressional feminists have undertaken a concerted effort to craft their policy proposals in "pro-family" language that deflects some conservative opposition, and they have been more willing than in the past to compromise on content to gain the broad political support needed for passage.

As a result, feminists have been able to achieve greater interparty coordination on women's rights issues. Initially, this type of coordination occurred on the least controversial issues, such as the right of abandoned spouses to receive child support (Law 19.408). In recent years, however, the most controversial feminist proposals, notably those on reproductive rights and abortion (bills 3197 and 3702), have enjoyed interparty support. Even more significant has been the diffusion of feminist ideals throughout the Left and, to a lesser but still significant extent, the PDC and the RN. There is now a group of male representatives who consistently sponsor or co-sponsor feminist legislation. These efforts have been bolstered by an improvement in the legislative resources given to Congress to develop legislation and by the creation of stable policy networks with a small number of feminist NGOs, lawyers, and academics, who have assisted with the drafting of legislation.

Increasing the visibility of feminist NGOs would bolster these nascent alliances. Feminist representatives lament the lack of feminist mobilization in favor of policy reforms, but they also point to the influence feminist activism can play in shaping public opinion and pressuring the government for reform. For example, representatives María Antonieta Saa and Fanny Pollarolo, who played a critical role in building support for the 1995 divorce bill, argue that even the low levels of feminist mobilization around the divorce bill had an impact on the opposition. During the two days of floor debate on the bill in the Chamber in 1997, women did constitute a noticeable presence in the visitors' gallery of the Chamber, and both representatives claimed that even this low-level involvement influenced the congressional debates. Saa cites the fact that right-wing legislators wanted the floor vote to be secret (this motion was denied) as evidence that they felt the pressure of the women's presence. Former representative Mariana Aylwin agrees that public opinion, and the threat of public disapproval, matters to legislators. By way of example, she explains that in the course of the debate on Chile's proposal for the 1995 International Women's Conference in Beijing, she became furious that fellow Christian Democrats had signed on to a right-wing Senate proposal attacking the conference.[1] In response, she held a press conference

---

1. For more on Chile's platform for the Beijing Conference, see Haas 2000.

denouncing those party members and encouraging women to hold them accountable. "It mattered to them," she says. "The next day they ripped me apart, but it mattered to them a lot. When you threaten them with women's votes, then they back off."[2]

The Election of Michelle Bachelet: New Opportunities for Feminist Policymaking

> Who would have thought twenty, ten, five years ago, that Chile would elect a woman president? . . . Thank you for inviting me to lead this journey.
> —President-Elect Michelle Bachelet, victory speech, Santiago, January 15, 2006

An analysis of the past sixteen years of policymaking on women's rights suggests that under a Bachelet administration, an increase in executive support could have had a major impact on reform efforts. The frustrations of feminists both within and outside government over the slow pace of reform, however, complicated by weak party support for feminist policy initiatives, interbranch conflicts between Congress and the executive, and a strengthening conservative opposition, posed significant obstacles in a number of policy areas. Bachelet's potential to advance significant policy reform on women's rights must be analyzed within the broader context of Chilean politics and as part of Bachelet's larger political agenda. Having a feminist in the Moneda represented an enormous political opportunity for progressive reform, but the very strength of the executive branch, which helps insulate it from outside pressures, also poses long-term risks for feminist policymaking and for broader democratic consolidation in Chile.

During her tenure as president,[3] Bachelet aggressively promoted women's rights issues in a number of areas. She boosted the representation of women in public office and put executive strength behind the implementation of policy reforms passed prior to her election but ineffectively enforced. Perhaps most notable was her recognition of the gender impact of policies in areas like health, education, and welfare, not ostensibly targeted to women.

Upon assuming office in March 2006, Bachelet made good on her promise to promote women's political representation by filling 50 percent of her cabinet positions with women. Following two cabinet reshufflings, there

---
2. Mariana Aylwin, interview by author, January 1997.
3. Bachelet's term in office ended in March 2010.

were again more men than women heading executive ministries, but women were still represented in higher numbers than in past administrations. Bachelet abandoned the usual process of soliciting suggestions for ministers from the Senate, keeping the posts secret until shortly before her formal announcement. Introducing her cabinet, she declared, "This Cabinet is a historic step for equality between men and women. These are people with considerable intellectual, professional and political prestige [who are] up to the great challenges we have ahead."[4]

Bachelet also sought gender parity at the local level, appointing women to 50 percent of Chile's governorships.[5] While attending the Regional Women's Conference in Ecuador in 2007, Bachelet announced her intention to introduce a bill creating gender quotas for parliamentary and municipal positions. As noted above, her support for quotas signaled her commitment to increasing women's representation in elective office, even if a mandatory quota law at the national level does not look likely in the near future.

Bachelet has also been credited with strengthening existing laws that had been underfunded, unenforced, or stalled in Congress. Establishing the right to day care has been a difficult struggle for women's rights advocates. A 1995 law (19.408) established the creation of day-care centers for a narrow range of women workers (those who worked in large shopping malls), but day care remained unavailable or inadequate for the vast majority of working parents. In her first few months in office, Bachelet created eight hundred new day-care centers. She also put executive pressure behind a decade-old bill allowing women to nurse their infants at work (Law 20.166). The bill had passed the Chamber of Deputies but had been stalled in the Senate since 1996; it finally passed in 2007. Bachelet also signaled her support for a bill that sought to improve on the law by mandating that private space be made available to nursing mothers at work (bill 4212).

Domestic violence policy is another area that received a decisive push from Bachelet. The Intrafamily Violence Law was passed in 1994 and represented the first coherent public policy to address violence in the home. While seen as a huge victory for the women's movement, Sernam, and feminists in Congress, the law has also been widely criticized for its narrow scope, lack of protection for victims, and the absence of shelters and other viable supports for victims that would make the law workable in practice. Years

---

4. "Chile's First Woman President Unveils 'Historic' Cabinet," Agence France Press, January 31, 2006, http://www.mywire.com/pubs/AFP/2006/01/31/1175773?extID = 10037&oliID = 229.

5. Local governors are still appointed in Chile.

after the passage of the law there was still only one shelter in Santiago for victims of domestic violence. Bachelet created new shelters and established a domestic violence hotline. She also strongly supported a 2007 bill on femicide (bill 4937), which includes specific provisions to protect women against domestic violence.

In a number of other areas Bachelet demonstrated her recognition of the unequal impact of government policies on women and men. In the area of health care, for example, she approved the construction of thirty new family health clinics, and free care for individuals over age sixty at public centers, both of which will benefit poor women who are the primary caretakers of their families. Her pension reform (Law 20.172) includes provisions that make it easier for nonbreadwinners (usually women) to gain access to their spouses' pensions and additional provisions to incorporate single mothers more effectively into the pension program.[6]

Arguably, Bachelet's most controversial policy decision in the area of women's rights was her executive decision to provide free emergency contraception to women fourteen and older. Chile has one of the highest abortion rates in Latin America, despite its illegality, and an estimated one-third of children are born outside marriage (Blofield 2006). Her decision to make emergency contraception available not only aroused the ire of her political opposition and the politically powerful Catholic Church, it also deepened divisions within the governing coalition (the Concertación), where many Christian Democrats disagreed strongly with this policy. In 2008 Chile's highest court banned emergency contraception, and Bachelet responded by introducing a "fertility freedom" bill to legalize emergency contraception. She submitted the bill to Congress in June 2009 and pushed hard for its passage by applying numerous urgency labels to the bill and by appealing personally to wavering lawmakers. The bill passed the Chamber of Deputies one month after its introduction, and it passed the Senate in January 2010. In one of her last acts as president, Bachelet signed the bill into law on January 19, 2010.

Clearly, Bachelet was aware that such policy decisions would cause tension within her governing coalition and strong opposition from the Right.

---

6. Angell and Reig (2006, 498) explain that "almost 40% of women in the labour force do not contribute to a pension fund, and of those that do, only a third will receive a pension greater than the minimum wage. Over two million women work only in the home and contribute to no pension scheme, but even worse off are the half a million who live in single parent households and who cannot hope to share the pension of a partner."

Her unapologetic commitment to gender equity signaled a change from past administrations, including that of her Socialist predecessor.[7] Yet there are clear signs of a political backlash against these feminist policies. Criticism over Bachelet's announcement that she would support a quota law illustrates the way in which the opposition spun her support for women's rights. RN senator Sebastián Piñera, who ran against Bachelet in the 2005 presidential election,[8] declared, "The president has been concentrating her efforts on issues which really do not interest the Chilean public. Where is the president when it comes to crime? Better education? The failed Transantiago plan? Frankly, I believe that the president is off somewhere, someplace Chileans do not want her to be."[9]

How much traction these criticisms have depends in part on the continuing evolution of public opinion, which appears to be liberalizing on women's rights issues. While Bachelet's policies on gender earned her praise from feminists, they also emboldened her political opposition. Other pressing problems also limited Bachelet's ability to pursue gender equality policies. Bachelet inherited a corruption scandal from the preceding administration, and her popularity plummeted in the wake of student and labor protests. Poverty in Chile remains deeply entrenched. Bachelet was forced to reshuffle her cabinet twice, once in the wake of the student protests over her education policy, and again following the Transantiago debacle. In the latter half of her term in office she faced a growing rebellion within the Concertación itself (from the so-called *díscolos*, or disobedient ones). Bachelet was uniquely positioned to integrate a concern for gender equity into her broader plans for policy reform. Her significant efforts signaled to the general public that women's rights are inseparable from the broader goals of a democratic society.

Finally, while it is clear that executive support for women's rights has the potential to succeed where congressional representatives alone have failed,

---

7. Although Ricardo Lagos put executive pressure behind efforts to legalize divorce, he reversed his earlier support for the decriminalization of abortion. His administration was criticized by feminists who felt he focused too much on "traditional" Socialist issues, such as labor, and not enough on women's rights.

8. Piñera was elected president in 2010, replacing Bachelet.

9. Quoted in "Bachelet Proposes Greater Female Participation in Chile's Government," *Santiago Times*, August 22, 2007. The Transantiago plan was a major reform of Santiago's mass transit system. It was begun under President Lagos and was launched by President Bachelet in 2007. In its first year of operation, the transit reform came under widespread criticism for poor planning and mismanagement. The Transantiago plan is considered a major failure of Bachelet's first year in office.

executive strength carries risks for long-term feminist policymaking and, by extension, for the evolving character of Chilean democracy. It is critical to continue to evaluate the effect that executive dominance has on the political participation of other policymaking actors, particularly the women's movement, political parties, and congressional supporters of women's rights. It is also worth considering how this executive dominance will affect the long-term institutional health and policy influence of Sernam itself.

Clearly, executive-sponsored legislation enjoys greater success than independent congressional efforts, owing to the significant formal and informal institutional advantages of the executive branch. But the power of the executive creates a tendency for it to develop its own policy agenda, without the participation of congressional representatives or interested groups in civil society. In the case of women's rights legislation, this often means that Sernam develops its own bills and then seeks the support of feminist representatives (and feminist NGOs) after a bill's introduction. While executive strength can help propel a bill through Congress over the protests of the opposition, the executive's power to develop legislative proposals independently of other actors weakens the broader policymaking networks that are necessary for sustained attention to women's rights. When the executive fails to seek the participation of civil society and congressional feminists at all stages of the policy process, those linkages will wither. This leaves the feminist policy agenda particularly vulnerable to a change in government administration. Should a member of the UDI be elected president, for example, a conservative would head Sernam, and the ministry's policy agenda would almost surely be fundamentally altered. If broader policymaking networks have not been sustained, there will be few opportunities to block the executive from rolling back the gains that have been made.

A critical consideration when evaluating the quality of democracy anywhere must be the degree to which democratic governments welcome the participation of women. This is particularly relevant in Latin America, where over the past few decades women's movements across the region have emerged to challenge legal, cultural, and economic discrimination and to fight for the right to help shape the public policies that affect their lives. The ability of actors inside and outside government to participate in the policymaking process determines the possibility of forming long-term policy networks on women's rights issues. Important and relevant on its own terms, the Chilean case also adds to our knowledge of gender and politics elsewhere and expands our understanding of the policymaking process in different political, institutional, and cultural contexts. The institutional and cultural factors I analyze in Chile have applicability to Latin America more broadly, where intragovernmental power struggles and conservative political forces have a long history. In Chile as throughout the world, effective network building among feminists inside and outside the state remains the greatest hope and the biggest challenge to more effective feminist policymaking.

The Chilean case illustrates the impact of institutional balance of power and intergovernmental conflict on the state's relationship with the women's movement and on the type of legislation that is ultimately successful. I argue that these factors merit examination not only in Latin America, where intergovernmental power struggles have a long history, but across cases of feminist policymaking in Europe and North America.

Research on women's rights policy development in Latin America is a fruitful area for further comparative research. Latin American cases provide variation on a number of variables that would allow us to explore the opportunities for successful policymaking strategies on women's rights in a variety of political, social, and economic contexts. Institutionally, the comparison of federal systems in such countries as Argentina, Brazil, and Mexico would illuminate the advantages and disadvantages of pressuring for policy reform in a decentralized political system. The strength of the Left, a key variable in building political support for women's rights initiatives, varies widely across the region. Other institutional factors that vary across Latin America and strongly influence feminist policymaking opportunities are the strength of the party system (beyond more basic questions of overall governmental stability), the need (or incentive) for interparty coalitions and alliances, the strength of the executive branch relative to the Congress, and the existence of mechanisms for promoting women's representation, such as party- or national-level electoral quotas for women candidates. Finally, the existence of "woman's policy machinery" is critical for maintaining government focus on women's rights and providing a point of access to the state for feminist groups in civil society. Executive-level women's ministries exist in a number of Latin American countries, but they vary considerably in structure, degree of political independence from the rest of the government, legislative influence, and connection with the country's feminist community.

At the level of civil society, the strength and political orientation of Latin American women's movements are critical components. Comparative research consistently demonstrates that substantive policy reform requires outside pressure from NGOs. Without a women's movement agitating for political change, policy reforms are either nonexistent or become largely symbolic gestures. Women's movements, and feminist policy communities, exist to various degrees across Latin America. While all of these movements struggle with posttransition funding cuts, internal fragmentation, and political marginalization, they continue to play an important role in the politicization of women's rights issues, in raising public awareness of women's rights, and in pressuring governments for policy reform. As feminist communities in Latin America focus increasing attention on policymaking, the political strategies of the region's evolving women's movements call for new comparative research.

Conservative opposition to reform is stronger in Latin America than in the United States and most of western Europe, but this too differs greatly across Latin American cases. In particular, comparative research on the roles that religious institutions and religious belief play in shaping public discourse on women's rights would illuminate the obstacles to deeper reform and suggest strategies for successful policymaking in conservative cultural contexts. Such research would be applicable to North America and Europe, where, despite higher levels of secularization, religion continues to play an influential—if underacknowledged—role in determining the possibilities for expanding women's equality.

Finally, Latin America's continuing challenges in the area of economic development present particular obstacles and opportunities for promoting women's rights. The inextricable link between women's equality and broader questions of basic development in much of Latin America stands in sharp contrast to the framing of women's rights issues in the postindustrial democracies, but it has much in common with other regions of the world where women are mobilizing for change.

APPENDIX 1
WOMEN'S RIGHTS LEGISLATION, 1990–2008*

Bill or Law	Issue	Date Introduced (month/day/year)	Sponsor	Extraordinary Session	Urgency	Passed Chamber	Passed Senate
Law 19.010	domestic workers	7/17/1990	Sernam	yes	no	yes 1990	yes 1991
Bill 157	domestic violence	9/13/1990	Congress (Left)	yes	no	no	**
Bill 197	sex discrimination	11/6/1990	Congress (Left)	yes	no	no	
Bill 234	domestic workers	1/8/1991	Congress (Left)	no	yes	no	
Bill 302	sex discrimination	3/7/1991	Congress (Left)	no	no	no	
Bill 355	divorce	5/16/1991	Congress (Left)	yes	no	no	

(continued)

Bill or Law	Issue	Date Introduced (month/day/year)	Sponsor	Extraordinary Session	Urgency	Passed Chamber	Passed Senate
Bill 374	paternity laws	6/11/1991	Congress (Left)	no	no	no	
Law 19.335	marital property	8/6/1991	Sernam	yes	yes	yes 1993	yes 1994
Law 19.325	family violence	8/21/1991	Congress (Left)	yes	yes	yes 1993	yes 1994
Bill 499	therapeutic abortion	9/17/1991	Congress (Left)	yes	no	no	
Bill 719 (Senate)	paternity laws	6/9/1992	Congress (Left)	no	no		no
Bill 871	sexual assault	11/25/1992	Congress (Right)	yes	no	no	
Bill 953	divorce	4/1/1993	Congress (Left)	no	no	no	
Law 19.617	sexual assault	8/3/1993	Sernam	yes	yes	yes 1995	yes 1997
Bill 1065	sex discrimination	8/17/1993	Congress (Left)	yes	no	no	
Bill 1090	divorce	9/14/1993	Congress (Left)	yes	no	no	

Law 19.585	paternity laws	10/10/1993	Sernam	yes	yes	yes 1994	yes 1998
Bill 1189	sex discrimination	4/21/1994	Congress (Left)	no	no	no	
Law 19.688	pregnant students	7/5/1994	Congress (Left)	yes	no	yes 1994	yes 2000
Law 19,408 (Senate)	child care	9/13/1994	Congress (Left/PDC)	no	no	yes 1995	yes 1995
Bill 1370	divorce	10/4/1994	Congress (PDC/Left)	no	no	no	
Law 19.741	child support	10/11/1994	Congress (Left-Right)	yes	no	yes 1997	yes 2001
Bill 1419	sexual assault and harassment	10/24/1994	Congress (Left-Right)	yes	no	yes 2004	yes 2005
Bill 1515/ 2202 (DS 1.640)	violence against women (CEDAW)	1/17/1995 7/14/1998	Sernam	yes	no	yes 1998	yes 1998
Law 19.611	sex discrimination	5/4/1995	Sernam	yes	yes	yes 1997	yes 1999
Bill 1631	wage discrimination	6/14/1995	Congress (Left/PDC)	no	no	no	
Bill 1707	marital property	10/4/1995	Congress (Left)	no	no	no	

(continued)

Bill or Law	Issue	Date Introduced (month/day/year)	Sponsor	Extraordinary Session	Urgency	Passed Chamber	Passed Senate
Bill 1719 (Senate)	marital property	10/19/1995	Congress (Left)	no	no	no	yes 1996
Law 20.166	nursing infants at work	11/23/1995	Congress (Left)	yes	no	yes 1996	yes 2007
Law 19.947	divorce	11/28/1995	Congress (Left-Right)	yes	no	yes 1997	yes 2004
Law 19.591	prohibiting pregnancy tests; expanding day-care options	11/29/1995	Sernam	yes	no	yes 1996	yes 1998
Bill 1838	sex discrimination (CEDAW)	4/17/1996	Sernam	no	no	yes 1998	yes 1997
Bill 1994	electoral quotas	3/13/1997	Congress (Left/PDC)	no	no	no	
Bill 2030 (Senate)	child care	5/20/1997	Congress (Left)	yes	no		no
Bill 2087	intrafamily violence	9/9/1997	Congress (Left)	no	no	no	
Law 20.066	intrafamily violence	4/7/1999	Congress (Left)	yes	yes	yes 2003	yes 2005
Law 19.739 (Senate)	age/sex discriminination	8/11/1999	Congress (Left)	yes	no	yes 2001	yes 2000

APPENDIXES   189

Bill	Topic	Date	Origin				
Bill 2608	reproductive rights	10/19/2000	Congress (Left-Right)	yes	no	no	
Bill 2665	sexual harassment	1/18/2001	Congress (Left-Right)	no	no	no	
Bill 2667	sex discrimination (CEDAW)	3/6/2001	Sernam	no	no	yes 2001	no
Bill 3020	electoral quotas	8/6/2002	Congress (Left/PDC)	no	no	no	
Bill 3197	therapeutic abortion	1/23/2003	Congress (Left-Right)	no	no	no	
Bill 3206	electoral quotas	3/13/2003	Congress (Left-Right)	no	no	no	
Bill 3702	reproductive rights	10/7/2004	Congress (Left-Right)	no	no	no	
Bill 4106	intrafamily violence	3/15/2006	Congress (Left-Right)	n/a†	no	no	
Law 20.172	pensions	5/16/2006	Executive	n/a	yes	yes 2007	yes 2007
Bill 4212	nursing infants at work	6/6/2006	Congress (Left-Right)	n/a	no	no	
Bill 4277 (Senate)	reproductive rights	6/27/2006	Congress (Left)	n/a	no		no
Bill 4356	pay equity	7/19/2006	Congress (Left-Center)	n/a	no	no	

(continued)

Bill or Law	Issue	Date Introduced (month/day/year)	Sponsor	Extraordinary Session	Urgency	Passed Chamber	Passed Senate
Bill 4465	granting mothers jurisdiction over children in their custody	9/5/2006	Congress: (Left-Center)	n/a	no	no	
Bill 4751	therapeutic abortion	12/19/2006	Congress (Left)	n/a	no	no	
Bill 4845	therapeutic abortion	1/18/2007	Congress (Left)	n/a	no	no	
Bill 4930	child support	4/3/2007	Congress (Left-Right)	n/a	no	no	
Bill 4937	femicide	4/3/2007	Congress (Left-Center)	n/a	yes	no	
Bill 4985	no-fault divorce	4/12/2007	Congress (Left)	n/a	no	no	
Bill 5200	intrafamily violence	7/17/2007	Congress (Left-Center)	n/a	no	no	
Bill 5241	minimum marriage age	8/2/2007	Congress (Left)	n/a	no	no	
Bill 5235	intrafamily violence	8/2/2007	Congress (Right)	n/a	no	no	
Bill 5472	violence against pregnant women	11/13/2007	Congress (Left)	n/a	no	no	

Bill 5569	intrafamily violence	12/13/2007	Congress (PDC/Indep.)	n/a	no	no
Bill 5680	sexual harassment	1/3/2008	Congress (Left)	n/a	no	no
Bill 5726	incest	1/16/2008	Congress (Left-Right)	n/a	no	no
Bill 5727	marital rape	1/16/2008	Congress (Left)	n/a	no	no
Law 20.418‡	emergency contraception	6/30/2009	Executive (president)	n/a	yes	yes
					2009	2010

SOURCE: HTTP://SIL.SENADO.CL/.

N = 62

* As of March 15, 2008.

** An empty cell indicates that the bill was never introduced in that house of Congress.

† Not applicable: the extraordinary legislative session was abolished as part of the constitutional reforms of 2005.

‡ This final bill was introduced after the period examined here but is included because of its central importance as a final legislative effort of outgoing president Michelle Bachelet.

APPENDIX 2
CONGRESSIONAL REPRESENTATION BY PARTY AND COALITION, 1990–2010

Coalition or Party	1990–1994 Chamber	1990–1994 Senate*	1994–1998 Chamber	1994–1998 Senate	1998–2002 Chamber	1998–2002 Senate	2002–2006 Chamber	2002–2006 Senate	2006–2010 Chamber	2006–2010 Senate
Concertación Coalition										
Christian Democrat (PDC)	39	13	37	13	39	14	22	12	21	6
Socialist (PS)	18	4	15	5	11	4	12	5	15	8
Party for Democracy (PPD)	7	1	15	2	16	2	21	3	19	2
Radical Democratic (PRD)**	5	3	2	1	4		6		7	3
Social Democrat (PSD)		1								
Humanist Green Party (PH)	1		1							
Independent (I-Concertación)							2		3	
Total	70	22	70	21	70	20	63	20	65	19
Right Coalition or Party										
National Renovation (RN)	32	13	29	11	23	7	19	7	20	8
Independent Democratic Union (UDI)	14	2	15	3	17	5	34	9	33	9
Center-Center Union (UCC)			2							
Independent (I-Right)		1	4	3	9	6	4		1	0
Total	46	16	50	17	49	18	57	16	54	17
Other	4				1			2	1	2
Congress Total	120	38	120	38	120	38	120	38	120	38

* Until 2005, in addition to elected representatives, there were nine appointed senators.
** The PRD and PSD combined to form the PRSD in the second democratic administration.

APPENDIX 3
WOMEN'S REPRESENTATION BY PARTY AND COALITION, 1990–2010

Coalition or Party	1990–1994 Chamber	1990–1994 Senate*	1994–1998 Chamber	1994–1998 Senate	1998–2002 Chamber	1998–2002 Senate	2002–2006 Chamber	2002–2006 Senate	2006–2010 Chamber	2006–2010 Senate
Concertación Coalition										
Christian Democrat (PDC)	1	1	1	2	2	1	3	1	1	1
Socialist (PS)	1		2		2		1		3	
Party for Democracy (PPD)	1	1	3		3		5		5	
Radical Democratic (PRD)**										
Social Democrat (PSD)										
Humanist Green Party (PH)	1									
Independent (I-Concertación)									1	
Total	4	2	6	2	7	1	9	1	10	1
Right Coalition or Party										
National Renovation (RN)	2		2		4		2		3	
Independent Democratic Union (UDI)					1	1	2	1	4	1
Center-Center Union (UCC)	1				1					
Independent (I-Right)			1				1			
Total	3		3		6	1	5	1	7	1
Other							1		1 (PAR) †	
Congress Total	7	2	9	2	13	2	15	2	18	2

* Until 2005, in addition to elected representatives, there were nine appointed senators. In 2005 the system of designated senators was abolished.

** The PRD and PSD combined to form the PRSD in the second democratic administration.

† Partido de Acción Regionalista de Chile (Regional Action Party of Chile).

APPENDIX 4
REVIEW COMMITTEES FOR WOMEN'S RIGHTS LEGISLATION, 1990–2008

Bill or Law	Issue	Date Introduced (month/day/year)	Sponsor	Review Committee	Passed Chamber	Passed Senate
Law 19.010	domestic workers	7/17/1990	Sernam	Labor[1] jointly with Constitution[2]	yes 1990	yes 1991
Bill 157	domestic violence	9/13/1990	Congress (Left)	Human Rights	no	
Bill 197	sex discrimination	11/6/1990	Congress (Left)	Constitution, co-review with Family[3]	no	
Bill 234	domestic workers	1/8/1991	Congress (Left)	Labor	no	
Bill 302	sex discrimination	3/7/1991	Congress (Left)	Constitution	no	
Bill 355	divorce	5/16/1991	Congress (Left)	Constitution	no	
Bill 374	paternity laws	6/11/1991	Congress (Left)	Constitution	no	
Law 19.335	marital property	8/6/1991	Sernam	Constitution	yes 1993	yes 1994

(continued)

198 APPENDIXES

Bill or Law	Issue	Date Introduced (month/day/year)	Sponsor	Review Committee	Passed Chamber	Passed Senate
Law 19.325	family violence	8/21/1991	Congress (Left)	Constitution jointly with Human Rights[4]	yes 1993	yes 1994
Bill 499	therapeutic abortion	9/17/1991	Congress (Left)	Constitution	no	
Bill 719 (origin: Senate)	paternity laws	6/9/1992	Congress (Left)	Constitution		no
Bill 871	sexual assault	11/25/1992	Congress (Right)	Constitution; Family denied co-review	no	
Bill 953	divorce	4/1/1993	Congress (Left)	Constitution	no	
Law 19.617	sexual assault	8/3/1993	Sernam	Constitution, jointly with Family	yes 1995	yes 1997
Bill 1065	sex discrimination	8/17/1993	Congress (Left)	Human Rights; Labor denied	no	
Bill 1090	divorce	9/14/1993	Congress (Left)	Constitution, jointly with Family from 1995	no	
Law 19.585	paternity laws	10/10/1993	Sernam	Constitution, co-review with Family	yes 1994	yes 1998
Bill 1189	sex discrimination	4/21/1994	Congress (Left)	Constitution	no	
Law 19.688	pregnant students	7/5/1994	Congress (Left)	Family; Education[5] in the Senate	yes 1994	yes 2000
Law 19.408 (origin: Senate)	child care	9/13/1994	Congress (Left/PDC)	Labor	yes 1995	yes 1995

APPENDIXES 199

Bill 1370	divorce	10/4/1994	Congress (PDC/Left)	Constitution, jointly with Family in 1996	no	
Law 19.741	child support	10/11/1994	Congress (Left-Right)	Family; Constitution in the Senate	yes 1997	yes 2001
Bill 1419	sexual assault and harassment	10/24/1994	Congress (Left-Right)	Constitution; Labor co-reviews from 1997	yes 2004	yes 2005
Bill 1515/2202 (DS 1.640)	violence against women (CEDAW)	1/17/1995 7/14/1998	Sernam	Foreign Relations[6]	yes 1998	yes 1998
Law 19.611	sex discrimination	5/4/1995	Sernam	Constitution yes 1997	yes 1999	
Bill 1631	wage discrimination	6/14/1995	Congress (Left/PDC)	Constitution	no	
Bill 1707	marital property	10/4/1995	Congress (Left)	Family; Constitution co-reviews from 2001	no	
Bill 1719 (origin: Senate)	marital property	10/19/1995	Congress (Left)	Constitution, jointly with Family in Chamber	no	yes 1996
Law 20.166	nursing infants at work	11/23/1995	Congress (Left)	Labor	yes 1996	yes 2007
Law 19.947	divorce	11/28/1995	Congress (PDC/Left)	Constitution, jointly with Family in Chamber	yes 1997	yes 2004
Law 19.591	prohibiting pregnancy tests; expanding day-care options	11/29/1995	Sernam	Labor	yes 1996	yes 1998
Bill 1838	sex discrimination (CEDAW)	4/17/1996	Sernam	Foreign Relations	yes 1998	yes 1997
Bill 1994	electoral quotas	3/13/1997	Congress (Left/PDC)	Constitution	no	

(continued)

Bill or Law	Issue	Date Introduced (month/day/year)	Sponsor	Review Committee	Passed Chamber	Passed Senate
Bill 2030 (origin: Senate)	child care	5/20/1997	Congress (Left)	Labor		no
Bill 2087	intrafamily violence	9/9/1997	Congress (Left)	Family	no	
Law 20.066	intrafamily violence	4/7/1999	Congress (Left)	Family, co-review with Constitution	yes 2003	yes 2005
Law 19.739 (origin: Senate)	age/sex discrimination	8/11/1999	Congress (Left)	Labor	yes 2001	yes 2000
Bill 2608	reproductive rights	10/19/2000	Congress (Left-Right)	Health	no	
Bill 2665	sexual harassment	1/18/2001	Congress (Left-Right)	Family	no	
Bill 2667	sex discrimination (CEDAW)	3/6/2001	Sernam	Foreign Relations	yes 2001	no
Bill 3020	electoral quotas	8/6/2002	Congress (Left/PDC)	Internal Affairs[7]	no	
Bill 3197	therapeutic abortion	1/23/2003	Congress (Left-Right)	Health	no	
Bill 3206	elecoral quotas	3/13/2003	Congress (Left-Right)	Family, co-review with Internal Affairs	no	
Bill 3702	reproductive rights	10/7/2004	Congress (Left-Right)	Constitution	no	

Bill	Topic	Date	Origin	Committee	Passed	Year
Bill 4106	intrafamily violence	3/15/2006	Congress (Left-Right)	Family	no	
Law 20.172	pensions	5/16/2006	Executive	Labor	yes	2007
Bill 4212	nursing infants at work	6/6/2006	Congress (Left-Right)	Labor, co-review with Health	no	
Bill 4277 (Senate)	reproductive rights	6/27/2006	Congress (Left)	Constitution, co-review with Health		
Bill 4356	pay equality	7/19/2006	Congress (Left-Center)	Labor, co-review with Family	no	
Bill 4465	grants mothers jurisdiction over children in their custody	9/5/2006	Congress (Left-Center)	Constitution	no	
Bill 4751	therapeutic abortion	12/19/2006	Congress (Left)	Health	no	
Bill 4845	therapeutic abortion	1/18/2007	Congress (Left)	Constitution	no	
Bill 4985	no-fault divorce	4/12/2007	Congress (Left)	Constitution	no	
Bill 4930	child support	4/3/2007	Congress (Left-Right)	Family	no	
Bill 4937	femicide	4/3/2007	Congress (Left-Center)	Constitution	no	
Bill 5200	intrafamily violence	7/17/2007	Congress (Left-Center)	Constitution	no	
Bill 5241	minimum marriage age	8/2/2007	Congress (Left)	Science & Technology	no	

(continued)

Bill or Law	Issue	Date Introduced (month/day/year)	Sponsor	Review Committee	Passed Chamber	Passed Senate
Bill 5235	intrafamily violence	8/2/2007	Congress (Right)	Family	no	
Bill 5472	violence against pregnant women	11/13/2007	Congress (Left)	Constitution	no	
Bill 5569	intrafamily violence	12/13/2007	Congress (PDC/Indep.)	Family	no	
Bill 5680	sexual harassment	1/3/2008	Congress (Left)	Internal Affairs	no	
Bill 5726	incest	1/16/2008	Congress (Left-Right)	Family	no	
Bill 5727	marital rape	1/16/2008	Congress (Left)	Family	no	
Law 20.418	emergency contraception	6/30/2009	Executive (president)	Health (Chamber); Constitution, co-review with Health (Senate)	yes 2009	yes 2010

N = 64

Complete names of relevant committees:
1. Labor and Social Security.
2. Constitution, Legislation, and Justice (in the Senate: Constitution, Legislation, Justice, and Regulations).
3. Family (Chamber of Deputies only); unless otherwise noted, these bills are reviewed by the Constitution Committee should they reach the Senate.
4. Human Rights (in the Senate: Human Rights, Nationality, and Citizenship).
5. Education, Culture, Science, and Technology.
6. Foreign Relations, Interparliamentary Affairs and Latin American Integration (Senate: Foreign Relations).
7. Internal Affairs, Administration, and Regulations (Senate: Internal Affairs).

REFERENCES

Acosta-Belén, Edna, and Christine E. Bose. 1995. *Women in the Latin American Development Process*. Philadelphia: Temple University Press.
Agor, Weston. 1971. *The Chilean Senate: Internal Distribution of Influence*. Austin: University of Texas Press.
Aldunate, Adolfo, Angel Flisfisch, and Tomas Moulian. 1985. *Estudios sobre el sistema de partidos en Chile*. Santiago: Flacso-Chile.
Alvarez, Sonia E. 1990. *Engendering Democracy in Brazil*. Princeton: Princeton University Press.
———. 1994. "The (Trans)formation of Feminism(s) and Gender Politics in Democratizing Brazil." In *The Women's Movement in Latin America: Participation and Democracy*, 2d ed., ed. Jane S. Jaquette, 13–64. Boulder Colo.: Westview Press.
———. 1997. "Contradictions of a 'Woman's Space' in a Male-Dominant State: The Political Role of the Commissions on the Status of Women in Post-Authoritarian Brazil." 2d ed. In *Women, International Development, and Politics: The Bureaucratic Mire*, ed. Kathleen A. Staudt, 59–100. Philadelphia: Temple University Press.
———. 1998. "Latin American Feminisms 'Go Global': Trends of the 1990s and Challenges for the New Millennium." In *Cultures of Politics/Politics of Culture: Revisioning Latin American Social Movements*, ed. Sonia E. Alvarez, Evelina Dagnino, and Arturo Escobar, 293–324. Boulder, Colo.: Westview Press.
———. 1999. "Advocating Feminism: The Latin American Feminist NGO 'Boom.'" *International Feminist Journal of Politics* 1 (2): 181–209.
———. 2000. "Translating the Global: Effects of Transnational Organizing on Local Feminist Discourses and Practices in Latin America." *Meridians: A Journal of Feminisms, Race, Transnationalism* 1 (1): 29–67.
Alvarez, Sonia E., Patricia M. Chuchryk, Marysa Navarro-Aranguren, and Nancy Saporta Sternbach. 1992. "Feminisms in Latin America: From Bogotá to San Bernardo." *Signs* 17 (2): 393–434.
Ames, Barry. 1987. *Political Survival in Latin America*. Berkeley and Los Angeles: University of California Press.
Angell, Alan, and Cristóbal Reig. 2006. "Change or Continuity? The Chilean Elections of 2005/2006." *Bulletin of Latin American Research* 25 (4): 481–502.
Aylwin, Mariana, and Ignacio Walker. 1995. *Divorcio: Argumentos de una posición*. Santiago: LOM.
Bacchetta, Paola, and Margaret Power, eds. 2002. *Right-Wing Women: From Conservatives to Extremists Around the World*. New York: Routledge.
Bacchi, Carol J. 1996. *The Politics of Affirmative Action: Women, Equality, and Category Politics*. London: Sage Publications.
Bagihole, B. 1994. *Women, Work, and Equal Opportunity*. Aldershot, UK: Avebury.

Baldez, Lisa. 2001. "Coalition Politics and the Limits of State Feminism." *Women and Politics* 22 (4): 1–28.

———. 2002. *Why Women Protest: Women's Movements in Chile.* New York: Cambridge University Press.

———. 2004. "Elected Bodies: Gender Quotas for Female Legislative Candidates in Mexico." *Legislative Studies Quarterly* 29 (2): 231–58.

———. 2008. "Political Women in Comparative Democracies: A Primer for Americanists." In *Political Women and American Democracy*, ed. Christina Wolbrecht, Karen Beckwith, and Lisa Baldez, 167–80. New York: Cambridge University Press.

Baldez, Lisa, and John Carey. 1999. "Presidential Agenda Control and Spending Policy: Lessons from General Pinochet's Constitution." *American Journal of Political Science* 43 (1): 29–55.

Banaszak, Lee Ann. 1996. *Why Movements Succeed or Fail.* Princeton: Princeton University Press.

Banaszak, Lee Ann, Karen Beckwith, and Dieter Rucht, eds. 2003. *Women's Movements Facing a Reconfigured State.* Cambridge: Cambridge University Press.

Barrig, Maruja. 1997. *De cal y arena: ONGs y movimiento de mujeres en Chile.* Santiago: Mimeo.

Bashevkin, Sylvia. 1996. "Tough Times in Review: The British Women's Movement During the Thatcher Years." *Comparative Political Studies* 28 (4): 525–52.

Basu, Amrita, ed. 1995. *The Challenge of Local Feminisms: Women's Movements in Global Perspective.* Boulder, Colo.: Westview Press.

Beckwith, Karen. 1992. "Comparative Research and Electoral Systems: Lessons from France and Italy." *Women and Politics* 12 (1): 1–33.

Bergqvist, Christina, et al., eds. 1999. *Equal Democracies? Gender and Politics in the Nordic Countries.* Oslo: Scandinavian University Press.

Bertelsen Repetto, Raul, José Luis Cea Egaña, Francisco Cumlido Cereceda, Humberto Nogueira Alscala, Osvaldo Oelckers Camus, Jorge Tapia Valdes, and Alejandro Vergara Blanco. 1993. *Diagnostico historico juricido cel poder legislativo en Chile, 1960–1990.* Valparaíso: Centro de Estudios y Asistencia Legislativa.

Betsalel, Claudio. 1994. "Divorcio: Por la ley de Dios." *Ercilla*, May 6.

Billson, Janet Mancini. 1994. "Keepers of the Culture: Attitudes Toward Women's Liberation and the Women's Movement in Canada." *Women and Politics* 14 (1): 1–34.

Blanc Renard, Neville, Humberto Nogueira Alcala, Emilio Pfeffer Urquiaga, and Mario Verdugo Marinkovic. 1990. *La constitucion chilena.* Vol. 1. Valparaíso: Centro de Estudios y Asistencia Legislativa.

Blofield, Merike H. 2001. *The Politics of "Moral Sin": A Study of Abortion and Divorce in Catholic Chile Since 1990.* Santiago: Flacso Nueva Serie.

———. 2003. *Inequality and Moral Politics: Abortion and Divorce in Chile, Spain, and Argentina in Comparative Perspective.* PhD diss., University of North Carolina, Chapel Hill.

———. 2006. *Moral Politics: Abortion and Divorce in Spain, Chile, and Argentina.* New York: Routledge.

Blofield, Merike H., and Liesl Haas. 2005. "Defining a Democracy: Reforming Laws on Women's Rights in Chile." *Latin American Politics and Society* 47 (3): 35–68.

Bock, Gisela, and Pat Thane, eds. 1991. *Maternity and Gender Policies: Women and the Rise of the European Welfare State, 1880s–1950s.* London: Routledge.

Borchorst, Anette. 1994. "Welfare State Regimes, Women's Interest, and the EC." In *Engendering Welfare States*, ed. Diane Sainsbury, 26–44. London: Sage Publications.
———. 1999. "Feminist Thinking About the Welfare State." In *Revisioning Gender*, ed. Myra Marx Ferree, Judith Lorber, and Beth B. Hess, 99–127. Thousand Oaks, Calif.: Sage Publications.
Borner, Jutta, Mariana Caminotti, and Jutta Marx. 2007. *Las legisladoras*. Buenos Aires: Siglo XXI Ediciones.
Bratton, Kathleen A. 2005. "Critical Mass Theory Revisited: The Behavior and Success of Token Women in State Legislatures." *Politics and Gender* 1 (1): 97–125.
Bratton, Kathleen A., and Leonard P. Ray. 2002. "Descriptive Representation, Policy Outcomes, and Municipal Day-Care Coverage in Norway." *American Journal of Political Science* 46 (2): 428–37.
Brenner, Johanna. 1993. "U.S. Feminism in the Nineties." *New Left Review* 200:101–59.
Brito, Eugenia. 1997. "El discurso sobre 'la crisis moral.'" In *Discurso, genero y poder—discursos publicos: Chile, 1978–1993*, ed. Olga Grau, Eugenia Brito, Riet Delsing, and Alejandra Farías, 49–64. Santiago: LOM-ARCIS.
Bronfman Vargas, Alan, Felipe de la Fuente Hulaud, and Fernando Parada Espinoza. 1993. *El Congreso Nacional: Estudio constitucional, legal y reglamentario*. Valparaíso: Centro de Estudios y Asistencia Legislativa.
Brownmiller, Susan. 1975. *Against Our Will: Men, Women, and Rape*. New York: Simon and Schuster.
Burrell, Barbara C. 1994. *A Woman's Place Is in the House: Campaigning for Congress in the Feminist Era*. Ann Arbor: University of Michigan Press.
Bystydzienski, Jill M. 1992. "Women and Politics in Norway." *Women in Politics* 8 (3–4): 73–95.
———. 1995. "Women's Equality Structures in Norway: The Equal Status Council." In *Comparative State Feminism*, ed. Dorothy McBride Stetson and Amy G. Mazur, 186–202. Thousand Oaks, Calif.: Sage Publications.
Bystydzienski, Jill M., and Joti Sekhon. 1999. *Democratization and Women's Grassroots Movements*. Bloomington: Indiana University Press.
Cáceres, Ana, Isabel Cárcamo, Patricia Provoste, and Gloria Salazar. 1993. *¿Cómo les ha ido a las mujeres en la democracia?* Santiago: Instituto de la Mujer.
Carey, John M. 2002. "Parties, Coalitions, and the Chilean Congress in the 1990s." In *Legislative Politics in Latin America*, ed. Scott Morgenstern and Benito Nacif, 222–53. New York: Cambridge University Press.
Carey, John M., and Matthew S. Shugart, eds. 1998. *Executive Decree Authority*. Cambridge: Cambridge University Press.
Casas, Lidia B. 1996. *Mujeres procesadas por aborto*. Santiago: LOM.
Castillo Vicencio, Arturo, and Telmo Meléndez. 1994. "Divorcio: Polemico desencuentro." *Ercilla*, May 6, 26–28.
Castles, Francis G. 1993. *Families of Nations: Patterns of Public Policy in Western Democracies*. Aldershot, UK: Dartmouth.
———. 2006. "On Religion and Public Policy: Does Catholicism Make a Difference?" *European Journal of Political Research* 25 (1): 19–40.
Caul, Miki. 1999. "Women's Representation in Parliament: The Role of Political Parties." *Party Politics* 5 (1): 79–98.
———. 2001. "Political Parties and the Adoption of Candidate Gender Quotas: A Cross-National Analysis." *Journal of Politics* 63 (4): 1214–29.

Centro de Estudios de la Mujer. 1996a. "Educar o no educar . . . el dilemma de la educación sexual." *Argumentos para el Cambio* 7 (September): 1–4.

———. 1996b. "¿Quien le tiene miedo a la ley de divorcio?" *Argumentos para el Cambio* 11 (January–February): 1–4.

Chant, Sylvia, and Nikki Craske. 2002. *Gender in Latin America*. New Brunswick: Rutgers University Press.

Chapman, Lynne. 1997. Review of *Lives on the Edge: Single Mothers and Their Children in the Other America*, by Valerie Polakow, and *Mothers on the Job: Maternity Policy in the U.S. Workplace*, by Lise Vogel. *Women and Politics* 18 (1): 99–103.

Chinchilla, Norma, and Liesl Haas. 2006. "*De Protesta a Propuesta:* The Contributions and Challenges of Latin American Feminism." In *Latin America After Neoliberalism*, ed. Eric Hershberg and Fred Rosen, 252–75. New York: New Press.

Chuchryk, Patricia M. 1994. "From Dictatorship to Democracy: The Women's Movement in Chile." In *The Women's Movement in Latin America: Participation and Democracy*, 2d ed., ed. Jane S. Jaquette, 65–108. Boulder, Colo.: Westview Press.

Cichowski, Rachel A. 2000. "Gender and Policy in Comparative Perspective." *Women and Politics* 21 (1): 107–15.

Cockburn, Cynthia. 1995. *Women and the European Social Dialogue: Strategies for Gender Democracy*. European Commission, Equal Opportunities Unit, V/5465/95-EN.

Conferencia Episcopal de Chile. 1989. *Certeza, coherencia y confianza: Mensaje a los catolicos chilenos en una hora de transicion*. Santiago: Area de Comunicaciones de la Conferencia Episcopal de Chile.

———. 1993. *Matrimonio, indisolubilidad, divorcio: Algunos estudios*. Santiago: Area de Comunicaciones de la Conferencia Episcopal de Chile.

Considine, Mark, and Iva Ellen Deutchman. 1996. "Instituting Gender: State Legislators in Australia and the United States." *Women and Politics* 16 (4): 1–19.

Constable, Pamela, and Arturo Valenzuela. 1991. *A Nation of Enemies: Chile Under Pinochet*. New York: W. W. Norton.

Conway, M. Margaret, Gertrude A. Steuernagel, and David W. Ahern. 1995. *Women and Public Policy: A Revolution in Progress*. 2d ed. Washington, D.C.: CQ Press.

Costain, Anne. 1992. *Inviting Women's Rebellion: A Political Process Interpretation of the Women's Movement*. Baltimore: Johns Hopkins University Press.

Craske, Nikki. 1999. *Women and Politics in Latin America*. New Brunswick: Rutgers University Press.

Craske, Nikki, and Maxine Molyneaux, eds. 2002. *Gender and the Politics of Rights and Democracy in Latin America*. New York: Palgrave Macmillan.

Dahlerup, Drude. 1988. "From a Small to a Large Minority." *Scandinavian Political Studies* 11 (4): 275–98.

Dandavati, Annie G. 1996. *The Women's Movement and the Transition to Democracy in Chile*. New York: Peter Lang.

Darcy, R., Susan Welch, and Janet Clark, eds. 1994. *Women, Elections, and Representation*. Lincoln: University of Nebraska Press.

Davis, Rebecca Howard. 1997. *Women and Power in Parliamentary Democracies*. Lincoln: University of Nebraska Press.

Deacon, Desley. 1990. *Managing Gender: The State, the New Middle Class, and Women Workers, 1890–1930*. New York: Oxford University Press.

De Avelar, Sonia. 1994. "Women in Parliament and Governmental Decision-Making in Latin America." Manuscript.

De Figueres, Karen Olsen. 2002. "The Road to Equality—Women in Parliament in Costa Rica." http://www.idea.int/publications/wip/upload/CS_Costa_Rica.pdf.

Delsing, Riet. 1997. "El problema del divorcio en Chile." In *Discurso, genero y poder—discursos públicos: Chile, 1978–1993*, ed. Olga Grau, Eugenia Brito, Riet Delsing, and Alejandra Farías, 179–92. Santiago: LOM-ARCIS.

Diaz, Adolfo Castillo. 1995. *Mujer y parlamento en Chile*. Santiago: Colección IDEAS.

Disney, Jennifer Leigh, and Joyce Gelb. 2000. "Feminist Organizational 'Success': The State of U.S. Women's Movement Organizations in the 1990s." *Women and Politics* 21 (4): 39–76.

Documentos del episcopado: Chile, 1974–1980. 1982. Santiago: Ediciones Mundo.

Documentos del episcopado: Chile, 1984–1987. 1988. Santiago: Ediciones Mundo.

Dogan, Mattei. 1995. "Erosion of Class Voting and of the Religious Vote in Western Europe." *International Social Science Journal* 47:525–38.

Dolan, Julie. 1998. "Support for Women's Interests in the 103rd Congress: The Distinct Impact of Congressional Women." *Women and Politics* 18 (4): 81–94.

Dominguez, Jorge I., ed. 1994a. *Parties, Elections, and Political Participation in Latin America*. New York: Garland.

———. 1994b. *The Roman Catholic Church in Latin America*. New York: Garland.

———. 1998. *Democratic Politics in Latin America and the Caribbean*. Baltimore: Johns Hopkins University Press.

Dominguez, Jorge I., and Abraham F. Lowenthal, eds. 1996. *Constructing Democratic Governance: South America in the 1990s*. Baltimore: Johns Hopkins University Press.

Dore, Elizabeth, ed. 1996. *Gender Politics in Latin America*. New York: Monthly Review Press.

Downs, Anthony. 1957. *An Economic Theory of Democracy*. New York: HarperCollins.

Duverger, Maurice. 1954. *Political Parties*. New York: John Wiley.

Eisenstein, Hester. 1992. *Gender Shock: Practicing Feminism on Two Continents*. Boston: Beacon Press.

———. 1996. *Inside Agitators: Australian Femocrats and the State*. Philadelphia: Temple University Press.

Ellickson, Mark C., and Donald E. Whistler. 2000. "A Path Analysis of Legislative Success in Professional and Citizen Legislatures: A Gender Comparison." *Women and Politics* 21 (4): 77–100.

Elman, Amy, ed. 1996. *Sexual Politics and the European Union: The New Feminist Challenge*. Providence: Berghahn Books.

Escobar, Arturo, and Sonia E. Alvarez, eds. 1992. *The Making of Social Movements in Latin America: Identity, Strategy, and Democracy*. Boulder, Colo.: Westview Press.

Esping-Anderson, Gosta. 1990. *The Three Worlds of Welfare Capitalism*. Princeton: Princeton University Press.

Fals Borda, Orlando. 1992. "Social Movements and Political Power in Latin America." In *The Making of Social Movements in Latin America: Identity, Strategy, and Democracy*, ed. Arturo Escobar and Sonia E. Alvarez, 303–16. Boulder, Colo.: Westview Press.

Farías, Alejandra. 1997. "Sobre educación de la sexualidad." In *Discurso, genero y poder—discursos públicos: Chile, 1978–1993*, ed. Olga Grau, Eugenia Brito, Riet Delsing, and Alejandra Farías, 271–300. Santiago: LOM-ARCIS.

Ferraro, Augustín E. 2006. "Informal Parliamentarism in Latin America: Coalition Politics and Parliamentary Influence on the Public Bureaucracy in Chile." Manuscript.

Ferree, Myra Marx, and Patricia Yancey Martin. 1995. *Feminist Organizations: Harvest of the New Women's Movements*. Philadelphia: Temple University Press.

Fisher, Jo. 1993. *Out of the Shadows: Women, Resistance, and Politics in South America*. London: Latin American Bureau.

Fitzsimmons, Tracy. 2000. *Beyond the Barricades: Women, Civil Society, and Participation After Democratization in Latin America*. New York: Garland.

Fleet, Michael, and Brian H. Smith. 1997. *The Catholic Church and Democracy in Chile and Peru*. Notre Dame: University of Notre Dame Press.

Flora, Cornelia Butler, and Helen I. Safa. 1992. "Production, Reproduction, and the Polity: Women's Strategic and Practical Gender Issues." In *Americas: New Interpretive Essays*, ed. Alfred Stepan, 109–36. New York: Oxford University Press.

Franceschet, Susan. 2003. "States and Women's Movements: The Impact of Chile's Servicio Nacional de la Mujer on Women's Activism." *Latin American Research Review* 38 (1): 9–40.

———. 2005. *Women and Politics in Chile*. Boulder: Lynne Rienner.

———. 2008. "The Politics of Domestic Violence Policy in Latin America." IAPR Technical Paper Series no. TP-08001. http://www.iapr.ca/files/iapr/iapr-tp-08001_0.pdf.

Franzway, Suzanne, Dianne Court, and R. W. Connell. 1989. *Staking a Claim: Feminism, Bureaucracy, and the State*. Cambridge: Polity Press.

Freeman, Jo. 1975. *The Politics of Women's Liberation: A Case Study of an Emerging Social Movement and Its Relation to the Policy Process*. New York: David McKay.

Friedman, Elisabeth J. 2000. "State-Based Advocacy for Gender Equality in the Developing World: Assessing the Venezuelan National Women's Agency." *Women and Politics* 21 (2): 47–80.

Frohmann, Alicia. 1990. *Puentes sobre la turbulencia: La concertación política latinoamericana en los ochenta*. Santiago: Flacso-Chile.

Frohmann, Alicia, and Teresa Valdés. 1993. *Democracy in the Country and in the Home: The Women's Movement in Chile*. Santiago: Flacso.

———. 1995. "Democracy in the Country and in the Home: The Women's Movement in Chile." In *The Challenge of Local Feminisms: Women's Movements in Global Perspective*, ed. Amrita Basu, 276–301. Boulder, Colo.: Westview Press.

Fuenzalida, Orozimbo. 1997. "Carta sobre el divorcio." *La Epoca* (Santiago), January 28.

Gaete, Carlos E. 1988. *Evangelizar la política: Magisterio de la iglesia en Chile, 1973–1988*. Santiago: CESOC.

Galligan, Yvonne, and Manon Tremblay, eds. 2005. *Sharing Power: Women, Parliament, and Democracy*. Aldershot, UK: Ashgate.

Gamson, William. 1975. *The Strategy of Social Protest*. Chicago: Dorsey Press.

Gardiner, Frances, ed. 1997. *Sex Equality Policy in Western Europe*. London: Routledge.

Gardiner, Frances, and Monique Leijenaar. 1997. "The Timid and the Bold: Analysis of the 'Woman-Friendly State' in Ireland and the Netherlands." In *Sex Equality Policy in Western Europe*, ed. Frances Gardiner, 57–86. London: Routledge.

Geddes, Barbara. 1996. "Initiation of New Democratic Institutions in Eastern Europe and Latin America." In *Institutional Design in New Democracies: Eastern Europe and Latin America*, ed. Arend Lijphart and Carlos H. Waisman, 15–42. Boulder, Colo.: Westview Press.

Gelb, Joyce, and Marian Lief Palley. 1996. *Women and Public Policies: Reassessing Gender Politics.* Charlottesville: University Press of Virginia.

Geller-Schwartz, Linda. 1995. "An Array of Agencies: Feminism and State Institutions in Canada." In *Comparative State Feminism*, ed. Dorothy McBride Stetson and Amy G. Mazur, 40–58. Thousand Oaks, Calif.: Sage Publications.

George, Alexander. 1979. "Case Studies and Theory Development: The Method of Structured, Focused Comparison." In *Diplomacy: New Approaches in History, Theory, and Policy*, ed. Paul Gordon Lauren, 43–68. New York: Free Press.

Gierzyniski, Anthony, and Paulette Budreck. 1995. "Women Legislative Caucus and Leadership Campaign Committees." *Women and Politics* 15 (2): 23–36.

Gill, Anthony. 1998. *Rendering unto Caesar: The Catholic Church and the State in Latin America.* Chicago: University of Chicago Press.

Goldstein, Leslie Friedman. 1989. *The Constitutional Rights of Women: Cases in Law and Social Change.* Rev. ed. Madison: University of Wisconsin Press.

González, Sandra, and María Isabel Norero. 1989. *Los derechos de la mujer en las leyes chilenas.* Santiago: CESOC.

González, Victoria, and Karen Kampwirth, eds. 2001. *Radical Women in Latin America: Left and Right.* University Park: Pennsylvania State University Press.

Grau, Olga, Eugenia Brito, Riet Delsing, and Alejandra Farías, eds. 1997. *Discurso, genero y poder—discursos públicos: Chile, 1978–1993.* Santiago: LOM-ARCIS.

Grupo Iniciativa Mujeres. 1994. *Mujeres: Cuidadanía, cultura y desarrollo en el Chile de los noventa.* Santiago: Grupo Iniciativa Mujeres.

———. 1997. *Acta de la primera sesión: Las mujeres en el ejercicio del poder y la toma de decisiones.* Santiago: Foro Nacional para el Seguimiento de los Acuerdos de Beijing.

Guadagnini, Marila. 1995. "The Latecomers: Italy's Equal Status and Equal Opportunity Agencies." In *Comparative State Feminism*, ed. Dorothy McBride Stetson and Amy G. Mazur, 150–67. Thousand Oaks, Calif.: Sage Publications.

Guttmacher Institute. 1996. "An Overview of Clandestine Abortion in Latin America." *Issues in Brief*, December. http://www.guttmacher.org/pubs/ib12.html.

Guzmán, Virginia, and Eugenia Hola. 1996. *El conocimiento como un hecho político.* Santiago: Ediciones CEM.

Guzmán, Virginia, Eugenia Hola, and Marcela Ríos. 1999. "Interlocución estado y sociedad en la implementación del Plan de Igualdad de Oportunidades para las mujeres." Santiago: Ediciones CEM.

Haas, Liesl. 1999. "The Catholic Church in Chile: New Political Alliances." In *Latin American Religion in Motion*, ed. Christian Smith and Joshua Prokopy, 43–66. New York: Routledge.

———. 2000. "Institutional Politics and the Expansion of Women's Rights in Chile." PhD diss., University of North Carolina, Chapel Hill.

———. 2001. "Changing the System from Within? Feminist Participation in the Workers' Party in Brazil, 1989–1995." In *Radical Women in Latin America: Right and Left*, ed. Victoria González and Karen Kampwirth, 249–72. University Park: Pennsylvania State University Press.

———. 2006. "The Rules of the Game: Feminist Policymaking in Chile." *Revista Política* 47 (Winter): 199–225.

Hart, Vivien. 1993. *Bound by Our Constitution: Women, Workers, and the Minimum Wage*. Princeton: Princeton University Press.

Hinojosa, Magda. 2004. "Chilean Women in Municipal Politics: Explaining Representation from the UDI." Paper presented at the twenty-fifth conference of the Latin American Studies Association, Las Vegas, Nevada, October 7.

Hipsher, Patricia. 1996. "Democratization and the Decline of Urban Social Movements in Chile and Spain." *Comparative Politics* 28 (3): 273–97.

Hobson, Barbara. 1990. "No Exit, No Voice: Women's Economic Dependency and the Welfare State." *Acta Sociologica* 33:235–50.

Hobson, Barbara, and Mieko Takahashi. 1997. "The Parent-Worker Model: Lone Mothers in Sweden." In *Lone Mothers in European Welfare State Regimes*, ed. J. Lewis, 121–39. London: Jessica Kingsley.

Hoff, Joan. *Law, Gender, and Injustice: A Legal History of U.S. Women*. New York: New York University Press, 1991.

Hofmann, C. 1994. *Issue Brief on Quota Systems for Women's Political Participation*. Quezon City, Philippines: Women in Politics Program, Congressional Research and Training Service.

Hola, Eugenia, and Gabriela Pischedda. 1993. *Mujeres, poder y política*. Santiago: Ediciones CEM.

Hoskyns, Catherine. 1996a. "The European Union and the Women Within: An Overview of Women's Rights Policy." In *Sexual Politics and the European Union: The New Feminist Challenge*, ed. Amy Elman, 13–22. Providence: Berghahn Books.

———. 1996b. *Integrating Gender: Women, Law, and Politics in the European Union*. New York: Verso.

Htun, Mala. 1998. "Women's Political Participation, Representation, and Leadership in Latin America." Issue brief. Cambridge: Weatherhead Center for International Affairs, Harvard University.

———. 2002. "Puzzles of Women's Rights in Brazil." *Social Research* 69 (3): 733–51.

———. 2003. *Sex and the State: Abortion, Divorce, and the Family Under Latin American Dictatorships and Democracies*. New York: Cambridge University Press.

Htun, Mala, and Mark P. Jones. 2002. "Engendering the Right to Participate in Decision Making: Electoral Quotas and Women's Leadership in Latin America." In *Gender and the Politics of Rights and Democracy in Latin America*, ed. Nikki Craske and Maxine Molyneaux, 32–60. New York: Palgrave Macmillan.

Huber, Evelyne, and John D. Stephens. 2000. "Partisan Governance, Women's Employment, and the Social Democratic Service State." *American Sociological Review* 65 (3): 323–42.

Ingelhart, Ronald. 1977. *The Silent Revolution*. Princeton: Princeton University Press.

———. 1997. *Modernization and Postmodernization: Cultural, Economic, and Political Change in Forty-Three Societies*. Princeton: Princeton University Press.

Ingelhart, Ronald, and Pippa Norris. 2003. *Rising Tide: Gender Equality and Cultural Change Around the World*. Cambridge: Cambridge University Press.

Instituto Libertad. 1991. *Boletin Semanal* 2, no. 14 (May 13–19): 6.

Iriarte Ribas, Claudia. 1994. *Mujer y legalidad en Chile: Una propuesta de cambio*. Santiago: Instituto de la Mujer.

Iverson, Torben, and Frances Rosenbluth. 2006. "The Political Economy of Gender: Explaining Cross-National Variation in the Gender Division of Labor and the Gender Voting Gap." *American Journal of Political Science* 50 (January): 1–19.

Jaquette, Jane S., ed. 1991. *The Women's Movement in Latin America: Feminism and the Transition to Democracy*. Boulder, Colo.: Westview Press.

———, ed. 1994. *The Women's Movement in Latin America: Participation and Democracy*. 2d ed. Boulder, Colo.: Westview Press.

———. 1995. "Rewriting the Scripts: Gender in the Comparative Study of Latin American Politics." In *Latin America in Comparative Perspective: New Approaches to Methods and Analysis*, ed. Peter H. Smith, 111–33. Boulder, Colo.: Westview Press.

Jaquette, Jane S., and Sharon L. Wolchik, eds. 1998. *Women and Democracy: Latin America and Central and Eastern Europe*. Baltimore: Johns Hopkins University Press.

Jelen, Ted G., Sue Thomas, and Clyde Wilcox. 1994. "The Gender Gap in Comparative Perspective." *European Journal of Political Research* 25:171–86.

Jenson, Jane. 1982. "The Modern Women's Movement in Italy, France, and Great Britain: Differences in Life Cycles." *Comparative Social Research* 5:341–75.

———. 1986. "Gender and Reproduction, or Babies and the State." *Studies in Political Economy* 20:9–45.

Jones, Mark P. 1996. "Increasing Women's Representation via Gender Quotas: The Argentine Ley de Cupos." *Women and Politics* 16 (4): 75–98.

———. 1998. "Gender Quotas, Electoral Laws, and the Election of Women: Lessons from the Argentine Provinces." *Comparative Political Studies* 31 (1): 3–21.

———. 2004. "Quota Legislation and the Election of Women: Learning from the Costa Rican Experience." *Journal of Politics* 66 (4): 1203–23.

Jones, Mark P., and Patricio Navia. 1999. "Assessing the Effectiveness of Gender Quotas in Open-List Proportional Representation Electoral Systems." *Social Science Quarterly* 80 (2): 341–55.

Kaplan, Gisela. 1992. *Contemporary Western European Feminism*. New York: New York University Press.

Kelber, Mimi, ed. 1994. *Women and Government: New Ways to Political Power*. Westport, Conn.: Praeger.

Kirkwood, Julieta. 1982. *Feminismo y participación política en Chile*. Santiago: Flacso-Chile.

———. 1986. *Ser política en Chile: Las feministas y los partidos*. Santiago: Flacso-Chile.

———. 1987. *Feminarios*. Santiago: Ediciones Documentas.

Kittilson, Miki Caul. 2006. *Challenging Parties, Changing Parliaments: Women and Elected Office in Contemporary Western Europe*. Columbus: Ohio State University Press.

Kolinsky, Eva. 1991. "Political Participation and Parliamentary Careers: Women's Quotas in Germany." *West European Politics* 14 (1): 56–72.

———. 1993. "Party Change and Women's Representation in Unified Germany." In *Gender and Party Politics*, ed. Joni Lovenduski and Pippa Norris, 113–46. London: Sage Publications.

Koven, Seth, and Sonya Michel, eds. 1993. *Mothers of a New World: Maternalist Politics and the Origins of Welfare States*. New York: Routledge.

Krook, Mona Lena. 2006. "Gender Quotas, Norms, and Politics." *Politics and Gender* 2 (1): 110–18.

———. 2010. *Quotas for Women in Politics: Gender and Candidate Selection Reform Worldwide*. New York: Oxford University Press.

Laakso, Markku, and Rein Taagepera. 1979. "The 'Effective' Number of Parties: A Measure with Application to Western Europe." *Comparative Political Studies* 12 (1): 3–27.

Laitin, David D. 1986. *Hegemony and Culture.* Chicago: University of Chicago Press.

Lang, Regina. 1989. *Frauenquoten: Der einen Freud, des anderen Leid.* Bonn: Verlag J. H. W. Dietz Nachf.

Larraín, Luis. 1996. *Divorcio y políticas públicas.* Santiago: Instituto Libertad y Desarrollo.

Laver, Michael, and Kenneth A. Shepsle. 1996. *Making and Breaking Governments.* New York: Cambridge University Press.

LeDuc, Lawrence, Richard Neimi, and Pippa Norris, eds. 1996. *Comparative Democratic Elections.* London: Sage Publications.

Leijenaar, Monique. 1997. *How to Create a Gender Balance in Political Decision-Making.* Brussels: European Commission, Directorate-General for Employment, Industrial Relations and Social Affairs.

Levine, Daniel H., ed. 1993. *Constructing Culture and Power in Latin America.* Ann Arbor: University of Michigan Press.

Lewis, Jane, and Gertrude Astrom. 1992. "Equality, Difference, and State Welfare: Labor Market and Family Policy in Sweden." *Feminist Studies* 18:59–86.

Lijphart, Arend. 1984. *Democracies: Patterns of Majoritarian and Consensus Government in Twenty-one Countries.* New Haven: Yale University Press.

———. 1994. *Electoral Systems and Party Systems: A Study of Twenty-seven Democracies, 1945–1990.* New York: Oxford University Press.

Lijphart, Arend, and Carlos H. Waisman, eds. 1996. *Institutional Design in New Democracies: Eastern Europe and Latin America.* Boulder, Colo.: Westview Press.

Linz, Juan J., and Alfred Stepan. 1996. *Problems of Democratic Transition and Consolidation: Southern Europe, South America, and Post-Communist Europe.* Baltimore: Johns Hopkins University Press.

Linz, Juan J., and Arturo Valenzuela, eds. 1994. *The Failure of Presidential Democracy.* Baltimore: Johns Hopkins University Press.

Lipset, Seymour M., and Stein Rokkan. 1967. *Party Systems and Voter Alignments: Cross-National Perspectives.* New York: Free Press.

Londregan, John B. 2000. *Legislative Institutions and Ideology in Chile.* New York: Cambridge University Press.

Lovenduski, Joni. 1996. *Women in Politics.* Oxford: Oxford University Press.

Lovenduski, Joni, and Pippa Norris, eds. 1993. *Gender and Party Politics.* London: Sage Publications.

Lovenduski, Joni, and Vicky Randall. 1993. *Contemporary Feminist Politics: Women and Power in Britain.* Oxford: Oxford University Press.

Lycklama a Nijeholt, Geertje, Virginia Vargas, and Saskia Wieringa, eds. 1998. *Women's Movements and Public Policy in Europe, Latin America, and the Caribbean.* New York: Garland.

Macaulay, Fiona. 1998. "Localities of Power: Gender, Parties, and Democracy in Chile and Brazil." In *Women and Empowerment: Illustrations from the Third World,* ed. Haleh Afshar, 86–109. New York: St. Martin's Press.

Mackay, Fiona. 1996. "The Zero Tolerance Campaign: Setting the Agenda." *Parliamentary Affairs* 49:206–20.

MacKinnon, Catherine. 1989. *Toward a Feminist Theory of the State.* Cambridge: Harvard University Press.

Madrid Meza, Ral. 1996. "Cuestión de estado." *La Nación*, June 7, 36.
Magar, Eric, Marc R. Rosenblum, and David Samuels. 1998. "On the Absence of Centripetal Incentives in Double-Member Districts: The Case of Chile." *Comparative Political Studies* 31 (December): 714–739.
Mahon, E. 1996. "Women's Rights and Catholicism in Ireland." In *Mapping the Women's Movement*, ed. Mónica Threlfall, 184–215. London: Verso.
Mainwaring, Scott, and Timothy R. Scully, eds. 1995. *Building Democratic Institutions: Party Systems in Latin America*. Stanford: Stanford University Press.
Mainwaring, Scott, and Matthew S. Shugart, eds. 1997. *Presidentialism and Democracy in Latin America*. New York: Cambridge University Press.
Mansbridge, Jane. 2005. "Quota Problems: Combating the Dangers of Essentialism." *Politics and Gender* 1 (4): 622–38.
Matear, Amy. 1997. "Desde la protesta a la propuesta: The Institutionalization of the Women's Movement in Chile." In *Gender Politics in Latin America*, ed. Elizabeth Dore, 84–100. New York: Monthly Review Press.
Matland, Richard E. 1993. "Institutional Variables Affecting Female Representation in National Legislatures: The Case of Norway." *Journal of Politics* 55 (3): 737–55.
———. 1994. "Putting Scandinavian Equality to the Test: An Experimental Evaluation of Gender Stereotyping of Political Candidates in a Sample of Norwegian Voters." *British Journal of Political Science* 24 (2): 273–92.
———. 1998. "Women's Representation in National Legislatures: Developed and Developing Countries." *Legislative Studies Quarterly* 23 (1): 109–25.
Matland, Richard E., and Donley T. Studlar. 1996. "The Contagion of Women Candidates in SMD and PR Representation Electoral Systems: Canada and Norway." *Journal of Politics* 58 (3): 707–33.
Matland, Richard E., and Michelle M. Taylor. 1997. "Electoral System Effects on Women's Representation: Theoretical Arguments and Evidence from Costa Rica." *Comparative Political Studies* 30 (2): 186–210.
Mattei, Laura R. Winsky. 1998. "Gender and Power in American Legislative Discourse." *Journal of Politics* 60 (2): 440–61.
Mazur, Amy G. 1995. *Gender Bias and the State: Symbolic Reform at Work in Fifth-Republic France*. Pittsburgh: University of Pittsburgh Press.
———. 1999. "Feminist Comparative Policy: A New Field of Study." *European Journal of Political Research* 35 (4): 483–506.
———. 2001. *State Feminism, Women's Movements, and Job Training: Making Democracies Work in the Global Economy*. New York: Routledge.
———. 2002. *Theorizing Feminist Policy*. Oxford: Oxford University Press.
McAdam, Doug, John D. McCarthy, and Mayer N. Zald. 1996. *Comparative Perspectives on Social Movements: Political Opportunities, Mobilizing Structures, and Cultural Framings*. Cambridge: Cambridge University Press.
Medina, Jorge. 1995. *De nuevo el tema del divorcio vincular*. Valparaíso: Arzobispado de Valparaíso.
Mezey, Susan Gluck. 1994. "Increasing the Number of Women in Office: Does It Matter?" In *The Year of the Woman: Myths and Realities*, ed. Elizabeth Adell Cook, Sue Thomas, and Clyde Wilcox, 255–70. Boulder, Colo.: Westview Press.
Miller, Francesca. 1991. *Latin American Women and the Search for Social Justice*. Hanover: University Press of New England.
Misra, Joya, and Frances Akins. 1998. "The Welfare State and Women: Structure, Agency, and Diversity." *Social Politics* 5:259–85.

Misra, Joya, and Leslie King. 2004. "Women, Gender, and State Policies." In *The Handbook of Political Sociology*, ed. Thomas Janoski, Rober Alford, Alexander Hicks, and Mildred Schwarz, 526–45. New York: Cambridge University Press.

Mlynarz, Danae, and Roxana Muñoz. 2003. "Familia, trabajo y participación política panorámia de la situación en la última década en Chile." Santiago: Colección IDEAS.

Molina, Natacha, and Patricia Provoste, eds. 1997. *Veredas por cruzar*. Santiago: Instituto de la Mujer.

Molyneux, Maxine. 1985. "Mobilization Without Emancipation? Women's Interests, the State, and Revolution in Nicaragua." *Feminist Studies* 11 (2): 227–54.

Montes, Juan Esteban, Scott Mainwaring, and Eugenio Ortega. 2000. "Rethinking the Chilean Party System." *Journal of Latin American Studies* 32 (2): 795–825.

Morgenstern, Scott, and Benito Nacif, eds. 2002. *Legislative Politics in Latin America*. New York: Cambridge University Press.

Muñoz, Adriana. 1987. *Fuerza feminista y democrática: Utopia a realizar*. Santiago: Instituto de la Mujer.

Murphy, Patricia. 1997. "Domestic Violence Legislation and the Police: The Role of Socioeconomic Indicators, Political Factors, and Women's Political Activism on State Policy Adoption." *Women and Politics* 18 (2): 27–53.

Navarro-Aranguren, Marysa. 1992. "The Construction of a Latin American Feminist Identity." In *Americas: New Interpretive Essays*, ed. Alfred Stepan, 137–51. New York: Oxford University Press.

Nohlen, Dieter. 1996. "Electoral Systems and Electoral Reform in Latin America." In *Institutional Design in New Democracies: Eastern Europe and Latin America*, ed. Arend Lijphart and Carlos H. Waisman, 43–55. Boulder, Colo.: Westview Press.

Norris, Pippa. 1997. "Equality Strategies and Political Representation." In *Sex Equality Policy in Western Europe*, ed. Frances Gardiner, 43–56. New York: Routledge.

———. 2000. "Women's Representation and Electoral Systems." In *The International Encyclopedia of Elections*, ed. R. Rose, 348–51. Washington, D.C.: CQ Press.

Norris, Pippa, and Ronald Ingelhart. 2001. "Cultural Obstacles to Equal Representation." *Journal of Democracy* 12 (3): 126–40.

Norris, Pippa, and Joni Lovenduski. 1994. *Political Recruitment: Gender, Race, and Class in the British Parliament*. Cambridge: Cambridge University Press.

North, Douglass. 1990. *Institutions, Institutional Change, and Economic Performance*. Cambridge: Cambridge University Press.

O'Connor, Julia S. 1993. "Gender, Class, and Citizenship in the Comparative Analysis of Welfare State Regimes: Theoretical and Methodological Issues." *British Journal of Sociology* 44 (3): 501–18.

———. 1996. "From Women in the Welfare State to Gendering Welfare State Regimes." *Current Sociology* 44:1–24.

O'Connor, Julia S., Ann Shola Orloff, and Sheila Shaver. 1999. *States, Markets, Families: Gender, Liberalism, and Social Policy in Australia, Canada, Great Britain, and the United States*. Cambridge: Cambridge University Press.

Orloff, Ann Shola. 1991. "Gender in Early U.S. Social Policy." *Journal of Policy History* 3:249–81.

———. 1993. *The Politics of Pensions: A Comparative Analysis of Britain, Canada, and the United States, 1880–1940*. Madison: University of Wisconsin Press.

———. 1996. "Gender in the Welfare State." *Annual Review of Sociology* 22:51–78.

Outshoorn, Joyce. 1995. "Administrative Accommodation in the Netherlands: The Department of the Coordination of Equality Policy." In *Comparative State Feminism*, ed. Dorothy McBride Stetson and Amy G. Mazur, 168–85. Thousand Oaks, Calif.: Sage Publications.
Oviedo, Carlos. 1991. *Morality, Youth, and Permissive Society.* Santiago: Arzobispado de Santiago.
Pascall, Gillian. 1997. *Social Policy: A New Feminist Analysis.* London: Routledge.
Peters, Anne. 1999. *Women, Quotas, and Constitutions: A Comparative Study of Affirmative Action for Women in American, German, European Community, and International Law.* Dordrecht: Kluwer.
Pierson, Paul. 2000. "Three Worlds of Welfare State Research." *Comparative Political Studies* 33 (6–7): 791–821.
Piven, Frances Fox, and Richard A. Cloward. 1993. *Regulating the Poor: The Functions of Public Welfare.* New York: Vintage Books.
Polakow, Valerie. 1993. *Lives on the Edge: Single Mothers and Their Children in the Other America.* Chicago: University of Chicago Press.
Power, Margaret. 2002. *Right-Wing Women in Chile: Feminine Power and the Struggle Against Allende, 1964–1973.* University Park: Pennsylvania State University Press.
Pringle, R., and S. Watson 1992. "Women's Interests and the Post-Structuralist State." In *Destabilizing Theory: Contemporary Feminist Debates*, ed. Michele Barrett and Anne Phillips, 53–73. Cambridge: Polity Press.
Provoste, Patricia F. 1995. *La construccion de las mujeres en la política social.* Santiago: Instituto de la Mujer.
Rabkin, Rhoda. 1996. "Redemocratization, Electoral Engineering, and Party Strategies in Chile, 1989–1995." *Comparative Political Studies* 29:335–56.
Ragin, Charles, and David Zaret. 1983. "Theory and Method in Comparative Research: Two Strategies." *Social Forces* 61 (3): 731–54.
Rai, Shirin M., ed. 2003. *Mainstreaming Gender, Democratising the State?* Manchester: Manchester University Press.
Rai, Shirin M., and Geraldine Lievesley, eds. 1996. *Women and the State: International Perspectives.* London: Taylor and Francis.
Randall, Vicky. 1987. *Women and Politics: An International Perspective.* 2d ed. Chicago: University of Chicago Press.
Randall, Vicky, and Georgina Waylen, eds. 1998. *Gender, Politics, and the State.* London: Routledge.
Requena-Bichet, M. 1990. "The Problem of Induced Abortion from the Standpoint of Human Rights." Baltimore: Johns Hopkins Bloomberg School of Public Health.
Richards, Patricia. 2004. *Pobladoras, Indigenas, and the State: Conflict over Women's Rights in Chile.* New Brunswick: Rutgers University Press.
Ríos Tobar, Marcela. 2003. "Chilean Feminism(s) in the 1990s: Paradoxes of an Unfinished Transition." *International Feminist Journal of Politics* 5 (2): 256–80.
Rochon, Thomas R., and Daniel A. Mazmanian. 1993. "Social Movements and the Policy Process." *Annals, AAPSS* 528 (July): 75–87.
Rojas, Juanita. 1991. "Divorcio: ¿Se acabará la mentira?" *Analysis,* June 3–9, 5–6.
Ross, Jen. 2004. "Chileans Facing up to Domestic Violence." Women's eNews, December 31. http://www.feminist.com/news/vaw38.html.
Rozell, Mark J. 2000. "Helping Women Run and Win: Feminist Groups, Candidate Recruitment, and Training." *Women and Politics* 21 (3): 101–16.

Rule, Wilma. 1987. "Electoral Systems, Contextual Factors, and Women's Opportunities for Election to Parliament in Twenty-three Democracies." *Western Political Quarterly* 40 (3): 477–98.

Rule, Wilma, and Joseph F. Zimmerman. 1994. *Electoral Systems in Comparative Perspective: Their Impact on Women and Minorities*. Westport, Conn.: Greenwood Press.

Sainsbury, Diane, ed. 1994. *Gendering Welfare States*. London: Sage Publications.

———. 1996. *Gender, Equality, and Welfare States*. Cambridge: Cambridge University Press.

———. 1999. *Gender and Welfare State Regimes*. Oxford: Oxford University Press.

Sawer, Marian. 1995. "Femocrats in Glass Towers? The Office of the Status of Women in Australia." In *Comparative State Feminism*, ed. Dorothy McBride Stetson and Amy G. Mazur, 22–39. Thousand Oaks, Calif.: Sage Publications.

Sawer, Marian, and Abigail Groves. 1994. *Working from Inside: Twenty Years of the Office of the Status of Women*. Canberra: Australian Government Publishing Service.

Schild, Veronica. 1998. "New Subjects of Rights? Women's Movements and the Construction of Citizenship in New Democracies." In *Cultures of Politics/Politics of Culture: Revisioning Latin American Social Movements*, ed. Sonia E. Alvarez, Evelina Dagnino, and Arturo Escobar, 93–117. Boulder, Colo.: Westview Press.

Schneider, Cathy Lisa. 1995. *Shantytown Protests in Pinochet's Chile*. Philadelphia: Temple University Press.

Scully, Timothy R. 1992. *Rethinking the Center: Party Politics in Nineteenth- and Twentieth-Century Chile*. Stanford: Stanford University Press.

———. 1995. "Reconstituting Party Politics in Chile." In *Building Democratic Institutions: Party Systems in Latin America*, ed. Scott Mainwaring, 200–246. Stanford: Stanford University Press.

———. 1996. "Chile: The Political Underpinnings of Economic Liberalization." In *Constructing Democratic Governance: South America in the 1990s*, ed. Jorge I. Dominguez and Abraham I. Lowenthal, 99–117. Baltimore: Johns Hopkins University Press.

Scully, Timothy R., and Samuel Valenzuela. 1993. "De la democracia a la democracia: Continuidad y variaciones en las preferencias del electorado y en el sistema de partidos en Chile." *Estudios Públicos* 51:195–228.

Shugart, Matthew Soberg, and John M. Carey. 1992. *Presidents and Assemblies: Constitutional Design and Electoral Dynamics*. Cambridge: Cambridge University Press.

Siavelis, Peter. 1997. "Continuity and Change in the Chilean Party System: On the Transformational Effects of Electoral Reform." *Comparative Political Studies* 30 (6): 651–74.

———. 2000. *The President and Congress in Postauthoritarian Chile: Institutional Constraints to Democratic Consolidation*. University Park: Pennsylvania State University Press.

———. 2002. "Exaggerated Presidentialism and Moderate Presidents: Executive-Legislative Relations in Chile." In *Legislative Politics in Latin America*, ed. Scott Morgenstern and Benito Nacif, 79–113. New York: Cambridge University Press.

Siavelis, Peter, and Arturo Valenzuela. 1996. "Electoral Engineering and Democratic Stability: The Legacy of Authoritarian Rule in Chile." In *Institutional Design in*

New Democracies: Eastern Europe and Latin America, ed. Arend Lijphart and Carlos H. Waisman, 77–101. Boulder, Colo.: Westview Press.

Simon, Rita J., and Gloria Danziger. 1991. *Women's Movements in America: Their Successes, Disappointments, and Aspirations.* New York: Praeger.

Sklar, Katherine Kish. 1993. "The Historical Foundations of Women's Power in the Creation of the American Welfare State, 1830–1930." In *Mothers of a New World: Maternalist Politics and the Origins of Welfare States*, ed. Seth Koven and Sonya Michel, 43–93. New York: Routledge.

Skocpol, Theda. 1992. *Protecting Soldiers and Mothers.* Cambridge: Harvard University Press.

Smith, Brian H. 1982. *The Church and Politics in Chile: Challenges to Modern Catholicism.* Princeton: Princeton University Press.

Smith, Peter H., ed. 1995. *Latin America in Comparative Perspective: New Approaches to Methods and Analysis.* Boulder, Colo.: Westview Press.

Staudt, Kathleen A., ed. 1997. *Women, International Development, and Politics: The Bureaucratic Mire.* Philadelphia: Temple University Press.

———. 1998. *Policy, Politics, and Gender: Women Gaining Ground.* West Hartford, Conn.: Kumarian Press.

———. 2002. "Dismantling the Master's House with the Master's Tools? Gender Work in and with Powerful Bureaucracies." In *Feminist Post-Development Thought*, ed. Kriemild Saunders, 57–69. New York: Zed Books.

Staudt, Kathleen A., and William G. Weaver. 1997. *Political Science and Feminisms: Transforming Political Science?* New York: Twayne.

Stephen, Lynn. 1997. *Women and Social Movements in Latin America: Power from Below.* Austin: University of Texas Press.

Stetson, Dorothy McBride. 1995. "Human Rights for Women: International Compliance with a Feminist Standard." *Women and Politics* 15 (3): 71–95.

———, ed. 2002. *Abortion Politics, Women's Movements, and the Democratic State: A Comparative Study of State Feminism.* Oxford: Oxford University Press.

Stetson, Dorothy McBride, and Amy G. Mazur, eds. 1995. *Comparative State Feminism.* Thousand Oaks, Calif.: Sage Publications.

———. 2000. "Women's Movements and the State: Job-Training Policy in France and the U.S." *Political Research Quarterly* 53 (3): 597–623.

Studlar, Donley T., and Ian McAllistar. 2002. "Does Critical Mass Exist? A Comparative Analysis of Women's Legislative Representation Since 1950." *European Journal of Political Research* 41 (2): 233–53.

Swers, Michelle L. 2002. *The Difference Women Make: The Policy Impact of Women in Congress.* Chicago: University of Chicago Press.

Taagepera, Rein, and Matthew S. Shugart. 1989. *Seats and Votes: The Effects and Determinants of Electoral Systems.* New Haven: Yale University Press.

Tabak, Fanny. 1983. *Autoritarismo e participação política da mulher.* Rio de Janeiro: Edições Graal.

Tarrow, Sydney. 1983. *Struggling to Reform: Social Movements and Policy Change During Cycles of Protest.* Ithaca: Cornell University Press.

———. 1991. *Struggle, Politics, and Reform: Collective Action, Social Movements, and Cycles of Protest.* Ithaca: Cornell University Press.

———. 1998. *Power in Movements: Social Movements and Contentious Politics.* 2d ed. Cambridge: Cambridge University Press.

Thomas, Sue. 1994. *How Women Legislate.* New York: Oxford University Press.
Tilly, Charles. 1985. "Models and Realities of Popular Action." *Social Research* 52 (4): 717–47.
Tremblay, Manon. 1998. "Do Female MPs Substantively Represent Women? A Study of Legislative Behaviour in Canada's Thirty-fifth Parliament." *Canadian Journal of Political Science* 31 (3): 435–65.
Tuominen, Mary. 1997. "Exploitation or Opportunity? The Contradictions of Child-Care Policy in the Contemporary United States." *Women and Politics* 18 (1): 53–80.
Turshen, Meredith, and Biavel Holcomb, eds. 1993. *Women's Lives and Public Policy: The International Experience.* Westport, Conn.: Praeger.
Urzúa Valenzuela, Germán. 1992. *Historia política de Chile y su evolución electoral (desde 1810 a 1992).* Santiago: Editorial Juridica de Chile.
Vaccaro, Victor. 1997. "Denuncian presiones por divorcio." *La Tercera* (Santiago), January 22.
Valdés, Teresa. 1998. "Mechanismos nacionales: Estrategias para el avance desde el movimiento de mujeres." Manuscript.
Valdés, Teresa, and Miren Busto, eds. 1994. *Sexualidad y reproducción: Hacia la construcción de derechos.* Santiago: CORSAPS and Flacso-Chile.
Valdés, Teresa, and Alicia Frohmann. 1993. *Democracy in the Country and in the Home: The Women's Movement in Chile.* Santiago: Flacso.
Valdés, Teresa, and Marisa Weinstein. 1997. "Corriendo y descorriendo tupidos velos." *Chile 96: Análysis y Opiniones:* 67–78.
Valenzuela, Arturo. 1994. "Party Politics and the Crisis of Presidentialism in Chile: A Proposal for a Parliamentary Form of Government." In *The Failure of Presidential Democracy,* ed. Juan J. Linz and Arturo Valenzuela, 91–150. Baltimore: Johns Hopkins University Press.
Valenzuela, María Elena. 1987. *La mujer en el Chile militar.* Santiago: CESOC.
———. 1991. "The Evolving Roles of Women Under Military Rule." In *The Struggle for Democracy in Chile, 1982–1990,* ed. Paul W. Drake and Ivan Jaksic, 161–87. Lincoln: University of Nebraska Press.
———. 1998. "Women and the Democratization Process in Chile." In *Women and Democracy: Latin America and Central and Eastern Europe,* ed. Jane S. Jaquette and Sharon L. Wolchik, 47–74. Baltimore: Johns Hopkins University Press.
———. 1999. "El desafío de hacer política feminista desde el estado." In "Feminismos fin de siglo." Special issue, *Mujer/Fempress.*
Valiente, Celia. 1995. "The Power of Persuasion: The Instituto de la Mujer in Spain." In *Comparative State Feminism,* ed. Dorothy McBride Stetson and Amy G. Mazur, 221–36. Thousand Oaks, Calif.: Sage Publications.
———. 1997. "State Feminism and Gender Equality Policies: The Case of Spain (1983–95)." In *Sex Equality Policy in Western Europe,* ed. Frances Gardiner, 123–38. London: Routledge.
Valverde, Mariana. 1991. *The Age of Light, Soap, and Water: Moral Reform in English Canada, 1885–1925.* Toronto: McClelland and Stewart.
Van Kersbergen, Kees. 1995. *Social Capitalism: A Study of Christian Democracy and the Welfare State.* New York: Routledge.
Velasco Letelier, Eugenio. 1993. *Familia, divorcio y moral.* Santiago: Editorial Juridica de Chile.

Vogel, Lise. 1993. *Mothers on the Job: Maternity Policy in the U.S. Workplace.* New Brunswick: Rutgers University Press.

Wägnerud, Lena. 2006. "Norway's Parliament—Not Equal." Kilden Information Centre for Gender Research in Norway. http://kilden.forskningsradet.no/c52778/nyhet/vis.html?tid=52946 (accessed April 1, 2010).

Walker, G. 1990. "The Conceptual Politics of Struggle: Wife Battering, the Women's Movement, and the State." *Studies in Political Economy* 33 (Fall): 63–90.

Waylen, Georgina. 1994. "Women and Democratization: Conceptualizing Gender Relations in Transition Politics." *World Politics* 46 (3): 327–54.

———. 1996a. "Democratization, Feminism, and the State in Chile: The Establishment of Sernam." In *Women and the State: International Perspectives,* ed. Shirin M. Rai and Geraldine Lievesley, 103–17. London: Taylor and Francis.

———. 1996b. *Gender in Third World Politics.* Boulder, Colo.: Lynne Rienner.

———. 1997. "Women's Movements, the State, and Democratization in Chile: The Establishment of Sernam." In *Getting Institutions Right for Development,* ed. Anne Marie Geotz, 90–103. London: Zed Books.

———. 2000. "Gender and Democratic Politics: A Comparative Analysis of Consolidation in Argentina and Chile." *Journal of Latin American Studies* 32:765–93.

Weldon, S. Laurel. 2002. *Protest, Policy, and the Problem of Violence Against Women.* Pittsburgh: University of Pittsburgh Press.

Wieringa, Saskia. 1996. *Subversive Women: Women's Movements in Africa, Asia, Latin America, and the Caribbean.* London: Zed Books.

Zilci, Sonia. 1994. "Divorcio: El 'lobby' de los curas." *Hoy,* May 9–15.

INDEX

abortion, 2
   Center's position on, 128
   in Chile, 121–23
   currents of thought on, in Chile, 125–29
   drafting bill for, by Open Forum on Health and Sexual and Reproductive Rights, 134–38
   Left's position on, 127–28
   legacy of attempts to decriminalize, 141–43
abortion laws
   attempts to reform, 119–20
   Catholic Church position on, 128
   feminist learning from failure to reform, 138–41
   framing debate for, 123–25
   legislative history, 129–34
activism, women and, 43
Aguiló, Sergio, 77, 101, 102–5
Albornoz, Laura, 61n13, 63, 118, 174
Allamand, Andrés, 156
Allende, Isabel, 79, 163
alliances. *See* Networks
Alvear, Soledad, 61, 61n13, 73n28, 108, 122, 165, 173
Andrade, Carmen, 61n13
annulments, civil, 146
Arancibia, Armando, 129
Aylwin, Mariana, 69, 78, 78n34, 82, 109, 137–38, 140, 151, 151n6, 158, 173, 176–77
Aylwin, Patricio, 1n1, 100

Bachelet, Michelle, 44n20, 60, 61n13, 63, 66, 120, 170–71
   appointing men to governorships and, 178
   commitment to gender equity and, 180
   creation of day-care centers by, 178
   domestic violence policy and, 178–79
   election of, 1, 1n1, 169
   feminist policymaking and, 177–83
   health care and, 179
   provision of emergency contraception and, 179
   violence against women and, 117–18
   women's representation to cabinet positions and, 177–78

Baez, Verónica, 139
Bilbao, Josefina, 61, 61n13, 62, 128, 174
Bosselin, Hernán, 76, 76n31, 133, 149, 162
Burgos, Jorge, 76
Bustos, Juan, 76

Camus, Carlos (bishop of Linares), 160n23, 161, 162
Caro, Cristián (auxiliary bishop of Santiago), 161, 163
Casa de la Mujer, 105
Casas, Lidia, 85n41, 135, 137
case studies, 9
Catholic Church. *See also* religion
   abortion position of, 128–29
   divorce issue and, 159–64
   influence of, on Congress, 84–88
   political power of, 45, 46–47, 46n22
Center-Left Concertación, 55
Chadwick, Andrés, 1–8
Chamber of Deputies. *See also* Congress
   committee system of, 75–79
   Constitution Committee of, 75, 76
   Family Committee of, 75, 77–79
   feminist leadership in, 79
   Labor Committee of, 75, 76–77
Chile
   abortion in, 121–23
   as bellwether for women's rights in Latin America, 4–7
   as example of evolution of women's rights, 6
   feminist policy agenda in, 7–9
   overview of contemporary politics in, 55–56
   policymaking dynamics in, 50–51
   state of women's rights in 1990 in, 2
Chilean democracy, feminism and, 3
Christian Democratic Party (PDC), 55, 66–67
   abortion legislation and, 122
   abortion position of, 128
   counterproposal of, for divorce bill, 152–54
   divorce reform position of, 147–48
   women representatives in, 73
   women's rights policy and, 68–70

civil annulments, 146
Civil Marriage bill. *See also* divorce
　floor debates on, 157–59
　institutional support for, 155–57
　passage of, 154–55
committee system, of Congress, 74–77
Concertación. *See* National Concertation for Democracy (Concertación)
Congress. *See also* executive branch; political parties; Senate
　executive branch and, 45–48
　feminist leadership in, 79
　influence of Catholic Church on, 84–88
　review committees of, 74–77
　staffing and legislative assistance for, 83–84
　support for women's rights and, 64–66
　women's access to power in, 74–79
　women's representation in, 72–74
Constitution Committee, 75, 76, 104
Cristi, María Angélica, 67, 107, 140, 175
culture, women's rights and, 45

day-care centers, 178
Department for the Coordination of Equality Policy (the Netherlands), 35
designated senators, 80–81
d'Hondt voting system, 81
divorce, 2. *See also* New Civil Marriage Law (2004)
　bill legalizing (1995), 154–55
　Catholic Church and, 159–64
　conservative counterproposal to feminist bill legalizing, 152–54
　feminist representatives attempts to legalize, 151–52
　first post-transition bill for legalizing, 148–49
　floor debates on, 157–59
　legalization of, 120, 145–46
　need for legalizing, 146–48
　position of Christian Democrats on, 147–48
　second bill for legalizing, 149–50
　Senate passage of bill for, 164–65
　third bill for legalizing, 150
divorce law. *See* New Civil Marriage Law (2004)
domestic violence, 24
　election of Bachelet and, 178
domestic violence legislation. *See also* Intrafamily Violence Law (1994, VIF)
　initial failure of institutional cooperation for, 102–4
　introduction of, 100–102

strategic framing and negotiation for, 104–7
Dupré, Carlos, 152–53, 159
Duque, Isabel, 93

Elgueta, Sergio, 151
Equal Status Councils (Norway and Denmark), 35
Errázuriz, Francisco (bishop of Valparaíso), 163
Espina, Alberto, 156
executive branch
　legislation sponsored by, 181
　power of, 56–58 (*see also* Congress)

Family Action, 140
Family Committee, 75, 77–79
　Sernam and, 82
feminism, Chilean democracy and, 3
　creation of national-level ministries and, 25
　defining influence of, 23–27
　diversification of, 26–27
　domestic violence issue and, 24
　engagement with the state and, 27–33
　NGOs and, 31–32
　participation of, in Latin American politics, 24–25
　political dissolution of, 3
feminist community, factors negatively affecting, 3n4
feminist legislation, agenda for, in Chile, 7–9
feminist movement(s), 3n3. *See also* women's movement(s)
feminist NGOs, 30–31, 100, 176. *See also* nongovernmental organizations (NGOs); Open Forum on Health and Sexual and Reproductive Rights
　drafting of abortion bill and, 134–38
feminist policymaking. *See also* policymaking process
　challenged of understanding determinants of, 21–22
　coordination and, 49
　data collection for, 11–14
　election of Bachelet and, 177–83
　explaining successful, 14–15
　future of, 169–77
　influence of women's movement over, 88–93
　networks and, 93–94
　political learning and, 50–51
　research on, 9–11
　trends, 94–95
Fernández, Sergio, 108n17
Ferrada, Luis, 157–58
Frei, Eduardo, 111, 112

Fuenzalida, Orozimbo (bishop of San Bernardo), 160n23, 162, 163

gender, research on politics and, 9–11
gender quotas, 40–41, 43, 44n20, 74, 175
Goic, Carolina, 77
González, Luis, 158
González, Rosa, 73n29
government policies, public opinion and, 47–48
Guzmán, Jaime, 124n6, 126

Human Rights Committee, 104–5

Ibáñez, Carmen, 73n29
ideologies
  women's rights and, 38–40
  women's rights policy and, 66–72
Independent Democratic Union Party (UDI), 12
  women representatives in, 73
  women's rights policy and, 70–71
International Women's Health Coalition, 134–35
Intrafamily Violence Law (1994, VIF), 14–15, 60, 65, 89, 178
  feminist learning in wake of, 112–16
  feminist response to, 110–12
  institutional cooperation for, 100
  legacy of, 116–18
  overview of, 97–98
  passage of, 109–10
  Senate's modification of, 108–9
  Sernam's contribution to passage of, 113–15
  significance of, 98–99
ISIS International, 100, 105

Labor Committee, 75, 76–77
Lagos, Ricardo, 1n1, 13, 61, 62, 120, 141, 180n7
Larraín, Hernán, 145
Latin America
  Chile as bellwether for women's rights in, 4–7
  research on women's rights policy development in, 182–83
Lavandero, Jorge, 53
the Left. *See also* New Left
  abortion legislation and, 122, 127–28
  divorce reform and, 147
  feminists and, 38–40, 49–50
  legislative assistance and, 83
  as support of feminist policy reform, 66–67
  women's rights policy and, 67–68

Letelier, Juan Pablo, 129
Longton, Arturo, 164

Matus, Verónica, 91
Medina, Jorge (cardinal), 160n23, 161, 162, 163
Mez, Fernando, 77
Molina, Jorge, 107
Montes, Carlos, 129
Moreira, Iván, 164
Muñoz, Adriana, 64, 64n18, 76, 77, 79, 101, 102–5, 107, 108, 115, 117, 119, 120, 123, 137, 148, 151
  abortion legislation and, 127, 129, 139

National Concertation for Democracy (Concertación), 66
National Episcopal Conference, 129, 129n14
National Renovation Party (RN), 12
  women's rights policy and, 70–72
National Women's Service (Sernam), 55, 59–64
  abortion legislation and, 123, 139
  abortion position of, 128
  contribution of, to passage of VIF, 113–15
  creation of, 2, 3
  divorce law and, 166–67
  domestic violence legislation and, 102, 106–7
  downside of, 64
  feminist representatives and, 93–94
  framing and negotiating VIF and, 104–7
  funding of, 59–60
  increasing policy impact of, 172–74
  leadership of, 61
  legislative efforts of, 7–8
  paradox of, 91
  policymaking efforts of, 3
  policy proposals of, 62
  resources of, 60–61
  Senate and, 81–82
  success in passing legislation and, 62–64
Navas, Sara, 125
Network Against Violence, 100, 105
networks, policy, 49–51
  bolstering, 176
  feminist policymaking and, 93–95
New Civil Marriage Law (2004). *See also* divorce
  feminist learning in wake of, 165–67
  floor debate on, 157–59
  institutional support for, 155–57
  legacy of, 167
  legislative history of, 145–46
  Senate passage of, 164–65

New Left, 67–68. *See also* the Left
    feminists and, 39
NGOization, of women's movements, 30–31, 90–91
nongovernmental organizations (NGOs), feminist movements and, 31–32, 90–91. *See also* feminist NGOs

Office on the Status of Women (OSW, Australia), 35, 36
Open Forum on Health and Sexual and Reproductive Rights, 128, 139, 143. *See also* feminist NGOs
    draft of abortion bill by, 134–38
Oviedo, Carlos (cardinal), 160n23, 162, 163

Parliamentary Front for Life (Frente), 140
Party for Democracy (PPD), 66
    women's rights policy and, 67–68
PDC. *See* Christian Democratic Party (PDC)
Pérez, Cecilia, 61n13, 63, 117, 165, 174
Pérez, Lily, 72, 175
Piano, Adriana del, 61, 61n13, 165, 174
Piñera, Sebastián, 180, 180n8
policymaking process. *See also* feminist policymaking
    data collection for, 11–14
    influence of women's movement on, 88–93
    research on gender and, 9–11
policy networks, 49–51
political issues, defining, 2
political participation, women and, 43
political parties. *See also* Congress; executive branch; *individual political parties*
    balance of power among, and policy reform, 65–66
    broadening support for women's rights by, 174–77
    women's rights and, 38–40
Pollarolo, Fanny, 109, 137, 151, 161, 176
PPD. *See* Party for Democracy (PPD)
pregnancy tests, 2
Prochelle, Marina, 76
property rights laws, women and, 2
PS. *See* Socialist Party (PS)
public opinion, government policy and, 47–48

quantitative analysis, 9
quota laws, for women's representation, 40–41, 43, 44n20, 74, 175

religion, role of, in framing debates on women's rights, 45–47. *See also* Catholic Church

the Right
    abortion legislation and, 122
    divorce reform and, 147
    as feminist policy initiatives and, 66–67
    feminists and, 38–40
    women's rights policy and, 70–72
RN. *See* National Renovation Party (RN)
Rodríguez, Laura, 127, 129, 148–49, 151

Saa, María Antonieta, 76, 79, 109, 117, 127, 137, 151, 156, 176
Salazar, Hector, 128
Santos, José Manuel (archbishop of Concepción), 160, 162
Senate. *See also* Congress
    committee system of, 82
    designated senators of, 80–81
    informal mechanisms of influence in, 81–83
    Intrafamily Violence Law and, 108–9
    policymaking in, 79–83
    Sernam and, 81–82
Sernam. *See* National Women's Service (Sernam)
sexual assault laws, women and, 2
small-N comparative studies, 9
Smok, Carlos, 129
Socialist Party (PS), 66
    women's rights policy and, 67–68
Soto, Laura, 76, 77

Turres, Marisol, 76, 126–27

UDI. *See* Independent Democratic Union Party (UDI)

Valdés, Teresa, 91
Valenzuela, María Elena, 91, 111–12
Veloso, Paulina, 173
Vidal, Ximena, 77
Viera-Gallo, José, 163
VIF. *See* Intrafamily Violence Law (1994, VIF)
Vodanovic, Hernán, 76

Walker, Ignacio, 69, 151
Weber, Paulina, 111
women in office, impact of, 40–44
Women's Collective of La Florida, 105
Women's Institute in Santiago, 105, 130, 130n16
women's movement(s). *See also* feminist movement(s)
    Argentinean, 25
    Brazilian, 25